Take Back America

20 Simple Ways the Average American Can Help

Kim Roth, Angie Shell,
Sharon Blackwell, and
Galena Coleman

AuthorHouse™
1663 Liberty Drive, Suite 200
Bloomington, IN 47403
www.authorhouse.com
Phone: 1-800-839-8640

First published by AuthorHouse 6/9/2008

ISBN: 978-1-4343-9371-5 (sc)

Library of Congress Control Number: 2008905229

Printed in the United States of America
Bloomington, Indiana

This book is printed on acid-free paper.

Our book is dedicated to
Stanley and Rachael McCullough
two people who taught
all their family members
to love their country and take pride in their country.

We would also like to dedicate our book
to our own families who are the actual inspiration
for such an undertaking.
All of them have been very supportive and patient.

Kim Roth would like to thank her wonderful husband, Amos,
her two sons, Kenny and Chris, her daughter, Carla, and
her three grandsons, Cole, Tyler, and Colin, who light up her life.
And thanks to her dear cousin, Angie, for
all her work on the Bibliography.

Angie Shell would personally like to thank her husband, Mark,
her two sons, Nathan and Jesse, her daughter, Cassidy, and
her grandson, Ethan.

Sharon Blackwell would love to thank her husband, David,
her daughters, Kim and Carrie, her grandsons, Kenny and Chris,
her granddaughter, Carla, and her beautiful great-grandsons.

Galena Coleman would like to thank her husband, Vince,
and her three children, Alex, Rob, and Angie
for their encouragement. She would also like to thank
her niece, Kim, for all the extra work she put into editing this book.

A big special thanks to all who sold the bumper stickers
so that we could publish this book. Another big special thank you to all
family and friends who gave us the encouragement that we needed to
realize our dream of writing this book.

Table of Contents

INTRODUCTION

The authors of this book are not people of higher education, published authors, or highly successful business women. We are just ordinary women with ordinary lives with an extraordinary love for our country; in no way, shape, or form do we want to come across as hypocrites or having done everything right in our lives. Like many, we have tried to learn from our mistakes. We are just true Americans who would like to do something, anything to help our great country be all that it can be. Mainly, we are mothers, daughters, grandmothers, wives, sisters, and friends of many who are suffering because our government has not lived up to its end of the bargain. We pay our taxes, we are good citizens, but our futures and the future of our loved ones are being jeopardized by illegal immigration, faulty trade agreements, government waste, political corruption, wars that can't be won, and the beat goes on. Greed, egos, and power have become way more important than "justice for all". However, those who truly believe in America can rise up and "Take Back America".

Our book is meant to inspire, not offend. We realize everybody may not agree with everything we have to say, and we are fine with that as long as it inspires someone somewhere. We have had this book self-published because of the need for inspiration in our country at this time and during the upcoming presidential campaign season. In our hurry to do so, we also did not have it professionally edited. Please overlook our undotted i's and uncrossed t's and the occasional butchering of the English language. Many arguments were had on capitalization. There may be many inconsistencies in the book. Each chapter is written by a different author, so I generally refer to the writer of that chapter, whereas we generally refer to the American people or the authors as a group. Our intentions are good, even if the editing is not.

As you may have noticed, this book is dedicated to Rachael and Stanley McCullough, parents of Galena Coleman and Sharon Blackwell, grandparents of Angie Shell and Kim Roth. These two wonderful people instilled our sense of pride in our country because they knew it as a land of promises and opportunities; a land where hard work came with benefits and hopes for better futures, and most importantly, a land of freedom where people can be who they want to be. It is the love of our country that gives us the desire to write a book we hope will keep this country from becoming what others think it should be. America should be what Americans want it to be, a land full of opportunities, a place to build the "American Dream".

The idea of doing this book came about on a trip Angie and Kim took to New York City to attend a Farm-Aid Concert, a concert that benefits the family farmers in America. Driving from St. Louis to New York City gave us a look at a Nation in trouble. We were astonished by the horrors of our infrastructure along the way, especially in New York City. We were completely amazed by the lack of common courtesy given to us in the simplest situations. We could not communicate with the staff at our hotels; hotels located in America where the language spoken is English (which we both speak fluently). We wondered if the British had the same problem in London? The Japanese in Tokyo? The Chinese in Hong Kong? The French in Paris? We heard tour guides tell us that New York City is being bought up by the Arabs. We were disgusted by the waste we were confronted with everywhere we went except at the Farm-Aid concert where all trash was separated. We learned about the struggles our farmers face at the first ever Farm-Aid concert held in New York City. And we jokingly said to each other, we need to write a book entitled "Take Back America".

As individuals, all four of us have watched with foreboding as this country has spiraled out of control. Each and every American can be the link needed to "Take Back America". We have all enjoyed the benefits and freedoms of living in America. All true American Citizens are needed at this time in our history to stand up to keep America, American.

Common courtesy, respect for others, pride in our work and community, and work ethics should be "the norm". Principles and hard-working people shaped this nation not the rude, self-absorbed, disrespectful slackers a lot of us have become. But what is worse, there is another more frightening group, a group that preys on those less fortunate. Many people fit into this category in many different respects. We all have to start putting Americans first regardless of race or creed, whether young or old, successful or not so successful, rich or poor. So, dear readers, strap on your seat belt and get ready for a roller coaster ride of ideas and suggestions that can be easily accomplished by the average American. Since you are already reading this, it is obvious you are an exceptional American open to change as it WILL TAKE CHANGE to "Take Back America".

In closing, a quote from former President Bill Clinton, "There is nothing wrong with America that cannot be cured by what is right with America." So lend your patriotic spirit to help bring justice back to the people of this great nation, and in so doing, the rest of the world.

Kim Roth's Story, Views, and Motives

For me, patriotism has always come naturally. There has never been a doubt in my mind that I was very fortunate to have been born in the USA in St. Louis, Missouri in February of 1963, one of the last baby boomers. However, to my dismay, my patriotism has made me feel like an outcast many times and today I'm just confused. It seems that there is a revolution going on that makes Americans want to be unpatriotic (hard to believe it has only been a little over six years since 9/11). I want to be patriotic, but everything and everyone around me screams "It is all about ME". I'm as guilty as the next, but deep down inside I also know I am guilty of letting down my country, and the American Veterans that made this country the place I love so much, from sea to shining sea. It is this very reason that I hope to inspire Americans across this great Country to stand up and TAKE BACK AMERICA!!

From the very beginning, my life has never been an easy one. Born to an unwed mother in a time when such things were not accepted, my childhood was mostly a never-ending series of moves and changes, nothing was ever secure so far as I can remember. Even though my childhood was unstable, I feel very fortunate for my experiences during these times, because I encountered so many things that many people do not in a lifetime. Until I was 14, when we finally settled in Missouri, my education was done in countless schools which gave me a look at so many different aspects of America. Kindergarten was a blur of school after school; first grade was a little better. During my second grade year in Miami, Florida, I was the only white girl in a school of African-Americans and a few Cubans (I was just happy I got to stay in one school for a whole year). For three years after second grade, I lived a fairly normal life in Homestead, Florida; same school, same home, same parents. My stepfather was restless. We moved to Mississippi, then to Texas, Colorado, then back to Texas, and again back to Florida. My mother divorced my stepfather and decided we needed to get back to our roots where we could depend on the aid and comfort our family could provide. I have now lived in Missouri (except for three months back in Florida) since 1977 and am proud to call it home.

The move back to Missouri was bittersweet in many ways. Living with a single mom who worked several jobs did not leave me much supervision. When we moved back to Missouri, I had 24/7 supervision in a home that was completely different from anything I had experienced in my short life. This was a real family with real family values and religious beliefs that I had never really practiced. Unbelievably, it was comforting to feel a part of something, but disconcerting to lose my freedoms. It was also a relief to be away from a Stepfather who struggled with an addiction to alcohol and was abusive to my mother. When my mother found financial freedom, we moved out on our own, and again I was unsupervised much of the time. My new found freedom led to becoming a teenage mother myself.

At 16, I married a man I knew would never live up to my dreams of what a husband should be, but thought it was the best thing for my baby on the way. Since I had never known my biological father, it was something I really wanted for my own child. On April 30, 1980 my son was born and my whole life changed. The overwhelming love I felt for this new little guy was such a new experience to me. I wanted a life so much better for my child. I wanted him to have the things I never had such as security, two parents with his best interests at heart, a home, a foundation, etc. Two young kids raising a kid rarely worked back then, still don't to this day. We gave it our best shot, but alas, had to admit defeat and that is exactly what it felt like to me. Divorcing my first husband still remains to this day one of the hardest things I have ever done, but the best thing I ever did for myself and my child.

After spending several years as a single mom, luck finally came my way when I met a man who would give me what I had been looking for most of my life; a stable home full of love, commitment, and security. It is a second marriage for both of us, both of us bringing kids into the equation. It wasn't perfect or easy at first, but we have become a family that we are both proud to be a part of. We have three wonderful children between us who are productive, responsible citizens. We are so proud of each and every one of them. Thankfully they have given us grandchildren that brings such unbelievable joy to us it is hard to put into words. It is this family, and our extended family that makes me want a hopeful future for all.

At 44, I fulfilled one of my life-long dreams. I got to do the "Big Apple". What's more, I was able to share one of my lifelong ambitions and the ultimate vacation with someone I love very much, someone who was just as enthusiastic as me, my cousin Angie, one of the co-authors of this book. New York City has always intrigued me in many ways, but mainly for its place in our Nations history. To see the Statue of Liberty from so many angles as our boat pulled into her dock was everything I imagined and more. Overwhelming feelings of pride for my country just flooded my body causing my eyes to mist with tears of joy. Visiting Ground Zero, sight of 9/11, and attending the ceremonies was unlike anything I have ever experienced. My heart bleeds for all Americans who lost so much that awful day. I experienced so much in New York City, good and bad, but that trip will never be forgotten and always treasured. And it was the beginning of this book.

After all the curve balls life has thrown at me, I would like to think that I am a better person for it. There are many things that I have not mentioned in this short biography, many things that no person should really have to deal with, but I like to believe that you learn from mistakes and the mistakes of others and move on. Too many people like to use the past as an excuse for unacceptable behavior. I have always tried not to dwell on things I cannot change (sometimes not so successfully). In order to have a hopeful future for our families and loved ones, I am afraid there are many challenges to address in our everyday lives. Each and every one of us has to become more involved in the roads we pave to the future. Our Government paves the future for many others but seems to forget who is footing the bills. Our Country should be putting Americans first. Basically, I am not a very motivated person. One of my favorite mottos is "I work to live, I don't live to work", but I could become real motivated for my country and my children and grandchildren. Maybe our new motto should be: Let's work as Americans to "TAKE BACK AMERICA"!

Angie Shell's Story, Views, and Motives

Currently, I am a stay-at-home mom. I have worked during the past years in the insurance industry (I know that ranks right up there with the IRS), but I was good at it. With all its duties, staying at home and running a household is as challenging as any job I have ever done. Paying the bills, taking care of schedules, educating our children, and the day to day responsibilities of running a household do not stop at five p.m. You are on call all day and night. It may seem like a thankless job with no incentives or quarterly bonus, but without folks like us that stay at home and keep it going, others would not be able to work and fulfill their role in the family as easily. It is a give-and-take situation and in the long run, it is priceless, outweighing any monetary gifts an employer could offer. You stay-at-home moms know what I am mean. It is a job that doesn't get the credit it deserves, but it is essential in numerous ways.

The early years of my childhood were great. I was fortunate to have two parents in my home. There were family struggles, but never were there more than we could bear as a family. My parents gave me a strong foundation from which I pulled from in my adulthood to raise my own family. When I matured, I developed a new respect for my parents that you cannot have as a child. I give them credit for who me and my brothers are today. My two older brothers are your typical siblings. They loved to scare me, tease me, and all those things that make your parents crazy. I loved my brothers as a young girl of course, but as an adult, I realize how lucky I am to have them. They are special men in my life; I wouldn't want them to ever quit picking on their little sister.

After being married 23 years, my husband and I have three children and a grandson. We were your typical opposites attract scenario.

After many stupid arguments and head butting, I find we say the same things at the same time. It's strange to think that two opposites now find so many situations where we are on the same page. He is a loving caring man that has stuck by me and been so supportive no matter what the situation. We have had our ups and downs and turned many corners together, but every time I think "how are we going to make it till death do us part?", something happens that makes me realize I couldn't live without this man. So, by today's standards, I'd say we have a successful marriage, and I am blessed to have him.

If they would only realize it, my two sons who are grown young men could do anything they desired. It fills me with great pride to introduce them to others. Watching them grow into the individuals they are is something (as a parent) that gives me a sense of wonder. They, of course, have traits from me and my husband, but have taken those traits to become unique, caring, loving men that make a parent proud. Don't get me wrong; they have faults and sometimes do things that make me shake my head, but I am nearly sure we have all did that to our parents. I am grateful to have these healthy young men in my life and tremendously blessed to be able to call them my sons.

My daughter is now reaching teenage years and truly a beautiful girl inside and out, not because she is my child, but because she is truly gifted. She is an outstanding young lady. Her interests and hobbies are different from other children her age. Don't get me wrong, she still likes all the popular things and is your typical teenager, but she is knowledgeable beyond her years. This book has been of great interest to her. She wants to know why something is like it is. She wants to learn for the sake of learning. I have to admit she doesn't get all of that from me. She has voiced many times to me how proud she is of me for being a part of this book, and in so many ways, has been a real inspiration for me.

Life has come full circle. I've finally got the concept of spoiling the grandson and sending him home. There is really nothing like it. Buying the noisy toys and letting our children get to know all the fun we had with them (some may call this a payback) brings a smile to my face. Watching my children with their own children is a feeling like no other. My grandson is four and a real blast to be around. You have to love the honesty of a child. He has been around a lot of adults and has a great vocabulary (sometimes too good!). There is just not enough a person can say about the joy of being a grandparent.

My motivations to participate in this book are for the reasons I just told you about. My children and grandchildren may never know America in the way we have known it. Frankly I am worried, just looking around and seeing what is happening tells me we need some changes and fast. Being proud of our country, I want to see it the great land it used to be. I am not trying to tell you I have done everything right or made all the right decisions. I haven't. I have participated in the PTO, been a soccer mom, room mother, full-time employee, volunteered in various ways, voted, gone to church and so many things that we all do that I consider important. Looking back, it occurs to me that I have neglected a few things. I am not an authority on every topic in this book or any, if it comes right down to it, but I am an American just like you that wants a bright future for my family. I want to know I am doing my part to make that happen. Participating makes me feel good. It is time that I take full advantage of the rights that have been given to me from all those who have sacrificed. Maybe it is past time I became more involved, but it is never too late. I know I can't do it all, no one can, but there are some ideas in this book that all of us can do. I hope you feel the same way after you read it. God Bless America and keep her safe!

Sharon Blackwell's Story, Views, and Motives

If you are asking yourself who is this old lady who wants to tell me how to live, I am going to tell you. Really, you should not have asked because I am really going to tell you.

Born on June 13, 1946 in a real shack in Jefferson County Missouri, I am a real baby-boomer, among the first of my breed. My father was a factory worker for Pittsburgh Plate Glass (PPG), and my mother a stay-at-home mom (advantage me). My parents, unlike others in the same circumstances (factory worker with five children) had an insatiable lust for knowledge and a passion for nature and the beauty that is free for the looking. Because of my parents, there was always a sense of wonder of the world around us. If everyone could feel the same about this great country of ours, the world would be a better place.

But alas, good start or not, I screwed up my life completely before I found my way back. Pregnant at 16, I was a high school dropout. Hoping to make my parents feel better, I married a man I didn't love. It didn't make my parents feel better. At 19 I came back to St. Louis and took a job as a file clerk at Associated Retailers. This was the early days of computers (1964-66) so I got my GED at International Data Processing and started computer training. Boring! Early computers were not real interesting to me. So I left the company and took a job as a waitress: more money, more fun.

Sharing an apartment with my sister Sue helped us both do well financially. Then my sister met Frank who introduced me to my second husband, Gary, a lineman with an Associate Degree in Power Line Design. Let me tell you IBEW stands for "I've been every where", because we were everywhere. He moved my daughter and me around the country to many states and towns unknown to most people. He was an alcoholic, a drug addict, a gambler, a womanizer, and a wife beater; and in the end, a stalker of sorts. Life with him was either very happy or total hell; there was little in between. I learned about life and learned to answer my phone with a cheery "Sharon's rent-a-husband service". For the most part, I made my own living; I sold insurance at Gieco, I was a pest control tech for several companies and I was also a part-time waitress. While living in Florida, I decided one day that I had had enough! I packed his things (all of them) and dropped them off at his friend's house with a note to never call me again! I saw him occasionally over the years but never took him back.

I moved back to Missouri in 1978, got my real estate license in time for the last real estate crash. Eventually I found financial freedom when I went to work for PPG Industries. My dad said I would last six months because the work was too hard for me, but I retired July 1, 2006. During this time I met my soul mate David; kind, generous and supportive. We have been married for 27 years; it is "till death us do part". Without his warmth and humor, life would be intolerable. Through the trials of my younger life, I learned to appreciate a man I liked as well as loved. A good lesson, your mate should be your best friend.

The life I have lived has been strange and difficult and I have known people in all strata of society. Things I have learned is those who love learning nature and their country are in all walks of life and they are always interesting. You do not need a PHD to be smart and you don't have to be poor to recognize suffering. As a nation, we are suffering at the hands of greedy robber barons (look it up) and unscrupulous politicians. I am willing to help stop them! Are You? So come along on an adventure with us. Big change starts with small steps. We can make a better world with small changes. Are you game? If you are, give this some thought! There was a very talented young man in the early sixties that wrote a song called "A Simple Song of Freedom". He died later in the night it was first performed. But it became an anthem of my youth. Maybe it is time to bring it back because "we the people here don't want no war".

Galena Coleman's Story, Views, and Motives

I was born February 6, 1938 which makes me 70 years old going on 100. My spirit is young but my body keeps trying to race ahead. As you've probably surmised, I've had some health issues. No, I'm not going to bore you with my medical history. I just wanted to mention that I'm recovering from a hip replacement at the moment, so my contribution to this book has been more verbal then actually writing down the words.

We are of one mind on every issue written about in this book and I make a great one-woman cheering section. Considering the fact none of us are professional writers, I can honestly say, this book is well done. Since I haven't actually written the words, I'm allowed to say that.

I've been married fifty-four years. I'm very happy, and I am blessed that I still have my mate. Vince is bright and energetic at 75 years old. He retired from his job as parts manager (39 years) for a large trucking company. He soon found retirement boring and has driven a school bus for almost nine years. Because of his age, the testing he goes through every year gets more and more difficult, which is a good thing. Children are precious cargo.

I retired from selling real estate years ago because of my health problems. Since then, I've had many foreign exchange students, and it was a wonderful experience. I even worked at placing students in other homes for awhile, but found that was a little more stress than I could handle.

My children are great kids. Well, they're not kids anymore. Alex is 52, Rob, 49, and Angie, 45. They'll always be "the kids" to me. My children, my family, and my many friends are a great blessing. With ten grandchildren, eight great-grandchildren, and another on the way, I'm truly blessed.

Like any family, we have our ups and downs, have disagreements, make up, hug, kiss, and cry. Through it all, we grow stronger spiritually and emotionally. We need some adversity in our lives to grow. Let someone treat one of us badly and we come together as one. Don't mess with the Coleman Clan.

The circle of life is a powerful and beautiful thing. Being a religious woman, I hope God blesses each and every one of you in ways I cannot even imagine. Together we can preserve the good in this country. God bless you all! And God Bless America!

Reading the last two sentences of the above paragraph, I realize I sound like a political person. I'm not, but I do try to keep up with the happenings in this country, and in the world. Sadly, at times, the news is so depressing that I must turn off the TV. It's usually about this time I find my soap box and start preaching; I tell anyone who will listen what I would do if I had the political power Nancy Pelosi gained when she took office as Speaker of the House. First, I would have pushed to impeach President George Bush and Vice-President Dick Cheney. Then I would have charged them with high treason for crimes against humanity. Along with them, I would have charged Donald Rumsfield, Karl Rove, and Condoleezza Rice.

The above mentioned people have crossed the line of decency too many times. I will never understand why Nancy Pelosi failed to do her job. I have lived long enough to know this country is spiraling out of control. I blame all of the politicians, both Democratic and Republican, for failing the American people. There are degrees of blame though, and the Bush crowd has, and still is, raping this country. Why is our so-called democratic system not working?

In my opinion, we are no longer a true democracy; we are a democracy in name only. We still have the trappings of a democracy. We still vote, even though we can never be sure the person that actually won will take office; it sounds more like a banana republic to me. We can still peacefully march, hold up our signs, and shout our objections about almost anything. Too all appearances, we give the impression of a democracy in action.

We have no draft. Our government just hires mercenaries instead, pays them with our money. While our soldiers are getting, let us say $100 a day, the mercenaries are receiving about $1000 a day. I seriously doubt a mercenary would hesitate to shoot civilians if ordered to do so, or even one of our soldiers, if ordered. Ladies and Gentlemen, it is time that "We the People" "Take Back America".

We Americans are a courageous people; we always have been strong. When you don't know who the enemy is, how can you fight back? Hopefully, this book will show you the enemies face. We don't lack motivation; we're not ignorant sheep to be herded according to the will of the powers that be. We're Americans! We don't lack courage! Once we know the enemy, we'll put our country back in order. Together, we're strong, and don't you forget it!

Chapter 1

Realize One Person Can Make A Difference

"Never be afraid to do something new. Remember, amateurs built the ark; professionals built the titanic."
Anonymous quote from www.quotations.about.com

Take Back America came to be during a trip to New York City. It started out as a joke since none of us have ever written a book. The idea could not escape our minds, the more we thought, the more we hoped a book of this kind could be a real inspiration to the American public. One idea turned into another and another. All of us have watched as our country has taken a turn for the worse. Inflation has skyrocketed out of control to the point people can barely afford the gas to get back and forth to work or put food on their table. The United States has itself involved in too many wars, wars that aren't ours to fight. Too many innocent lives are being sacrificed for no viable reason causing much heartache in this country. Not only is the war taking lives but it is causing economic difficulties right here in the United States. Our government is letting our infrastructure fall apart to finance a conflict most citizens detest. Although we support our troops and pray for them, most U.S. citizens do not support this unwarranted fight that puts Americans in jeopardy. Worst of all, we are probably in a war caused by political corruption more than anything. It is not a secret that many in our government are considered unscrupulous, crooked, and do not have America's best interest at heart. For a long time now, America has been put at risk by people in high positions and our own government. They send our good-paying jobs overseas by awarding corporations incentives and tax breaks. Not only that, our leaders have allowed our borders to be breached to the point that the problem is out of control allowing illegal immigrants to steal American jobs pushing our unemployment rate even higher. The Government has allowed us to become dependent on the rest of the world for our oil instead of addressing the problem here in the United States. In so many areas of what the United States consumes, we are dependent on other nations. The situation is out of control! So, my dear readers, this is how this book came to be. Since our government seems to want to give away the American dream, we thought as individuals, wouldn't it be the true American dream if all Americans could unite at this time and "Take Back America"?

America has always been known for its fundamental family values, moral integrity, and responsible citizenship. Standing by our principles has become so overwhelming because of our hectic lives and the shifts we work; fitting the simplest things into our day is barely possible anymore. Therefore, many of the essential characteristics, that have made our country an inspiration to most, have been lost along the way. Without our show of patriotism, it looks like we take our country for granted. Most of us who live here and love our country have been neglecting our responsibilities as U.S. citizens. It is with this in mind that we give you this book to bring back the missing qualities we are lacking to "Take Back America", one individual at a time.

Many times I have heard people say, "I don't like how things are, but there is nothing I can do about it." Well.....I disagree. Why can't we make a difference? If you have an opinion and you have any motivation, you can make a difference. Just a complaint or an opinion is not enough; you have to take some kind of action. Remember, many people feel as you do. This can happen in many ways and on many different levels. I challenge you to read this book, find something that fits into your schedule, and begin. I think you will find it rewarding to participate in a society where one person can make a difference. Here are twenty examples of how an individual can make a difference that will hopefully motivate every individual to want to "Take Back America".

1. <u>Realize One Person Can Make A Difference.</u> First of all, each American has to come to the realization that one person

can make a difference if you put your mind to it. When we talk about one person making a difference, it tends to throw people off a little bit. Their first response is generally "No, I can't". Others believe that to make a difference in our nation, it has to be a huge number of people, and even more seem to believe it takes our government to lead us to achieve these changes. I say no. One person, with just one mind, can have an idea or a dream and set it into motion. The idea then gets shared with others, begins to grow, and soon this dream of one person is no longer a dream but a reality. It began with only one and blossomed. Can you think of some things in our history that began that way? What if Thomas Edison had never invented the light bulb? Can you imagine how different life would be? What if Alexander Graham Bell had never invented the telephone? His wife and mother were deaf which profoundly affected his work. Think how different life would be if the Wright Brothers had not invented the first successful airplane which later led to the invention of the first practical fixed wing aircraft. Let's not forget the invention of sliced bread and the machine in which the bread was wrapped in order to keep it from getting stale. This machine was invented by Otto Frederick Rohwedder and set off a trend leading to the toaster being developed. These gentlemen are forever etched in our history. To find out more about these inventors and other inventors, go to www.ideafinder.com. Not all of us are inventors or full of innovative ideas, however we all have information we can share with one another. Each and every one of us possesses skills that could benefit another person. The trick is to find out how to apply yours to the people around you. Let's start sharing these talents and making a difference one person at a time.

2. Educate Yourself And Your Family. Education pertains to many things not just academics. We need social skills to build our confidence and learn how to communicate with each other. An important part of education is learning to manage our time so the effort we put into our work is productive.

Never stop seeking knowledge. You are never too young or too old to learn. In today's world, it has become critical to have some kind of training or higher education to get a decent paying job. Don't be afraid to go after that skill or training. Put yourself out there, figure out what you want to do, what it will take to get there, and go for it! Just like Andre Agassi did when he founded a college prep academy and located it in an area of Las Vegas to help underprivileged children. Agassi is quoted from Bill Clinton's book, Giving How Each Of Us Can Change The World, as saying, "Tennis was a stepping-stone for me, changing a child's life is what I always wanted to do". Here is a prime example of how one person can make an impact, go to www.agassifoundation.org to learn more about his contributions that are making a difference in our country. And on a smaller level, a grandparent taking extra time to read, or teach a child to read, is a way one person can make a difference in education. One day, that child may read to an elderly citizen who needs company. By taking responsibility for our education and the education of our families, we will be one step closer to "Take Back America".

3. Be A Responsible Voter. Over the last few years, Americans have come to realize how important voting really is. During the 2008 primaries, voters have turned out in record numbers to cast their vote to ensure their voice counts. Even though it is pretty obvious that America is divided, having the right to vote and the right to campaign for our choice are rights we often take for granted. Women and African Americans had to fight for their right to vote. As four women writing this book, we would like to expound on the difference one person made in her struggle to attain the right to vote for all women. Susan B. Anthony made a lifelong commitment to this cause and while her dream was not realized in her lifetime, she was instrumental in getting the 19th Amendment passed in 1920. When this dream was finally realized, Carrie Chapman Catt had taken over for Susan B. Anthony. Catt is another individual who has made a difference not only in the

U.S. but across the world because after the 19th Amendment passed, women all over the world realized they could make a difference also. Now it is your turn, man or woman! You make a difference when you make an informed decision and vote. To help you make an informed decision, go to www.FactCheck.org in order to educate yourself on the facts of political candidates. Many other web-sites can be found to help you make an informed decision. Please remember, an uneducated vote is the same thing as not voting. Use your voting right responsibly, so you too, can make a difference.

4. Be Aware Of The Opposition. The opposition is not always what it appears to be or who we think it is. For years the people of our wonderful nation have been kept in the dark regarding Government activities. A great example of an elected official opposing the will of the people is when Richard Nixon was involved in Watergate. In this case, one person that made the difference by not allowing a corrupt President to hide his secrets any longer was a courageous, honest man named William Mark Felt, Deputy Director of the FBI, who spoke out for justice. Although he did this anonymously at first using the alias of "Deep Throat", he eventually shared his name and his story with America not too long ago. Because of his actions, our country got rid of many bad apples including the President and his Chief of Staff. Go to www.americanhistory.about.com for more information on this proud man. As individuals, we could pluck out the weeds at local levels before they take over the lawn. You will be able to help pluck out the weeds when you become an informed educated voter. So much good information can be found on the world-wide-web to enlighten you about what is going on in your community and in your country. Share the information with everyone to begin making a difference where the opposition is concerned. If we plan well and keep up with the political climate of the world, we are many and we can prevail, one person at a time. Join together and we can create a renaissance in the 21st century.

5. Be Proud You Are An American. Since we live in the greatest country on Earth, there is no reason to be anything but proud. We should be proud of the beauty that surrounds us with shining seas, majestic mountains, and prairies of waving grass. We should be proud of the richness of our farmland and the fact that we can feed so many with the bounty from those fields. We should be proud of the freedoms that the people of this land enjoy and be proud to protect those freedoms. We should be proud of this country, home to many pioneers of science. Neil Armstrong is one of those pioneers that made a difference. Before President John F. Kennedy's untimely death, he pledged an American would stand on the moon before the end of the decade. Neil Armstrong and the inventive people of NASA made that pledge a reality when on July 20, 1969 Neil Armstrong became the first man to set foot on the surface of the moon. His famous words "One step for man, one giant leap for mankind" resounded throughout the world. The proudest moment for America, however, is when Buzz Aldrin and Neil Armstrong planted our flag on the moon's surface–that moment made us all proud to be an American. Without his ambition and courage, the race to the moon would have taken much longer and Kennedy's dream would not have been realized. How can you not hold this man in high esteem? He was certainly proud to be an American. For more information, go to http://nssdc.gsfc.nasa.gov. Each time you fly an American flag, your pride shows. Each time you vote responsibly, your devotion shows. Each time you dare to try to change an unjust law, your courage shows. This is what it means to be a true American, one who loves, honors, and reveres their nation. Let your pride in your nation shine through, and everyone will know you are proud to be an American.

6. Take Pride In Your Work. People have conflicting ideas about this topic I believe. The way most companies have chosen to sacrifice quality over quantity has made workers take less pride in their work. Of course, we know this does not apply

to everyone. But, it has become a theme throughout the business world to make as many as possible instead of setting reasonable goals while maintaining quality. The working man becomes discouraged by these expectations and has a misguided idea that the quality no longer matters. We each have to make this a personal undertaking to change the way we think as employees and even more so as employers. Some of this can be blamed on the demands employers have made on us and some of it is our own fault. Americans should not abandon their work ethic so easily, and we should always do the best we can to uphold our own principles. If you don't want to do your job to the best of your ability, you can bet there will be someone out there willing to give it a shot. Many individuals in our history have excelled in their work ethics and their desire to be the best. Henry Ford is a good example of someone who obviously took pride in his work. He was the founder of the Ford Motor Company and the father of the modern assembly line used for mass production. The Model T automobile revolutionized the transportation industry in America. He has made a huge footprint on our history, to find out more about his contributions to modern technology, go to www.ideafinder.com. Someone else who wanted to do it better than anyone else is Adolphus Busch. He and his father-in-law, Eberhard Anheuser, co-founded a brewery that was to become the first of its kind. They created a network of rail side ice houses to deliver beer. He also had the industry's first fleet of refrigerated freight cars. However, success really came to Busch by finding a way to pasteurize beer so it could remain fresh to be shipped all over the world. If you ever get to St. Louis, Missouri, hopefully you will have time to tour this brewery, it is really quite interesting, and a great example of one person's drive to be the best he could be. All of us need to be more vigilant concerning the work we put out. We each can make a difference by taking pride in our work. We need to change this epidemic that has swept our nation, an epidemic that has left most Americans believing that going to work is a social event not a responsibility to their employer, their company, or their fellow workers. Personally, I know we are capable of beating this epidemic and making the United States known for the quality and productivity of its work force as it once was. In a world where so many things are out of control, this is definitely an area that each of us can make a difference.

7. <u>Be An American Consumer.</u> One of the most important things we need to do as individuals to "Take Back America" is learn to "Be An American Consumer". If we cannot come together for this common cause, it could have disastrous consequences for our country, worse than the effects we are feeling at this time. Our country needs its manufacturing base to keep the economy thriving. In order to keep our manufacturing base, we have to buy these products that are "Made In America". At this point, finding American made products has become nearly impossible. However, it does not mean we should abandon hope or allow this unnatural practice to continue. Why would you want most of your products to come from another country? The answer is no American should want this to happen because too many of us are feeling the consequences from these moronic practices already. The American unions have worked to eliminate these practices and keep American jobs here in the United States in the past and continue to do so today. They constantly struggle with the opposition while trying to accomplish their mission which is to advance its members interests in respect to wages, benefits, and working conditions. The union's reputation was tarnished by its link to organized crime in the past causing the American public to doubt its mission. Today more than ever, we need our unions to protect our rights and keep jobs in America. However, if we do not become American consumers, their work is for naught. One person who strives to make a difference for American workers is James P. Hoffa, General President of the Teamsters Union, and a member since he was 18 years old. He and the union are fighting hard to invigorate the American labor movement and end

policies that punish workers while making profits for big businesses. One of his goals is to make sure that the "Made In America" label is more prominent in the United States than the "Made In China" label. You can find more information at www.teamsters.org. For him and many others to realize this dream, we must buy American-made products and be the best American consumer possible. Believe me, while writing this book, I took a look around and found it terrifying how much I owned that was "Made In China" or in some country I never even realized existed. It was also a shocker when I made a concerted effort to buy American made products and couldn't. We realize that buying American products is not always possible and probably never will be, but we do know that we can turn this around if Americans demand and patronize "Made In America" labels more than any other.

8. Put Americans First. America is a can-do nation. It has always been and always will be if we have anything to do with it. At the beginning of World War 2 we were not prepared for a war the scope of what had to be fought. The people of our country geared up for war and did things no one thinks is possible today. Our men and boys went off to fight, and some of our women went to save their lives. One of those boys was Audie Murphy who was 17 years old when he enlisted by pretending to be 18. He became one of the most decorated veterans of World War 2 receiving 33 U.S. medals, five from France and one from Belgium. He fought the good fight and he made a difference, many lives were saved by his bravery. He then worked with veterans of Korea and Vietnam to help them with Post Traumatic Stress Disorder and he addressed the Government about increased health care benefits and mental-health disorders for our veterans. Even after he made a difference fighting in World War 2, he made a difference in the lives of Vietnam and Korean veterans. To find out more about this hero, go to www.audiemurphy.com. So after he made a difference, he made a difference. On a smaller scale, the women and older citizens that were left behind built the

machines, guns, ships and planes to fight the biggest war in the history of the World. The people of this era are known as the greatest generation, and they, as individuals, took the responsibility to make that war plan work. Each willingly sacrificed for the country they loved. We need to honor them, but even more we need to learn to serve our country and each other with the same passion and patriotism they showed. We need to recreate that state of mind in all of our citizens now. Let us study and realize what it takes to "Take Back America".

9. Respect American Culture And Language. For those of us who have lived a long life in our wonderful country, we are the lucky ones. We know what this country is truly about and mourn the loss of so much we held dear. We also know that there is much to be done to return to a life that values tradition and the values that make America great. Each of us has the opportunity to jump start our nation and returns it to its proper place in the world. In this election year, there have been many candidates vying to be known as the best American. While I do believe many are sincere in their minds, I think perhaps, John Edwards held our culture more dear than most. Senator Edwards was born June 10, 1953 in North Carolina. He would later serve as a U.S. Senator from his home state. He was picked as John Kerry's running mate in 2004 and even though that ticket lost, the former Senator Edwards continued to campaign to restart the labor movement in this country. He walked picket lines and sought to make life better for the working man. By working full time at the One America Committee (which he founded), taking part in many other causes to help those in need, and helping preserve American culture and tradition, he's a lawyer we should relate to and respect. While he may never be President, he has won the hearts of many. Go to www.johnedwards.com for more information. There are many not so well-known people who make a difference in keeping American culture on track. While attending a woman's

basketball game in Houston, Dana Steel (Readers Digest, May 2008, pg. 104) was shocked and upset by those who continued to talk and guzzle beer while the National Anthem played. Keeping this in mind, she teamed up with a friend, H.C. Thomas, to remind people of those who gave their lives to protect our freedom. She and Thomas created a plan to film U.S. servicemen in Iraq making patriotic statements that would play before the National Anthem at sporting events to encourage participation in the traditional respect shown to our flag and our National Anthem. These clips are offered free of charge to sports stadiums across the U.S. Perhaps people will be more respectful of our anthem when it is introduced by one of our men in uniform. Good Idea! The preceding is only two examples of people taking a stand to defend our culture one person at a time. Could your idea be the next to help "Take Back America"?

10. Help Secure Our Borders. The issue of illegal immigration in our country recently hit home for me when I read that many of our cities are running out of water! Our natural resources are being strained to the limit by a population so large this land cannot support it. We currently have millions of illegal immigrants in our country using our natural resources without regard to the consequences to our land and resources. In order to keep our country sustainable, we must secure our borders to help control our population. One of the best ways to do this is to stop illegal immigration and deport those already in our country, especially the criminal element who do not contribute to America in a productive manner. Illegal immigrants are basically using our country to prop up the economy of their country. The quality of life for the middle-class has been seriously undermined by those entering our country illegally. Lou Dobbs is a leader in the effort to secure our borders and stop illegal immigration. Dobbs graduated from Harvard where he got his degree in economics and has served on the board of many of the top journalistic societies in America. One of his many awards as a journalist includes

the George Foster Peabody Award for his coverage of the 1987 Stock Market crash. During one of his hard-hitting investigative newscast, Dobbs coined the phrase "The war on the middle class" which eventually led to a book of the same title. Proclaiming to be an independent populist, he has won the hearts of Middle America with his fact based fight on illegal immigration. Way to go Lou! Keep up the fight, this country needs more men of your caliber telling the truth to the citizens of the United States. Go to www.LouDobbs.com for more information on his work and learn how to join his crusade to "Help Secure Our Borders". On a smaller scale, Ramos and Compean are two border patrol agents who are currently serving prison sentences for doing their job. While on patrol, these two brave men shot a drug smuggler trying to escape. There was no doubt he was a drug smuggler because he abandoned a van full of marijuana. As he ran back to the border, he was shot in the buttock, but escaped anyway. The border patrol agents were convicted of unnecessary force and sentenced to prison for up to fifteen years but no less than ten. The drug smuggler was given immunity by the federal prosecutor to testify against Ramos and Compean. . After his testimony, he was turned loose to offend again while Ramos and Compean lost their jobs, their families, and their freedom. There have been many calls to commute their sentence and they have all been ignored by President Bush. Isn't it funny that his friend, Johnny Sutton, was the prosecutor of this case? The drug smuggler has since repeated the offense, been caught, and is currently in jail serving a three year sentence. As individuals, we should be outraged! Please write letters to your senators and representatives to help these men gain their freedom so they can go home to their families. Helping to secure our borders was their job, but when they did their job, justice did not prevail. Go to www.hecubus.wordpress.com http://www.wnd.comfor more information on this unjust situation. Our border patrol is stretched thin across our southern boundary. Many are fighting the border fence for ecological reasons such as the Mexican Free-tail

Bat whose migration they say will be affected. Excuse me, they fly, they do not walk across the border. The mass influx of illegal immigrants into this country is an ecological and economic disaster. All citizens of the United States must keep informed to prevent this major problem. You must act in any capacity and every way you can to bring this issue to a screeching halt. Each one of us must take responsibility and get involved before it is too late. Remember one person can make a difference.

11. <u>Don't Be Bitter, Be Pro-Active.</u> In order to "Take Back America", each individual must learn to approach difficult circumstances with courage and conviction instead of fear and denial. When we approach our problems in this manner, we can alter the outcome, and therefore, make a difference. John Walsh is an individual whose son was abducted and murdered at six years old. In his grief he felt the resolve to do something more positive about these kinds of situations. He took a pro-active stance to help prevent other children from suffering this same fate. John Walsh and his wife established the Adam Walsh Resource Center and were instrumental in bringing <u>America's Most Wanted</u> to television in 1988, an investigative reporting show he hosts that has helped capture nearly 1000 criminals in the past 20 years. If John Walsh had chose to be bitter, there would possibly be nearly 1000 criminals still roaming the United States and justice would not have prevailed. To learn more about the life's work of John Walsh, visit <u>www.amw.com.</u> So the next time a problem arises and you want to throw your hands up in the air, remember what John Walsh did. Figure out what the problem is, find a new way to approach it and take a pro-active stance. What you are able to accomplish by being pro-active may not take away your heartache or problem, but your actions may very well make a difference in America or in someone else's life. Wouldn't you rather change someone's life for the better than remain bitter?

12. Commit To Family Integrity. Family integrity can mean so many things to many different people. Family is defined as a group of people connected by blood or marriage and sharing common ancestry; as we all know, in today's world, family has become a little more than that. Integrity can be defined as an uprightness of character, honesty; the condition, quality, or state of being complete or undivided. Isn't it comforting that the two definitions kind of go hand in hand? The family unit is the main building block of a Nation; the Nation can be no stronger than its weakest link. Look at the difference in our country since divorce has become common place and the integral family the exception. There seems to be no commitment among the young today, the wedding hasn't even been paid for before the divorce papers arrive. The young have been swayed by the lack of family integrity that has swept our nation in the past decades. What happened to the days when June and Ward Cleaver were considered role models instead of a punch line? Maybe this example seems a little extreme, but they did represent the prevalent family values of their age. One of the greatest love stories in politics is that of Harry and Bess Truman, probably the happiest couple to ever live in the White House. Harry Truman was born in Lamar, Missouri to a farm family as one of three children. He worked at various jobs before entering the Missouri National Guard. When the U.S. entered World War One in 1917, he served in France attaining the rank of Captain. In 1919, he married Bess Wallace who he had known since childhood. A relative was quoted as saying "there never was but one girl in the world" for him. Both of them attended the same school from 5th grade through the end of high school. They had one daughter Mary Margaret in 1924 who was the apple of their eyes. He entered politics in 1922 and ascended to the presidency of the United States when Franklin D. Roosevelt died. He guided our country through the end of World War Two. Through the struggles of living a public life, they stood together, inseparable as a family. All that knew him and his family knew what family integrity was. If memory serves me,

their daughter released their love letters after her mother's death. The letters show a family that was totally devoted to each other's happiness. Harry Truman's campaign slogan was "Give 'em Hell Harry", in all reality, I think Harry gave everyone a little glimpse of heaven. Today, he and his wife lie side by side at the Harry S. Truman Library in Independence, Missouri, together, forever. Go to www.trumanlibrary.org for more information on this extraordinary family. On a more personal level, the person I think of most when I think of family integrity will always be my mother. A woman who came from a broken home when divorce was considered unthinkable, but when she married, it was till death do us part (when Dad died, they had been married for 63 years). She worked her way through the morass that was her childhood to raise five children who always knew they were cared for and loved. We came home from school with the wonderful smell of a dinner slow-cooking on a stove and a mom there to greet us. We were regaled with tales of family and friends from her childhood. She knew how to make us laugh and sometimes cry with stories of the depression and how they coped with it. Mom was never boring. She raised us with a sense of loyalty to family and love of nature. After all, are these things not the best things in life? Perhaps my take on this subject is a bit old fashioned and vary from the norm, but those who dare to be different and yet instill these values in others, their children and strangers are a powerful influence in this country and can help us "Take Back America".

13. Be Involved In Your Community. The definition of community is a social group of any size whose members reside in a specific locality, share Government, and often have a common cultural and historical heritage. Who do we love and like to spend time with? What actions are we willing to take to help others? Community really defines these questions and more. In the chapter devoted to this topic we discuss various ways each person can become involved ranging from the smallest of actions to the larger activities. An individual that comes to

mind that has taken the extra step in community involvement is Rev. Larry Rice. He is currently the director of a center to help people in need. The New Life Evangelistic Center in St. Louis, Missouri started out in a small church close to Lafayette Park back in the sixties. Rev. Rice's motivation is to follow what the Bible teaches. As a man of God, doing the work he believes in, he has ran into opposition. Many of man's great endeavors to change the way the system operates often run into those who wish to squash its efforts. Believe it or not, the city is actually trying to evict him from his downtown location. His interest in the environment and renewable energy sets him apart from others. Rev. Rice has fought to keep people from losing power to their homes, and because of this, solar power caught his interest as it is free. Recently, he purchased a house on the south side of St. Louis, and is now working on opening a training center which would enable homeless people to learn how to find employment in the solar power field. The project has provoked people in the neighborhood to speak out against the completion of his training center. The people of our nation need to remember our homeless problem is not going to disappear if we ignore it. I give thanks and appreciation to the Rev. Larry Rice for staying the course and fighting the good fight. To learn more information on Rev. Larry Rice and his center go to www.associatedcontent.com. Participating in our community as individuals every day can have a big impact. Working at food pantries or meals on wheels, visiting the elderly or sick, being a Big Brother or a Big Sister, or volunteering at a humane society are only a few of the things we can do. The first thing you must do is make up your mind you are going to get involved and then do it! We all can make a difference in our community; all we ask is that you try. Pulling together as a group, standing side by side as individuals, will again make America the strongest Nation in the World and a place we are proud to live and call home.

14. Commit To Personal Financial Security. You may ask yourself how my personal finance affects the rest of our country. Have you watched the news or read a newspaper lately? The sub-prime mortgage meltdown may be the best example of financial irresponsibility to ever hit the news. The people in our country suddenly decided they could afford houses that were in all reality, completely out of their price range. With creative (but unethical) financing, they were able to purchase homes for which they could never pay. The ripple effect of this fiasco has sent panic throughout the investment banking system. We have many good financial advisors available in our nation. One who is well-known is Suze Orman. She is called a force in the world of personal finance and "a one-woman financial advice powerhouse" by USA Today. Her lectures and seminars draw large crowds of people wanting to find ways to maximize their income through wise investing and savings. The books she writes are national best sellers, as her strategies help the "financially challenged" find a way to regain control of their money. For more information on this woman wonder of the financial counseling scene, go to www.suzeorman.com. There are many small success stories in this country; my Great Aunt Lorraine was one of them. Born dirt poor in rural Missouri, her mother died shortly after her birth. She married very young and had six children. At the same time, she put herself through school by working at the small arms plant in St. Louis, Missouri. She saved her salary, and when she was able, opened the most successful dress shop in her hometown. She did not stop there, when she and her husband retired, they joined the Peace Corps and did a two-year stint in Jamaica where she taught sewing and Uncle Moe taught electrical work. On returning to the United States, they joined Vista (Domestic Peace Corps), to teach these same skills to migrants in Texas. Unfortunately her husband suffered a stroke before they could complete this mission. She brought him home and cared for him until his death. Imagine me and my best cartoon voice saying "What a woman". My hat is off to you Lorraine; you made

a difference in so many lives. Hard work and good money strategies allowed this woman to pursue her dreams and live life to its fullest. If all Americans, as individuals, work hard, save money, and use good money strategies, each one of us can realize the same dream. After all, isn't life for living?

15. Have Faith And Practice What You Preach. Practicing what you preach and having faith are easy words to say, but more difficult to master. We all seem willing to voice our principles and convictions without hesitation. Following through with these beliefs is a true work in progress. The word preach is often misconstrued because most people relate it to a lecture or sermon. Practicing what you preach is a way of living by example. Strong convictions about family, religion, work ethic, and politics are principles you need to incorporate into your everyday life. It is unfair to criticize others when we are not making a concerted effort to live up to our own principles. Faith is also associated with religion, but it signifies more than that. Faith is trust, loyalty, confidence, and reliance. If we were honest with ourselves, many Americans have lost track of the core beliefs which made our country whole and function more smoothly. We are not referring to the obligations we have to close friends and family, we are talking about our American brothers and sisters. In today's day and age, it is difficult to trust anyone. Confidence in each other has become a thing of the past, so we tend to do things ourselves without wanting to rely on each other for help or support. In our hearts, we absolutely know that we have lost something precious. We need to regain this lost ground to strengthen our nation. Martin Luther King was a pivotal leader of his time. King practiced what he preached and had enough faith for those around him full of apprehension. He was a Baptist minister and became a civil rights activist early in his career. Perhaps the most famous event in his life came during the march on Washington in 1963 where he gave his famous "I Have A Dream" speech, a speech that inspired the people of this country to make a difference. The work of this one

individual actually inspired a President to write new civil rights legislation and make it a reality. King was the youngest recipient of the Nobel Peace Prize for his efforts to end segregation and racial discrimination through non-violent means. Go to www.nobelprize.org for more information on some more amazing people. Today, King is a legend for his individual efforts. There are many individuals who make a difference, one such person is Cindy Sheehan who became a war activist when her son was killed in the Iraq War. Her demonstrations against the war made her a global figure in the news. Cindy Sheehan had a cause, to end the war in Iraq. She attracted many followers, and although the war continues, she made many people aware of the horrors of this unnecessary war. She stood up for her beliefs and made a difference. If you "Have Faith And Practice What You Preach", you too, can make a difference because America needs more honest citizens to speak up and right the wrongs.

16. Have A Healthy Mind And Body. In order to keep health care from rising at its current astronomical rate, we all need to take responsibility for our health. The day of the two-donut, two cups of coffee breakfast should be a thing of the past. We all know how damaging these things are to our health. Finding a healthier way to eat can be the first step toward better health. You are what you eat, so if your current diet consists largely of junk food, you are doing yourself no favor. Fresh vegetables and complex carbohydrates should make up the bulk of your diet. When your body is in top condition and you exercise regularly, you are more likely to have good mental health also. Try to maintain recommended weight for your height. Your mental health and the health of your body are closely associated; keep one healthy, the other may follow. A leader in the field of preventative medicine is Dr. Sanjay Gupta who encourages personal responsibility for your health. Dr. Gupta is CNN's Chief Medical Correspondent and as such, addresses the major health concerns of our country. As a practicing neurosurgeon, his credentials are spotless.

He stays up-to-date in many other areas of medicine. When you watch CNN, you will find he gives us free lessons in health and tries to inspire all of us to take responsibility for our own health. His activities in pollution and the degrading of the atmosphere have also kept him in the forefront of the news. The documentary Planet In Peril was done by Dr. Gupta, Jeff Corwin, and Anderson Cooper, making us all aware of the health problems connected with pollution and global warming. Go to www.CNN.com and search for Dr. Sanjay Gupta for more information on how you can become a responsible healthy citizen. Along the same lines, there is a woman making a big difference too many people. Her name is Valerie Sobel. When her son, Andre, was diagnosed with brain cancer, she thought she was perhaps the unluckiest soul on earth until she met other patients and parents in the same cancer ward at the hospital. Many were single parents and had to make choices between house payments, work, or being with their children. It was a very sobering situation for her. Andre died in 1995 at age 19 and her grieving husband committed suicide the following year. Instead of staying home and feeling sorry for herself, she founded the Andre Sobel River of Life Foundation. They give money to single care-givers of seriously ill children at twelve U.S. hospitals. The program has now given over $4 million dollars (Readers Digest, May 2008, Pg. 115). Not many of you can make the kind of difference Dr. Gupta makes, but by taking responsibility for your own mind and body, you can make a difference. Only when we achieve a healthy mind and a healthy body can we have the energy and the stamina to fight the fight to "Take Back America".

17. Have Common Courtesy, Use Common Sense. Common sense and common courtesy have different meanings to a lot of us. Common sense can refer to an awareness or sound practical judgment that most people agree is proper. Unfortunately, everyone has a very different take on those words. Common courtesy implies a respectful or considerate act or an act of civility, respect or possibly reverence. As individuals, each of

us have our own opinions, so basically those interpretations effect us differently. I am going to give you two very different examples of how these meanings have been applied by outstanding citizens. A name you have heard many times is Todd Beamer, a passenger on Flight 93 on September 11, 2001, the day our country was attacked by cowardly terrorists. Beamer and several other passengers were instrumental in fighting back and bringing the hijacked plane to the ground. His efforts, along with the other passengers, were a judgment call that had the safety of our nation in mind. When they learned of the attacks on our country, they chose to get involved by using common courtesy and common sense for the benefit of others, ultimately costing them their lives. Common courtesy was used by having respect and reverence for the safety of their country, and common sense was used by deciding to crash the plane instead of letting the hijackers fly it into another U.S. landmark and thus saving hundreds of lives. They are heroes in my opinion and their sacrifice is a true example of uncommon valor and demonstrates that one person can make a difference. As a Nation, we are forever in their debt. Thank you to Todd Beamer, the passengers, and crew of Flight 93 for sacrificing your life for our country. Go to http://warbirdforum.com/beamer.htm for more information on this man who made a difference. The second example is on a very different scale. Amy Vanderbilt was an author on etiquette. Etiquette is, in general, thought to be a part of decorum and a code that governs the expectation of social behavior. She published a best seller titled Amy Vanderbilt's Complete Book Of Etiquette in 1952, and it is still in circulation today. It has since been updated, but its popularity is still considered a standard of etiquette writing. She has written novels and articles for many magazines. You can see how different these examples are, but both apply to "Have Common Courtesy and Use Common Sense". The lesson we can all learn from these individuals is to think before we speak or act. Americans need to have more regard for each other in these areas. It is something each of us can work on to make life better for those around us. So let's rally together and start treating others the way we want to be treated. The benefits will affect us all, along with our country. Remember, you reap what you sew.

18. Wake UP! Reduce, Reuse, Recycle. With so many ways to improve our country and our world, just saying the words reduce, reuse, and recycle seems too small. Believe me, it is not a small thing at all. It is not just a matter of landfill space, or taking the litter off our highways and byways. It is a matter of cleaner air, water, and atmosphere; it is a thing as big as the Earth. Face it folks, we are many years away from being able to move to another planet which makes taking care of Mother Earth a matter of the utmost importance. If you are filling a bag of trash everyday that is going to the landfill, wake up and do your part in saving our world for the coming generations. There are not too many things in our life that are more important. A person who is trying to make a big difference in how we treat our world is Jeff Corwin. Jeff Corwin has traveled the world trying to save Mother Earth from mankind, and as a well-known biologist and herpetologist, he creates documentaries for TV that show the problems man has created for the animals that share our space. He points out the problems caused by careless disposal of plastic and pleads with us to do better. His goal is to make life on earth better for all of us. For more information on Jeff Corwin, go to www.jeffcorwin.com. A young college student in New York City by the name Avery Hairston saw an area in which he could help. He got some friends together and founded a group called Re-light New York. The idea of his group was to replace incandescent light bulbs with compact florescent bulbs for the poor in New York City because they use less power and last longer. So far his group has replaced 21,000 light bulbs in New York. This young man raises funds from individuals and some corporations, but his group does all of the work. Here we have two individuals, one famous and one not, but they both make a big difference and perhaps will

keep Mother Earth livable. How can you make a difference when you reduce, reuse, and recycle? When you step up to the plate and get involved, as one of our famous cartoon characters says, "Can we fix it? Yes, we can!". As individuals, we are responsible for our part in saving the planet.

19. Be Aware Of How You Affect Global Warming. All over the world, there are still many doubting that doubt this so called theory of global warming. How anyone can really question what is going on all over the world really shocks me. I often wonder what it will take to convince people this is real. And do I really want to be here for that moment of truth? I imagine it will take some really startling activity to convince these folks this is not hocus pocus. Floods, hurricanes, volcanoes, tornadoes, earthquakes, and famine really ought to be making you doubt that this is a far out tale. Many of you will argue that these patterns of destructive weather have occurred since the creation of Earth. To those of you with this opinion, I want to ask you some questions. Through all the bizarre weather patterns that the Earth has endured, were there billions cars driving over millions of miles of paved highways? Were there so many factories you couldn't count them spewing pollution into the air we breathe? Were there smog alerts because of this pollution? Were trees being slaughtered by the millions (trees that help us breath)? Were natural habitats being destroyed for the sake of the all mighty dollar? Were resources being used faster than we could possibly replace them? Were our land and oceans being drilled for oil 24/7? We do have an entire chapter on this topic and I would challenge you to read it, look up some of the web-sites, do some checking on your own, and make an informed decision whether you feel this is really happening. Obviously I am a firm believer. However, we all are entitled to our own opinion as Americans. We just need to make sure it is an informed opinion. One person that made the difference on this subjects of course Al Gore, former Vice-President of the United States and past future President. He was determined to prove that Global Warming

is a reality. And he did. If you haven't seen the movie An Inconvenient Truth, please find it and watch it. Honestly, it is a very enjoyable documentary that captures your attention with the style he uses. He won the Nobel Peace Prize and two Academy Awards for his determination in bringing this problem to the front of everyone's conscience. Thank you, Mr. Gore, for taking so much time to try to save our planet. For more information about Al Gore and his work on global warming go to www.algore.com. Many people in our society today make a difference individually by turning off their TV's when not in the room, shutting the water off when they brush their teeth, turning down the thermostat, walking or car pooling instead of driving, using energy-efficient light bulbs, or participating in a carbon footprint program that offsets our individual pollution output (go to www.fightglobalwarming.com for a list of ways you can do this). It's simple; every one of us has a responsibility to participate in saving our planet.

20. Pass Your Enthusiasm Along. Have you ever been so excited about something you couldn't wait to tell someone your news? I believe everyone has felt this enthusiasm at least once in their life. When an idea is so good that you get this great feeling, don't keep it to yourself, tell everyone. You may be the one to start a powerful movement. With so many causes that need attention from people like you, we need every individual to take part in making our United States a great place to live. If you are an individual who has the strength to start a movement to "Take Back America", get many involved so that there is nothing we can't do? Think about it! Former President Bill Clinton is one of the best people in this country to generate enthusiasm. As a child from Arkansas he had the opportunity to meet John F Kennedy, it was a life altering experience. Early in his life he already knew what he wanted to do, he was going to make a difference. His wife Hillary, who he met in college, shared in the belief that they could make a difference. Shortly after their marriage, Bill Clinton became the youngest Governor in the United States. They

never looked back. Bill became the third youngest President of the United States in1993. He served for eight years and kept the Nation financially stable during his presidency. When he left office, he established the William J. Clinton Foundation and many other initiatives. The mission of his foundation is to "strengthen the capacity of people throughout the world to meet the challenges of global independence". In 2004, Bill Clinton released his autobiography My Life. Those of us who have read his book grew to know him as a warm and caring person. While reading his book, you feel as if he is in the room telling you his life story; his writing style is great. His second book since leaving office is titled Giving How Each Of Us Can Change The World, a look at his philosophy of charitable work. As you read this book, you learn of his enthusiasm on getting everyone on the planet involved in creating a better world for all. He truly believes that each individual can make a huge difference. In the book, you will see examples of companies and individuals that have made a difference in the lives of many. As you read about these individual efforts, you may find areas in which you can participate. Go to www.clintonfoundation.org/Giving to find out what his foundation is doing to make a difference. Someone not so famous that has made a difference is Hal Colston who founded the Good News Garage twelve years ago. In the years since he founded his program, he has provided three thousand vehicles to the needy in New Hampshire, Massachusetts, Connecticut, and Vermont. His thoughts are that if you have a job and you can't get there, you won't have a job long. So by taking donated cars and rebuilding them, he has made a difference and kept 83% his recipients working. Good job Hal! Whether your contribution is enormous or tiny or somewhere in between, each person on the face of the earth can change someone's life for the better. Being involved may be more difficult than standing back and doing nothing, but it's much more productive. Let's all pass our enthusiasm on to let others "Realize One Person Can Make A Difference" so that we can "Take Back America".

As you go through the rest of this book, you will probably notice that the first chapter is the most detailed and the longest. The authors of this book wanted to elaborate here to give you a glimpse of the material to be found in the rest of the book. We hopefully will grab your attention right off the bat, and inspire you to read on although we do not expect everyone to agree with the premise of this work, that would be impossible. The intent in writing this book is to motivate all of our readers to make it their personal ambition to join in our cause to "Take Back America". This is not a structured organization, this is just four average women who want to make a difference in the direction our country is headed. As Americans, we must all agree that change is necessary; we include ourselves along with all like-minded people. Ours is not a political statement as much as an appeal to all Americans to return to better values and unite our Nation to help the American Dream return. Our children and our children's children depend on us to make the future of the United States a bright one in which they can live full and happy lives. Try a few of our ideas and see if you can incorporate them into your life and inspire others to do the same. As citizens of this great land, we depend on each other to keep our nation great; perhaps our ideas will help us all achieve these goals. Here is a challenging question, Are you ready to help "Take Back America" one person at a time?

Chapter 2

Educate Yourself and Your Family

"A nation of well informed men who have been taught to know and prize the rights that God has given them cannot be enslaved. It is in the region of ignorance that tyranny begins."
Benjamin Franklin (1706-1790)

Education is a never ending process. We tend to think about it with our children, but it continues into adulthood as well. In many of our jobs, we have requirements for continuing education. We have to be certified for this or that particular reason. Every thing we learn allows us to arm ourselves with skills that cannot be taken from us. We want to make ourselves better so that we are indispensable at work. Nowadays, jobs are difficult to find without an education. Our children will have a difficult time finding a good job with a future of growth and a good benefit package without a good education. As parents, it is only natural to want to give our children every opportunity which includes helping them develop skills for a more secure future in the ever changing job market. One of the best ways to do that is to give them confidence, guidance, directions, and encourage them to pursue a line of education that can meet their needs and make them happy. The more we educate ourselves and our young, the stronger our nation will be. I want to see a stronger United States for myself, my children, and my grandchildren; I am sure you want the same thing.

1. <u>Be positive.</u> Be a positive parent and in turn you will have a more positive child. It is not easy in our demanding lives to remain positive. Let's face it, it is almost impossible to do 100% of the time. Again, what we need to aim for is the action

of trying. Our children will also recognize our efforts. When something goes wrong, and we know it will, our actions reflect who we are and form a picture in our children's mind on how they should react. I have not always been the best example of this, but I catch myself and try to change it. I think it's acceptable to explain to our children that we may not have handled a situation well and tell them how we could have approached it differently. We, as parents, aren't going to be perfect, nor should we expect ourselves to be. Educating our children on how a positive outlook will impact their lives in every way is the key to all future generations. Is the glass half empty or half full? In my world, it is now half full.

2. Play an active roll in your children's education. Regardless of where our children go to school, public or private, we cannot put all the burden of their education on the teachers and staff. We should play an active roll in what they are studying, what they are excelling in, and what they are struggling to learn. As Frank Smith, a published author on education, said, "It is infinitely more useful for a child to hear a story by a person than by computer. Because the greatest part of the learning experience lies not in the particular words of the story but in the involvement in the individual reading it." A teacher has so many students that it is difficult for any one student to get the personal attention he or she may need. As parents, we could help aide their education with some one-on-one time at home; but don't be too quick to provide the answers to their questions, teach them to research it on their own. There are some issues that the school system does not address and yet other issues that need further guidance. We need to teach our children the things schools do not, this can vary greatly depending on the curriculum your child has. Play an active role. If you feel an area is not being covered, take it upon yourself to fill in that gap with subjects such as ethics, morals, civics, or values. Apply these issues to the core curriculum they study daily. Let us arm our children with

information and choices that they will need to become well-rounded individuals to carry them into productive future.

3. Manage your time. Do many of you find your child does not make good use of their time? As an adult, I sometimes struggle with this myself. However, it is a skill that will benefit them now, and always. It will make them more responsible as well. Go to www.mindtools.com for information on some time management techniques. Here are some suggestions to help manage your time. Take a few minutes to prepare for the next day because it will save you time and make you more focused; make a plan and make it happen. Start your day a little earlier so you won't be rushed; this allows for any last minute changes. Take action on the things you have been putting off such as a report or chore, and do it. Use technology only when it saves you time or when it produces a positive result. Conquer your clutter, having to clean areas so you can work is a waste of time; it also makes your job more stressful. Eliminate distractions by turning off the radio or TV; this will help you stay focused, your work will be better and you will finish it faster. Do something when it is asked of you, don't put if off. Know yourself; you know what time of day you are most effective. When you plan the next day's activities, keep your peak times in mind. Finally, try to make it enjoyable. It will go faster and produce better work if you have a good attitude about it. Remember the wise and humorous words of Mark Twain, "The secret of getting ahead is getting started. The secret of getting started is breaking your complex overwhelming tasks into small manageable tasks, and then starting on the first one."

4. Take advantage of educational resources. The library is a great place to spend time as a family, do homework, or nurture the imagination. Most libraries offer many programs for a number of ages as well as adults. Today, we have some excellent resources available to us today. There are educational shows, movies such as An Inconvenient Truth, newspapers, magazines, and other forms of media that help keep us

current. The internet is not just for fun. There is a wealth of information available. We, as well as our children, need to be taught to use these resources. Relying on our educators or only watching the news is like half-way educating yourself. Take the next step, get involved, and educate yourself by checking out these easily accessible resources. Knowledge is power, so let's challenge ourselves to become more powerful.

5. Put Civics back in school. Civics is defined as the branch of political science dealing with civic affairs and the duties and rights of citizenship. So you really have to ask yourself why this is an endangered subject. The lack of knowledge Americans display on the subject and our own history is not a matter of debate. It has been established in survey after survey. Richard Dreyfuss, the well-known actor has made putting Civics back in school his crusade. Dreyfuss is teaching Civics as a college professor; believe me, it is not because this award-winning actor needs the money. Let's all give praise to this man for his crusade in helping "Take Back America", because we all need to know what it means to be an American in order to appreciate this precious gift. He says, "Our children are not learning about current events and how the government works. They need to be informed on what it means to maintain the system while sharing political space." Go to www.truthout.org for more information on his work in Civics. It is essential for our children to be taught this from an early age in order to establish their identity as an American citizen and a citizen that participates in government issues. Civics will also help our young, who are the future of our country, learn the vital liberties that make Americans so proud. There is nothing more important to our country's future than learning what has made us American and what we must do to maintain a democracy in America.

6. Question the difference in salaries between administrators and teachers. This is really quite simple, attend school board meetings and insist on equal pay. Gather as many parents as you can to attend with you. If you can get enough people,

they will have to meet the demands of the public. Remember that teachers are more responsible for shaping the lives of our children than the administrators. Why do they get paid more? Very few parents are acquainted with the names and responsibilities of school administrators. We elect the school board and they are responsible for hiring or appointing the administrators. Be aware of who we elect to run our schools because their decisions effect our children. As taxpayers we should demand more equal pay between administrators and teachers so that our children have a chance to be better educated. Quality teachers continue their education throughout their career. Unfortunately they have to pay for many of their classroom supplies (an issue that is completely unacceptable since they earn less than the administrators of the school who are responsible for balancing the budget which includes making sure the students have the supplies they need). They deserve a salary equal to their education and commitment because true commitment can only be attained by these teachers if they are paid a living wage. In order to show our appreciation to these fine teachers, we must persuade our school boards that merit raises are a better way to maintain a higher quality teacher. These dedicated teachers influence our children every day; think about all the stories you have heard of a public figure giving credit for their success to one of their childhood teachers that inspired them. Wouldn't you love for your child to remember his teachers in this capacity?

7. Be concerned about our educational reputation. Ignorance is not bliss. I'm sure everyone has seen Jay Leno or other shows that ask everyday people off the street questions which should be easily answered. Most answers to some of those questions make us all laugh which is their point. I've laughed as much as anybody. Truth of the matter, it really isn't funny because our nation has become lazy regarding education. While on a trip to New York City in 2007, my cousin and I took a guided tour of Central Park. We chose a two-seated bicycle carriage

tour with a guide that impressed us with his knowledge of the park which he shared with us while he peddled the bike. The tour was beautiful, interesting, and very informative. While talking with our guide, we found out he was from another country going to school here. He knew so much more about the park and the city than I ever dreamed of knowing. I realize he is trained to know these things, but it got me thinking that I didn't even know half that much about my own home area. We need to make sure we know more about our own surroundings so that we can pass this onto our children. As adults, we need to refresh our memories, because if Jay ever stops me on the street, I want to impress him and my children with my knowledge and education instead of being laughed at by millions. Hopefully I will know that France is not a neighbor of Australia or know the picture he is showing me is the President of the United States. If you are given your 15 seconds of fame, how do you want to be remembered?

8. Have game nights. Trivial Pursuit, Life, Monopoly, Scrabble, Yahtzee, Risk and Operation are some of the games that can be educational for you and your family. Educational games come in all shapes, sizes, and age levels. Not only will having a game night educate, but it will build comradery with your family that will create long-lasting memories. Some of these games can only take 15 minutes to an hour; they could easily fit into an evening at home. So instead of turning on the repeat sitcoms you have seen before, pop some popcorn, grab some juice, and create some memories with your family that can be an education in the process. Take the opportunity while they are young because the years slip by so quickly. If you're lucky, this habit will lead into a tradition as they transition into adulthood (many families like poker nights–poker is educational too). And don't forget about political games, they educate on the processes of our government (Risk, Landslide, and Strategy are just a few). Puzzles are a great way to spend time together and teach manual dexterity to the young and preserve it for the old. Remember, the more fun you make

education, the more likely they are to accept it willingly. Strong families are the key to "Take Back America".

9. Get involved in school. I know how hard it is to take the time to do it all, but some things are worth fitting into your schedule. While your children are in school, get involved in fund raisers, the parent teacher associations, room mothers or fathers, and participate in special events; this teaches your children that these values are important. Although your children act like it doesn't matter to them, it does!! Around their buddies they are too cool to show their appreciation, but it is something they will remember forever. As they get older, they will most certainly appreciate your efforts and involvement which will more than likely make them an involved parent. And you never know, you may enjoy the experience and find a hidden talent you didn't know you possessed. Get involved and be a valuable asset to our education system.

10. Appreciate hard-working teachers. It is really important to have a good relationship with your children's teachers. If your child is struggling with issues, it will be resolved easier if you have a good working relationship with the instructor. Teachers give a lot of their free time to enable their students to get extra help and have to get into their own pocketbooks for classroom supplies. These are traits that are very commendable and deserve appreciation. If I were a teacher in the school system at this time, I would feel undervalued. We as parents need to participate more to lighten their load. An apple for your teacher may seem old fashioned, but a token to show your appreciation is definitely in order. A greeting card for the holidays may not seem like much, but by adding a personal note inside you can make this teacher's day brighter. If you develop a good working relationship with your child's teacher, it can be a win-win situation. Your child will benefit from the cooperation, and the teacher will find their job easier (which we should all want to do). All of our efforts are an investment in our children's future.

11. Know your children's interests. Have you ever noticed that we tend to expect our children to be interested in the same things we were as kids? This is a common practice among parents. So many times we learn this may not be the case. Just because you played basketball in high school, doesn't mean your children will want to do the same. Remember that there are so many more choices available to our children today than when we were growing up. A few examples that come to mind are Ribbon dancing (they have this in the Olympics now), hip hop dancing, kick boxing, or skateboarding to name a few. The truth is that we need to encourage our children's to pursue their individual interests. Do not push them into things they have no desire to do. We had our time and cannot keep living it through our kids. Let them have their time to explore to find what they really like. Just keep in mind to always teach them to finish what they start. Enrolling in various classes and quitting without really giving it an effort, is not teaching our children the right message. Encourage your children to research what classes they want to take, and before paying, make sure they really do want to take classes. When they find what they like to do, be a loyal supporter of it, and give them the encouragement they need to pursue it. Some of these interests could be life-long hobbies or lead them into a more interesting career. Don't we all want our children to have a career they love? When you are interested in what you do, it is fun, not work.

12. Learn another language. Our nation has reached a point where it has become necessary to learn other languages. Although we believe English should be spoken in America, the job market requires the knowledge of other languages. I know this personally because I have filled out job applications and read ads in the classified sections looking for bilingual applicants. Other languages are taught in school; many other programs are available for all age groups. One of the more popular language skill programs is Rosetta Stone. You can go to www.rosettastone.com to get more information on this

program. Taking advantage of these programs can make you more valuable as an employee. Incorporating it into our children's education is necessary to help them get a head start in a world that has become so global. It is something all adults should strongly consider because you are never too old to learn a new language. Let's face it, the job market is tough; anything we do to help ourselves or our children will only benefit us all in the long run.

13. Home school the children who cannot thrive in regular school environments. Home schooling your child was not a very popular idea for awhile. People thought this was a strange way to educate your child...not anymore. This method of education has taken off and is growing by leaps and bounds. Associations have been founded for home schools by areas or counties. Many activities are available such as team sports, science fairs, spelling bees, choir, meetings for college prep that include both parents and students, and so much more. I was amazed to find so many resources were available. Support from other parents is easily found as well. These associations have minimal fees and the cost of teaching your child at home is cheaper than sending them to a public school. In my case, my daughter was having health issues so we decided to home school her for this reason. It doesn't take a rocket scientist to figure out that germs get passed back and forth from student to student. Unfortunately, students get sent to school with illnesses instead of being kept home until they are no longer contagious. Curriculum for home schooling is readily available. Anyone interested in teaching at home should contact the administrative office of the local school district; they should be able to give you the contacts you need to get started. If you can get the names of other parents who home school, their experience with different curriculums could be a wealth of information for you. In my experience, home school parents are always willing to share their knowledge, and I have felt welcomed by them. Since we live in uncertain times, this could be something you may want to consider. As for

my opinion of home schooling, I would say it has been a very rewarding experience. I think we are lucky to have so many choices on how to participate in our children's education.

14. Teach your children the value of money. When I left home, I had very little knowledge on how the real world worked and the money that was required to live on my own. It was quite overwhelming. In hind sight I should have been better prepared. Sheltering our children from some of the ugliness of the world has played a roll in setting young adults adrift in this crazy world. We are over protecting our children. Our young ones will become adults much sooner than we realize. Preparing them for adulthood should start early in their education. The values we teach them will stick with them as they mature. The value of a dollar doesn't mean much to our children (toddler to teenager). They tend to think we, as parents, are made of money, and they basically expect to be provided for in every way. This is not how it was dealt with years ago. Allowance should not be given, it should be earned. For extras that children invariably want, they should be taught to save up, and purchase these items themselves. It is a much needed lesson to prepare them for what lies ahead. We tend to make it too easy for our children. If we do not teach our children how to earn and handle their money, it will come back to haunt us in the end. Go to www.extension.umn.edu for more information on how to teach your child money habits for life. Teaching our children to realize the value of money and how to budget is an important step that could help us "Take Back America". After all, they are in charge of America's future.

15. Discuss politics and the election process at home. Imagine how our world could change if we began discussing politics at home with our children once they are old enough to read the newspaper or watch the news. It could make a difference in our nation's future. By being instructed on politics and how the election process works early in life, as adults, this could affect who gets elected to office, what bills are passed, how

foreign affairs are handled, and economics, etc. Politics are a tough topic; but if you talk with your child and break it up into small age-appropriate topics, it would make it more enjoyable to learn. Make up your own game on how the election process works. This may sound challenging, but an election process could be as basic as voting on the family vacation that year or campaigning to change something around the house. Make your child convince you of their argument. They are capable of doing the research and learning these skills is an absolute must. Go to www.professorhouse.com for more information on educating your children on politics. I was recently talking to many individuals in their early twenties, and it shocked me how little they knew about politics or had the desire to know. I also talked with a couple of people (I wish that number was greater) around the same age that really impressed me with their understanding of politics and current events. Our little boys and girls are going to make decisions for our country one day. Won't you be proud that you gave them the information they need to be a great success and a responsible voter?

16. Teach social skills. Social skills are a wide range of abilities. These skills are not automatic; you are taught them and learn them by example. Being patient, respectful, greeting others, taking turns, being a friend, being a good listener, helping others, being willing to try a new task, accepting criticism, and accepting differences are only a few of these skills. They need to be taught at home and in school at all ages beginning as early as possible. These concepts are not rocket science, but they are what give us the ability to get along with our fellow man and feel good about ourselves. Without these skills, communicating and interacting with one another wouldn't be easy or enjoyable. Social skills are very important in our society. I encourage you to get on-line and Google social skills or get a book on the topic. We could dedicate an entire chapter to this subject. The bottom line is the more social skills we have, the more confident we will be. They help us in every aspect of our lives, at work and play, in our personal

relationships, and so much more. Take the time, know these skills, and use them so others can learn from your example. These skills make people stand out and be noticed. Wouldn't it be great to have Americans believing in Americans? Wow..... how powerful this could be!

17. Do not procrastinate. Procrastination becomes a chain reaction. To understand the complete meaning of procrastination, go to www.psychologytoday.com. Many times I have put something off of importance that I was dreading, only to worry and feel guilty about my procrastination. If I had just done it to begin with, I wouldn't have wasted all that time worrying about it. You know what I am talking about!? It is a bad feeling that usually is accompanied by thoughts of negativity towards yourself for your failure. I can't suddenly fix all my bad habits at once, but I am certainly making an effort to do things when they need to be done. I'm not alone, am I? Procrastination has reached epidemic proportions in the last century. When you accomplish your tasks in a timely manner, you'll notice it actually feels good to get those things off your mind. It also may give you a feeling of empowerment; control if you will. Just start selecting a task a day, three or four a week, whatever feels comfortable, and before long you'll be on top of things. It also gives those around you, family, friends, and co-workers, confidence that you'll be responsible enough to do the things they ask of you. Only good things can happen with this change. Try it, consistency is the best policy.

18. Volunteer. How many people in our great nation have made the New Year's resolution to volunteer more? Not nearly enough. The great thing is it doesn't have to be a new year to begin volunteering. There are urgent needs for volunteers all year long. Some are not as urgent as others; they just need some kind of consistent help. What needs pop into your head? Nursing homes, Big Brothers, Big Sisters, churches, schools– the list is endless. With a few calls and a little research, you can find a cause that fits your views, and work it into your schedule. Think of the example you will set for your children.

You are showing them to think beyond themselves and for others. You are also teaching them a responsibility, making them better individuals, and ultimately better adults. When your actions are noticed by friends, other family members, or co-workers, you will also inspire others to donate their time. I only named a few options, and I challenge you to look for more. Find out what fits your lifestyle and let volunteering be a wonderful adventure you enjoy as a family or as an individual. If donating time is not an option, please donate money to organizations (too many to name) that desperately need all the help they can get. Go to www.kidshealth.org for more information on how to get started. Spreading the news about such organizations is another wonderful way to volunteer, not much time involved, but the results could be priceless.

19. Eat together as family. Some studies have found while a child is growing up sharing meals with their family, it improves their eating habits and they tend to eat more vegetables and fruits. By eating at home with family, you have the choice to cook with healthier ingredients. These are great reasons to eat as a family, but there are more benefits than just a healthy diet. Meal time has become one way of keeping up with each other's activities. It strengthens family ties and is a great way to pass on family cultural traditions. It also teaches our children how to sit down at a table and use their manners. We have all seen children at a restaurant that simply don't know how to behave at dinner tables. Maybe they have never sat down and ate as a family at home. Since we are so busy, it may seem like skipping a family dinner would be easier, but don't sacrifice this time with your family. Make it a tradition. Set a time for dinner and make everyone participate. If your schedule is crazy, you may need to vary this time from day to day. Do whatever it takes to keep it going. This is not simply just a meal. Pulling together as a family at home can help "Take Back America" one family at a time.

20. Teach our children to be stylish not fashionable. We encourage everyone to be their own person and create your own style. While these are all true statements and we should stick by them, we could also say that a little modesty goes a long way. You should not be judged for trying to be cool or following the latest fads. However, knowing the difference between what is stylish and what is tacky is very important. Just because one of our young female rock stars is wearing a see-through blouse with no undergarment doesn't mean we should all allow our children to dress that way or even think it's cool. We have to speak out against this type of trend that influences our children around the globe. Many schools have gone to uniforms or dress standards to eliminate the distraction caused by improper or overly provocative clothing. Think about it, we could improve our education system simply by teaching our children what style is.

Basically, our lives are centered around the education of our young. The more we know, the better equipped we are to handle ourselves. Our education begins when we are infants, and hopefully, it never ends. Before a baby can speak they learn that crying gets attention (some adults still practice this method). I have said it before, and I still firmly believe, whatever we can do to make ourselves stronger as a community, family, or as individuals will continue to make our nation stronger. Education allows us to get better paying jobs, thus strengthening our nation's employment. Remember that the skills you learn and any specialized training is valuable, and nobody can take away your knowledge.

Chapter 3

Be a Responsible Voter

"We the People of the United States, in Order to form a more perfect Union, establish Justice, domestic Tranquility, provide for the common defense, promote the general Welfare, and secure the Blessings of Liberty to ourselves and our Posterity, do ordain and establish this Constitution for the United States of America."

Preamble to the Constitution
Written by Thomas Jefferson (1743-1826)

"We the People" is a phrase every one in this country needs to remember, it has confirmed many times that many voices come from one voice and all those voices make a difference. We also have to be responsible educated voters. It is "We the People" who voted these clowns into office that have put our country in a terrible mess. If you have never voted, shame on you!!! Voting is a responsibility to yourself, your family, and your fellow Americans. If you choose not to vote, don't complain because you have lost that right. I challenge all Americans to "Be A Responsible Voter". For all responsible voters, thank you so much for participating in our democratic system, and please convince others to do the same so that we can "Take Back America".

1. Educate yourself politically. The information to help you make an informed decision and help you become a responsible voter is all around you. Newspapers, internet, and the library are just a few of the resources available to you. You can go to www.ontheissues.org for the facts on political candidates; this is but one of many web-sites to check out. With all the resources available today, there is no excuse for making an

uninformed decision. Before you enter the booth to vote, make sure you have reviewed the records of those running in the election. An informed vote is another step to "Take Back America".

2. Use the Congressional Record. If you own a computer, the Congressional Record can be easily found online at www.gpoaccess.gov. Every vote made, skipped, or proposed by every one of your lawmakers is there for you to see. Use this resource wisely. If you do not own a computer, use one at a library or you can request the Congressional Record be sent to your home as a hard copy. You will not find a more valuable resource for determining the voting record of incumbent politicians. Do not assume that a person who has held office for twenty years is necessarily voting in the best interests of his constituency. If their record does not suit you, it is time to vote them out. When you investigate these records, you are one step closer to being a responsible voter.

3. Read Newspapers. Newspapers can be a great inexpensive resource with tons of information about local and national politics even though most newspapers are biased toward one party or the other. You will still need to read news from both points of view in order to understand the bigger picture. Please remember do not believe everything you read, back up news stories by exploring their voting records which do not lie. Sometimes you need to walk a tightrope between opposing views to find the exact area of agreement. It can be fun or it can be boring; it's what you make of it, but it will keep you informed and current, which are qualities to help "Take Back America".

4. Familiarize yourself with the local Government. Government starts at city and county levels. Go to www.usa.gov/Agencies/Local.shtml to have access to information on your local governments. Learn about those running for office in your areas so that you can make an informed vote and educate others as to their strong and weak points. You may be able to

pluck out the weeds before they grow into state and national problems. Would you rather vote for a blooming flower or a blooming idiot?

5. Discuss your thoughts with friends and family. Try to reach a consensus on candidates that will do the best job for the beliefs and community of your friends and family. When you discuss politics, make it a friendly and educational time, but don't ever try to discuss politics when drinking is involved. Politics and religion are touchy subjects that require clear thought. Agree to keep it amiable, you will learn more and not alienate friends and family. Remember, this is America; everyone's opinion should be given consideration, even if you don't agree. Everyone has different opinions, but being able to discuss issues in a friendly manner may help sway someone who is on the borderline between two issues. If you keep an open mind during these discussions, everyone could learn more and become a more responsible voter.

6. Volunteer at local level campaigns. You can volunteer to put out signs and answer phones at your candidate's campaign headquarters. At the polls, you could work as an election judge, drive voters to the polls, or campaign outside the stations. Before elections ever happen, you could help "get out the vote" by making sure everyone is registered to vote. Most candidates at local levels have web-sites listed in the local newspaper or displayed on their campaign signs; go to their web-sites to learn how to volunteer. You could educate yourself about candidates and the political process just by volunteering. Win-win situation! In today's world, a small amount of time can make a big difference.

7. Study the candidate before voting. If you don't know a political candidate's stand on issues, do not vote for this person. Go to www.factcheck.org for details on candidates. Know the facts before you enter the booth because you could make a mistake that is not easily corrected, a mistake such as voting for a politician who has an endless supply of earmarks that will

add to the national debt. An earmark is an add-on to a bill that needs to be passed. The earmark is often for low priority projects that are very expensive, and are often well hidden in the text of the bill by the Representative who inserted it. How do you spot an earmark? It doesn't belong in the bill you're reading. A good example is the Alaskan bridge to nowhere–a bridge that was built to an island with a very low population. Speaker of the House, Nancy Pelosi, has tried to set a moratorium on earmarks until the budget deficit improves. So, study your candidates before you vote and "Be A Responsible Voter".

8. Assign questions to your children regarding politics. Politics begin at home for children. How politics is presented to them affects their beliefs for the rest of their lives. So be involved in your child's political upbringing. Start with little things. Who is the Mayor or County Commissioner? Then move on to the details of what their jobs encompass. Go to the bigger picture; who is the Governor, Senators, and Representatives of your state? From there, move to national politics and how they work. Discuss these issues during dinner; you can learn from them, and visa versa. Their curiosity and questioning minds will make them educated responsible voters, this may be the best thing we can do for our children's future.

9. Learn about Civics. If you need to know what Civics entails, it is time to learn. Civics explains the inner workings and procedures of our government. It is nearly impossible to be a responsible voter if you don't understand how the Government works. For some bizarre reason, Civics has been given a very low priority in public school curriculums, beginning with the first changes made in education by the first President Bush. Some unscrupulous politicians love for Americans to have no knowledge so that they can use the system for their own political agenda. Currently, the actor Richard Dreyfuss is spearheading an effort to return this subject to the public school curriculum and perhaps reverse the decline of the educational system in America. Convince people that

learning Civics and educating ourselves are the only way to keep America on its proverbial toes. Go to www.ischool.zm to learn about Civics and what it means to you. Tell a friend to tell a friend. Vote responsibly!

10. Help eliminate the Electoral College. If any American political system is totally outdated, it would be the Electoral College. It is a system that assigns electoral votes to candidates by giving them all delegates to whoever won the popular vote in the state. This method of electing a President has given us George W. Bush and three other Presidents who did not win the popular vote. The Electoral College is ponderous, expensive, time-consuming, and mostly does not reflect the will of the people. It also allows the media to influence the outcome of elections with their never-ending analysis of the polls. All Americans need to voice their opinions on eliminating the electoral college by speaking, writing, or e-mailing your Senators, Representatives, or the President of the United States. Perhaps, someday we can rid ourselves of this outdated system so that we can elect our candidates by popular vote only. So you can decide whether the Electoral College is in your best interest or not, go to www.America.gov for all the information you need to make an informed decision.

11. Know your union's stand on politicians and issues. If you are a union member, find out your union's opinion and research their recommendations. You can do this at http://eightiesclub.tripod.com/id296.htm If you agree, vote with them. However, keep in mind that the Teamsters advised voting for Ronald Reagan. Shortly thereafter, he dissolved PATCO (Professional Air Traffic Controller Organization); some say it was the beginning of the demise of the unions. Most of the time, your union leads you in the right direction and does what is right for the average working American. If you're not a union member, but like the concept and want to vote with labor, look on the internet for a union that is familiar to you to see if you agree with their views. Unions can help all of us make a

more informed decision where the middle-class is concerned, know before you vote.

12. Vote with your children's future in mind. How will this candidate affect their lives ten or twenty years from now? Make sure the candidates you back take into consideration the best interests for future generations. Fair trade policies, clean water and air, and good educational systems are among the issues that will affect their futures. If your candidate does not address these issues publicly, he probably has no interest regarding these important subjects. Therefore, the only interest you should have in that candidate is making sure he is defeated. Future generations and your children will thank you for your responsible vote.

13. Be a conscientious voter. If you have made mistakes in your life and who hasn't, a good honest well thought out vote can go a long way toward erasing them. With the power of your vote, you can help to heal wounds from past bad policy makers. If your family or friends are suffering due to bad trade agreements and economic policies, your vote could be the catalyst for change. Just think, your vote can make a difference to the people you love. Our vote is our voice!

14. Do not choose a candidate based on a good speech. Chances are very good that someone else has written the words and cued him on emotions to be expressed. Speeches are written and approved by handlers, much as a handler trains a dog. Basically, the speech writer is given ideas and issues to be discussed; the speech writer then puts these same ideas and issues into warm and fuzzy phrases to make them palatable to the American public, and provides fodder for the media. Please realize what comes out of his mouth came from another persons mind and does not always reflect his feelings. The present administration gave a good example of this through the speech George W. Bush made after 9/11 at ground zero. His efforts to make us feel safe did not find fertile ground. Does the Patriot Act consider the rights of the U.S. citizens?

Does the Department of Homeland Security make us all safer? NO! Instead we lost some freedoms and are less safe than we were on 9/11. Before you vote, know their records and how they pertain to their speeches. If records and speeches are polar-opposites, do you want this politician to represent you?

15. Do not vote for personalities or appearance. In our history, some very fine men lost their bid for election because some people voted for the good 'ol boy instead of a serious academic. Would you rather have a thinking person in office or someone who makes you laugh, smile or feel good? Politicians do not have to be eye candy either. They are serious public servants with very serious jobs to do. Looking good is not one of those serious jobs. Don't look at the package, look at its content. If the contents suit you, place your vote accordingly. If the package and the content are the same...BONUS!! No, seriously, politics are serious business for serious people who want their country to be the best it can be. Base your decisions on a politician's intellect, his stands on issues, his will to make a difference, and his ability to lead. After you make your well-informed vote, you will be the one to laugh last.

16. Don't let comedians influence your vote. Comedians make their living by making fun of candidates; these jokes are not always based on reality but usually taken out of context to make the candidate look silly. But remember, what is funny to some can be offensive to others. Who you watch and listen to is a personal choice. There are many comedians who are informed and can give you food for thought. Have a laugh, but do not use all this information as a basis for your vote. If you know your candidate well, you will realize if this was a slip of the tongue taken out of context or something you should seriously consider. Candidates spend 18 to 20 hours a day on the road addressing constituents. Therefore, they are constantly sleep deprived, and because of this, there may be many slips of the tongue. Know these blunders for what they are. Aren't we all guilty of a slip of tongue every now and

then? Boy I am so glad I am not in the public eye, because I would hate to be the butt of all the late-night talk show humor. Use the resources named in this chapter to make a well-informed decision. Make your choice based on facts not humor.

17. Oppose the unopposed. Use your write-in rights! If someone is on the ballot unopposed, how can that be an election? Only vote for the unopposed if you know the candidate's intellect, their ability to lead, and know they can make a difference. Otherwise, write in another candidate's name or better yet, run against them if you are qualified. When the unopposed do not receive all the votes, the numbers speak for themselves. It tells us that this person running unopposed is not considered to be the best for the job by all voters and gives others incentive to run against them in the future. Before you check the unopposed candidate's box, make sure you know they are the right person for the job.

18. Don't allow election fraud. Many of us share the belief that some past elections have not been completely fair. We have watched in horror as legal voters have been turned away from the polls because of faulty records. In some cases, ballots were not even delivered so that voters could vote before the polls closed. In one instance, a federal judge tried to extend voting hours because ballots were delivered late. She was threatened with jail for violating election laws because all polls are supposed to close at 7 p.m. Think about this, shouldn't the politicians who objected to this violation of election laws be concerned about every citizen's right to vote? Suspicious...I think so. Why were these bizarre things happening to our voters that have never happened before in our nation's history? Remember Florida and the "hanging chads"? Was that really necessary? Was it someone's way of avoiding the true outcome, or someone's way of controlling the outcome? What can you do to help? When you uncover shady practices in your precinct or town, complain loudly

because "the squeaky wheel gets the grease" leading to fair and accountable elections for every responsible voter.

19. Insist on a paper trail. If you have watched the news in the last seven years, you have heard about the faulty electronic machines. Even though the results are fast, these machines can be easily tampered with, hacked into, and election results totally changed. Could this be another sign of government waste and another way to pull the wool over our eyes? Some states are dropping several different brands of these machines and going back to paper ballots. They have realized that accuracy is better than efficiency. What's the big hurry anyways? It only takes days to count the votes, and most candidates do not take office in that space of time. Paper ballots can be counted and the people who count them are accountable. With the electronic voting machine, there is no paper trail and no way to keep track of what the vote really was. If you are as concerned as we are about keeping elections honest, file an absentee ballot this year so there will be a paper trail and your vote will definitely be counted. Continue to do so until your state accepts that we will not rely on these questionable machines to invoke the will of the people.

20. Celebrate your victories. The joy of getting your candidate and his ideas elected should invoke a certain amount of cautious joy. Celebrate! You worked hard to make yourself a responsible voter, now reap the benefits, but stay ever vigilant. The pen is mightier than the sword as they say. So when your politician strays, do not hesitate to let them know of your displeasure and then withdraw your support. But for now, know that you have worked hard for this outcome and a celebration is warranted.

Do you like mystery, sex, war, history, or comedy? Take a walk on the wild side! Politics has all this and more. Because all politicians are human, there will always be scandals of some nature to toss the media a bone. Bottom line, you have to learn to differentiate between what is truly bad and what is just human. You just have to know where to look and apply it to your vote. Does this sound like a lot of work? Well, it can be, but this is the stuff that makes America work, and reflects the will of "We the People". Voting is a means to an end; the end should be a better brighter America for all.

Chapter 4

Be Aware of the Opposition

"You can't start a fire, You can't start a fire without a spark,
This gun's for hire, Even if we're just dancing in the dark."

From the album Born In The U.S.A. in 1984
Lyrics from the song Dancing In The Dark
Words and music By Bruce Springsteen

There's a rather famous saying, "keep your friends close, but keep your enemies closer". These are good words to live by in this world gone mad. The opposition wears many faces. In the fight to "Take Back America", I sincerely hope we can shed some light in the dark areas so you can see the danger of inaction. When the plant I was working at shut down for three years in 1992, all employees had to take other jobs, and it was then that the dark areas of politics first came to light for me. Firestone Tire Plant was a good fit for me; I worked as night gate guard three nights a week. While there, one of the plant guards started telling me about a vast world-wide conspiracy loosely called the New World Order. The object of the New World Order is to have a one-world government and a one-world economy. For the chronological history of the New World Order, go to www.constitution.org/col/cuddy_nwo.htm. You might think to yourself "This is a good idea".... WRONG!! If you are an American that still longs for the return of the American dream, their objective is just about as bad as it can get. It does not entail bringing everyone in the world up to our standard of living, but redistributing our wealth to the rest of the world and totally eliminating the middle-class worldwide. And so my friend I ask you to read, study, and keep your eyes wide open. And be afraid....be very afraid!!

1. Study history. You will find evidence of some of these conspirators as far back as the crusades. At that time most of the world was ran as a feudal system, the wealthier ruling class and the serfs. Today, we would not be a part of the ruling class. Soon after the crusades began, a group called the Knights Templar came to the front as a powerful group. They gave pilgrims to the Holy Land protection, and also invented the first Traveler's Check by allowing pilgrims to deposit money with them in France, and draw it out when they reached the Holy Land. The Knights Templar became very powerful both in Europe and the Middle East, but the Catholic Church eventually became very jealous of their money and power causing the Pope to issue an edict disbanding the group. They were hunted down and killed by the hundreds, but some escaped to Scotland and kept their group together. This group has morphed into many forms over the centuries and is called by many names. For more information on the Knights Templar, go to www.ancientspiral.com/templar.htm.

2. Know the past, cause and effect. Those who do not study history are doomed to repeat its mistakes. In studying the history of Europe after the fall of the Roman Empire, you will find what is considered to be the most hideous treatment of the common man ever known. It is known as the Dark Ages because the majority of the people were held in bondage by the nobility. They had no rights whatsoever. They were tied to the land they were born, and could be whipped, branded, or killed for anything their masters deemed as a crime. Learn more about this part of history at www.geocities.com/soho/square/8171/dark.html. The advent of the New World Order is said to have the same goals in mind, no middle-class. Wake up America, we cannot let this happen!!!

3. Think about the Trilateral Commission. This is a group of political elitists. You know of many members: George H. Bush, Henry Kissinger, Bill Clinton, and many more. The list goes on to involve many of the world leaders, industrialists, scholars, and European Royalty. Why should we study this

group? One reason is that they have more to do with the price of oil than OPEC (Organization of Petroleum Exporting Countries) does. They plan the moves of industry around the world (such as moving industry to China from the U.S.), and their goal is a one-world government and economic system. Follow their movements in the news and on the internet at www.anitwar.com/berkman/trilat.html. A well-informed majority can fight back, and fight we must to "Take Back America".

4. Be aware of other elitist groups. There are many more groups in the world with the same goals as the Trilateral Commission. The Bilderbergers (find out about this group at www.sourcewatch.org) operate with the same goals and many of the same people. I really have not got much more to say about them, other than to watch and study their meetings and movements. In this way, you can know what to expect in the future.

5. Illuminate your mind. There is a very old group based in Italy called the Illuminati (find out more at www.educate-yourself.org/nwo/). I know you have heard of them in the movies. Guess what? They really do exist. In their minds, they are the greatest minds of all time and know much more than we do what is best for the world. One of their main objectives is to reduce world population to less than two billion people. Methods to be used are sterilization, stringent birth control, useless wars, famine, disease, and a world-wide population that gives up hope. Does this sound familiar? Watch the news and see these things happen around the world. These are not accidents of nature or coincidence, this is well-orchestrated pandemonium. Get the picture? If you don't, think about this: Hitler was an Illuminati.

6. Rid Washington of lobbyists & PACS (Political Action Committees). There are groups that are definitely more ordinary in nature, but by their very existence, threaten our way of life. We know one group by the hated name "lobbyist",

those greedy, money-grubbing, power-seeking leeches that buy our congressmen and senators. That may sound dramatic, but it is the ever-loving truth. These people haunt the inside of the Washington Beltway, stalk our elected representatives with hands full of money, and plan to make much more by influence peddling. Lobbyists try to justify their actions by pointing to a line in the Constitution that basically says private citizens have a right to seek compensation for losses caused by Government actions. I for one do not believe that our forefathers had this type of thing in mind when the Constitution was drafted. Find out more about lobbyists and PACs at www.opensecrets.org/pacs/pacfaq.php. We must write letters, e-mail, call, and protest until the insects scuttle back to their homes under the rocks. Come on folks, let's make some noise!!

7. Be aware of foreign lobbyists. Speaking of these vermin, did you realize some countries such as Mexico have people lobbying our elected representatives for favor? Go to www.democracyinaction.org to find out more on foreign lobbyists. And in the case of Mexico, they are working very well as more in the Senate and House are leaning towards amnesty for the millions of illegal immigrants already in our country. We have not fought a war; none the less, our country is being occupied by an army of illegals that will not have to fire a shot to destroy our nation. Do we really want to sit by and watch this happen?

8. Watch our government with Bald Eagle Eyes. Again, with the lobbyists! Do you realize that the Air Force just gave a $36 Billion contract to a French company, Air Bus of France, to build refueling tankers instead of hiring an American company that employs American workers? Go figure! For more on the Air Bus of France contract, go to www.nytimes.com and look at the 3/12/2008 edition. We now hire mercenary soldiers at approximately ten times the rate we pay our own soldiers and buy our Air Force tech from another country. George Washington and Abe Lincoln just rolled

over in their graves in perfect sync. Is there a way to stop this madness? Yes...but we all have to be more vigilant, study the people running for office, and make sure we vote only for the few public servants that will listen to the voice of the people. Being a responsible voter will make the politicians we elect conform to our majority opinion. When they stop listening, get rid of them by vote or recall.

9. Be aware of a group called La Raza. We have groups in this country that come here illegally, then protest, and lobby to prevent our government from enforcing our laws. It seems that no one from our southern hemisphere understands the word illegal. They have no respect for the laws of our sovereign Nation. La Raza is one of these organizations; you can find out about them at www.humanevents.com. I have seen one of their spokespersons on TV and I feel justified in saying the only points this woman had in her favor was a very loud voice, and the ill manners not to let anyone else speak. Follow this organization in the news and you will find they are supported in part by the Catholic Church. When donating to your church, be specific about where you want your money allocated. Please let your church know you do not support pro-illegal immigrant politics, and you will no longer give them your money to help them give away our country.

10. Honor the service of our ancestors. It is often painful when you know who the opposition is. One of the enemies is the President of the United States. Yes. I am talking about little Bush and his infamous sidekick, Dick "shot my friend in the face" Cheney. My family has been in this country since 1738 (they left Scotland to escape the tyranny of King George, maybe the name George is synonymous with the word tyranny), my ancestors fought in the Revolution, for the Union in the Civil War, and most wars since. My father passed away before this current bunch of traitors took office; thank goodness he did not have to see what has occurred in the past seven and a half years. He surely would have died from a broken heart because he would definitely feel like all

the past soldiers sacrificed their life for naught. We must all take care not to let this happen again, we must choose our leaders carefully so that the world will respect us again.

11. Pay no attention to "over-the-top" conservatives. This is for the over-zealous conservatives...you all know who you are. There just happens to be one person in particular I would like to address, Ann Coulter, author of How To Talk To A Liberal. The answer to her question, of course, is with more intelligence than she possesses. My dad taught us how to speak to people of her type: slowly, kindly, and in very small words. One never knows what caused her disability, but you shouldn't blame her too much. Just ignore her, and she will fade away. Most of these over-the-top conservatives seem to be misinformed and ignorant of the facts; therefore, listening to them can be deemed counter-productive. Political pundits with this limited range will soon lose their appeal to the public, if we just ignore them, they will fade away also.

12. Stop the super central highway. Want to take a drive? You will soon be able to drive from Central Mexico to Canada on an eight-lane super highway conceived to promote fair and free trade between Canada, the U.S., and Mexico. We all know the only people this will benefit are rich industrialists and the Mexican Government. It amazes me that Canada wants anything to do with this venture because there is no gain for them. Are they as dense about this as they thought we were when America re-elected George W. Bush? Go to www.theamericanresistance.com/sovereignty/sovereignty.htm for more information on super central highway. The Free Traders and the Trilateral Commission seem to think this is a very good idea which should send up the first red flag. Please let your reps know in no uncertain terms that you do not agree with a super central highway that will cause more problems with illegal immigration.

13. Try to stop the North American Union. Do you realize that behind our backs and behind the backs of the elected law

makers of this country, the traitor in the White House has been negotiating with Canada and Mexico to become a one-entity trading unit, much like the European Union? While he has no legal authority to do this, it has not stopped him. He has signed a letter of intent and agreement. This is much like the matter of Mexican truckers on U.S. highways. Congress has demanded that this inroad into our trucking industry stop on three occasions. They have been totally ignored. Are you starting to get the picture? A European Union and North American Union could be in the near future, each using one monetary system. These will soon be joined to create one, another step closer to the New World Order. Go to www.stopthenorthamericanunion.com/NAU for more information. America cannot allow this to happen!

14. Be aware of a group called Skull and Bones. There is a highly secretive society at Yale University called the Scull and Bones. This "club" of wealthy men from powerful families is the beginning of the ascension of the members into positions of power around the world. Go to www.cbsnews.com/stories/2003/10/02/60minutes/main576332.shtlm for more information about Scull and Bones. Members go on to belong to the Trilateral Commission and the Bilderbergers, both President Bushes belong to the Sculls. Since taking office, little Bush has allowed most good paying jobs, both in manufacturing and technical fields, to leave this country and gave them a tax-break to do it! The jobs that have since been created are poor-paying service jobs. The war on the middle-class intensifies daily! The Government tells us that inflation was 5% in 2007. We who shop for our families know it is more like 20%. The only thing that makes it appear less is using the drop in housing prices to offset rises in everything else. Does this sound like the elimination of the middle-class and a move closer to the New World Order? It does to me; now let's talk about what we need to do.

15. Prepare for shortages of essential products. All Americans need to practice and learn the old-fashioned survival

techniques our ancestors used, raising and storing food and commodities. Sound silly? Not at all, as prices rise, our dollar buys less and less. Food can be raised cheaply if you study gardening and combine the use of old knowledge with some newer developments. Try to downsize your home by buying a smaller place with a very low or no mortgage payment away from the city if possible. Store a stock of over-the-counter medications and keep your family as healthy as possible. Read everything you can on food gathering and frugal living. Have you noticed there are shortages in some things already? And as fuel prices rise, there will be more shortages. Buy ahead in such things as soap, detergents, and hygiene products. The prices are going to get very high. Store whatever you can, wherever you can in your home. As the rate of inflation rises, you will be glad you did, because it may save your life and the lives of your family.

16. Begin a quiet revolution. This will be a revolution of knowledge and decisive action to improve our government and reclaim our place as a great Nation and world leader. Because this cannot happen overnight, we will have to learn to endure hard times with the same grace and courage our ancestors did. If you follow the stock-market and money-market, you know we are teetering on the edge of a great depression (famine and disease...does this sound familiar?). We can overcome the hard times; it will make us stronger and wiser. We must work harder and smarter than ever before to give our children the tools they will need to live and thrive through a difficult time. If we all work with this common goal in mind, our children and grandchildren may never have to realize the realities of the New World Order.

17. Use American strengths to endure the hard times. As we begin to reclaim our proper place in the world, we will have to tap into the hidden strengths we all possess. Among those special things most Americans possess are humor and the ability to bounce back when we are down. We are a highly social people, and this is one thing that may make our lives

easier in bad times. A free exchange of ideas and solutions with friends, neighbors, and family can save money and time. Form groups to organize and conserve resources; it will be a source of encouragement as you draw on the strength of the group. Share fun and laughter for a new form of entertainment. Never forget you are an American, and you can overcome anything that is thrown at you.

18. Watch out for the enemy within. While we begin to rebuild this country, there are many things to make us wary. One of our biggest obstacles to overcome is those who say we cannot rebuild this country. We must not be trapped by pity for them. There are downers in every society, and as a group, we must learn to ignore them if we cannot help them. No one should be allowed to ruin the morale of a group fighting to keep a society productive and thriving.

19. Accomplish what others say is impossible. The idea of America must never change. Freedom of speech, religion, and all the other freedoms that are ensured by our Constitution must be preserved, or in some cases restored. The present Administration has trampled on the Constitution and our right to privacy. There has never been a President or Administration that has ignored the will of the people as George W. Bush and his cronies have. We cannot let the changes he made to policy stand. In this election year, we must work hard to find and elect a person of high moral standards, and a patriot in the full sense of the word. So work for this and pray for success, let us take back the real America.

20. Make our government work for us, not against us. The FBI, Homeland Security, NSA, and all other secret little people with all their little secret lives need to be kept under control. They are totally convinced that none of us should have a secret that they don't know. They listen to our phone calls, read our mail, and monitor our e-mail; they watch our bank accounts, and check our credit in the name of national security. I truly

> think they just enjoy being a pack of peeping Toms, looking into our lives for entertainment. For most of us, there can be no other reasonable explanation. There is little or no privacy left in this country; when you shop and use a credit or debit card, it is recorded, and you become a demographic on several mailing lists. Our government and businesses peek into our lives to keep us in line and to sell us more Chinese junk that we do not want or need. Just think...they are using Chinese technology to spy on American citizens. We must put a stop to this trend. Fight back, use cash when possible, and fall under everyone's radar, this is just another way to "Take Back America".

This has been a difficult chapter to write, pointing fingers at other Americans (no matter how deserving) is distasteful to me. Frightening people is also not pleasant. On the other hand, helping people get through these difficult times and the more difficult times that may lie ahead makes it worthwhile. I will never say this is my country right or wrong, I say when my country is wrong, it is time to fix it! Get your tools out, let's get to work.

Chapter 5

Be Proud You Are an American

"There is nothing wrong with America that cannot be cured by what is right with America."

Bill Clinton (1946-Present)

Remember where you were on September 11, 2001? I really do. Who doesn't? Day after day, every American wanted the world to know that we are the USA, and we will survive anything, even the most horrific terrorist act in history. And we did survive. September 11, 2001 was not that long ago. What happened? Do we have to be the target of terrorists for us to show our patriotism? One thing we should all remember is that we do live in one of the greatest countries in the world!! Is it perfect? Hell NO!! Will it ever be perfect? No...life is not perfect, neither are countries. There is no way to make 100% of a population completely happy! Do some research, find out what goes on around the world so you can learn to appreciate the freedoms we sometimes take for granted. Come on, we live in perfect freedom compared to most countries. This is our nation; stand beside her and guide her back to the greatness for which she is known.

1. Be Patriotic. A patriot can be defined as a person who loves and loyally and zealously supports and defends his own country. A more admirable trait is hard to find and a true patriot is priceless. No country can prosper without the love, loyalty, support and defense of its people. So it stands to reason that we all must become the most patriotic people in this time of decline in this great country of ours. A patriot stands by their country in good times and bad, and patriots are especially needed during the bad times. Dig deep in your heart for

all the reasons you should be thankful to walk this great land. Recite those reasons to others, and listen to the reasons that others share with you on why we should be proud to be patriots of the United States of America.

2. Be loyal to your country. Loyalty can be defined as a faithful allegiance to one's country and government, meaning that one should support and defend your country no matter what. Loyalty to your government does not always mean you agree with their actions but you must always defend and support your country. To uphold our values and morals that define us as Americans, we must all learn to be loyal to our fellow American. We cannot only stand together during good times; we must be especially united during the bad times. In these times of inflation, high gas prices, and rampant unemployment, one would think that we would be at odds with each other, instead there are more people everyday talking of patriotism and love of country and taking back America. If we all remain loyal during these hard times, standing united, we can achieve our goal to "Take Back America".

3. Know American history. Several years ago, my husband and I visited some friends we met in Mexico who live in London, England. We were so impressed with how much they knew about their homeland and how proud they were to share their knowledge. It seems to me, we need the same enthusiasm here in the U.S. Great history is everywhere in this wonderful country of ours; interesting, intriguing, engaging, amusing and fascinating facts are yours just by opening a book or by going to www.americanhistory.about.com. American history is important to all of us because what we learn from the past can help us face the future.

4. Teach all why you should "Be Proud You Are An American". In many ways, this should not have to be taught. In a perfect world, the young know to take pride in the country where they were born. I don't know if that is so true anymore; mostly what I see is people who want to take advantage of

this fine country. How do we instill a sense of pride in our country? First, we all must learn to respect each other and our differences, after all that is one of the greatest things about America, we can all be who we want to be as long as it is not criminal. Second, compare our freedoms to those of other countries. Third, show your pride for all generations to see. And last but not least, do whatever it takes to keep future generations involved in being a patriot of this great nation.

5. Know and teach what it means to be a responsible voter. Another of our greatest rights is the right to vote; it is something we take for granted and a right many across the world would love to have. In order for democracy to shine through, we must take this responsibility to heart since so much depends on our decisions and the decisions of others. Don't be the voter who lets the media and polls sway your opinions; make up your own mind by researching the candidates before you enter that booth. If you don't know about a candidate or issue, don't vote on it; better to let the informed vote for our futures. A responsible voter knows the issues and the candidates and makes informed decisions. And remember, even when your candidate does not win, you were still given the right to choose.

6. Display American flags wherever and whenever possible. After September 11, 2001, the display of American flags was never more prevalent, or at least not so much in my lifetime. I remember a commercial that sounded so menacing it caught your attention immediately. "They thought 9/11 would change everything" as they showed a normal average street that looked like it was probably in San Francisco. The screen goes black. "It did" as they show the same street with flags everywhere! It was an amazing sight! It filled you with a sense of pride beyond explanation! To this day, that commercial is still one of my favorites. Why does it take something horrific to display our pride in our country? No matter how many problems our nation faces, we are absolutely blessed to live in a country with so many freedoms. One of those freedoms

is being able to display our flags in so many ways: decals, stickers, window clings, t-shirts, patches, coats, and the best of all, old glory waving from a flag pole, there is not a more beautiful sight. Go to www.flagstoreusa.com for your patriotic merchandise made in America. Go get yours and display it proudly.

7. Celebrate all American holidays appropriately. The Presidents of this country, past and present, deserve to be honored for their service to our country. Martin Luther King, Jr. definitely should be honored for his effort to bring justice to all Americans. Memorial Day has fittingly been set aside for us to remember our loved ones who have passed on. We also have a special day for our flag, a new holiday for patriots (9/11), and a holiday to celebrate the day Christopher Columbus discovered America. And most importantly, Independence Day, the day America declared her freedom. No matter what the occasion, these holidays were developed for a reason and should be celebrated appropriately and with pride. Go to www.history.com to find out the history of these holidays. All these holidays are great reasons to "Be Proud You Are An American".

8. Do not litter. Keep your country beautiful. When your country is beautiful and clean, your pride shows without saying a thing. What is not beautiful is the trash littering our highways and country roads. During the winter which is drab and ugly anyways, litter becomes even more apparent because the vegetation does not hide it as well. As an example, some states spend over $5 million a year cleaning up their litter. Don't you think our tax dollars could be better spent? Go to www.stoplittering.com http://www.litteritcostsyou.com to find out more about the expense of litter. Find a system to keep your trash in your car until you get to a trash can. Do not allow trash to fly out of your windows or the back of your trucks. How can we sing "America the Beautiful" while littering her beyond belief? Please do your part to stop the madness!!

9. Buy American-made products. Is it possible to do all the time? No, but make a conscience decision to buy American products when at all possible. It's better to buy quality than quantity. Food made in the U.S. is inspected for safety, and it is so obvious that the same procedures are not followed in China. It is nearly impossible for all of China's imports to be inspected in the U.S. Do I even need to mention the toys from China? This should be enough to make you want to boycott "Made in China". If you are not convinced yet, there are more reasons, such as our precious fuel being wasted to transport all the goods (our country even produces the raw materials, ships them to China, China makes the product, and ships it back to us), lower environmental standards (adding to the problem of global warming), cheaper wages and loss of jobs for those of us in the U.S. (causing what could be a recession), and the knowledge that it is just as hard to find a "Made in the USA" sticker in China as it is to find here in the United States. Something is very wrong with this picture!!

10. Use American services. And we do not mean American Express since they no longer use American people for customer service representatives. Is that an oxymoron or what? Americans can no longer speak to American Express customer service representatives in America. Unfortunately, this is only one example of probably thousands. Whenever possible, use services that are located in the United States. When this is not possible, express your displeasure to the company that they should have their services located in our country or at least employ people that we can understand to address our needs and problems. Use your voice and your pocketbook to sway companies back to the shores of the country where that company became so successful in the first place.

11. Honor veterans on Veteran's Day. America would not be America if we did not have such courageous men and women willing to sacrifice everything including their lives so that we could walk this beautiful land in freedom. The least we could

do is honor them on the day that has been set aside for all our brave soldiers. You can go to www.military.com/veteransday/history.htm for more information on this great holiday. Please find a way to show your appreciation on this special day. You can have fun and honor our veterans in the same day. Try to teach all you can what these special men and women have done to keep America free!

12. Visit American historic sites. So many sites, so little time!! Every one of us has that problem. Some things are just worth the time, however. To find out how to spend your time wisely, go to www.historyplace.com/tourism/usa.htm. On my recent trip to New York City, I took time to visit the Statue of Liberty. The emotions that flooded my body are unexplainable as our ferry passed by her; it is definitely one of the highlights of my life and time spent wisely. I will be forever grateful for this experience. Most Americans would feel the same if they spent the time visiting great American historic sites; nothing is more inspiring if you are a true patriot.

13. Impress upon foreign immigrants the importance of the American way. So many people would not want to move to this great land if it weren't for the freedoms we share. Yet these same people come to our country, then complain, and lobby against those freedoms. Convince foreign immigrants that accepting our differences is what America is based on and what made this country so inviting to others. Americans are willing to accept your differences as long as you accept ours and do not try to change them to suit your needs. Changing America will change the very idea of America. You came here to live the American way: independence not known in many places, opportunities for those who are not afraid to work, roads to travel, exciting places to go, fun things to do, and the freedom to do so. What more can you ask for? I would like to ask the foreign immigrants of this country, legal or not, to appreciate and respect the American way!! After all, you moved here to our country, we did not move to yours.

14. Record your family histories. What have your families done to show pride in America? For example, have they fought in wars, invented a product, been in Government, led in westward expansion, struck gold in California, abolished slavery? Even if they weren't involved in such elaborate parts of our history, many people led interesting lives. Is there a horse thief or bank robber in your past? Did they ride for the Pony Express? All these facts are a part of your history and are worth knowing and preserving for the future generations. Many genealogy programs are available to help you do so, one of them is www.familysearch.org. Talk with your elder family members to get information, some of their stories are flat-out intriguing. You will be able to find out exactly when your family moved to America. Take the time to do this, you will find it very rewarding. After you have your genealogy researched, share it with all your family. Make it a tradition at Thanksgiving to tell one interesting story about an ancestor to keep the family history alive and give you one more reason to "Be Proud You Are An American".

15. Take patriotism to work with you. Let's face it; most Americans go to work to earn money to live. It's not a lot of fun for most, but it is an unavoidable part of life. Why not make the best of it? Show pride in your work no matter how menial–we are all a piece of a big puzzle that makes this country prosper day to day. If we can all make the best of it and do the best we can, these actions will show true patriotism. Take these ideas to work with you and make these actions as contagious as the flu. Wouldn't you rather catch the fever that could "Take Back America" than the virus that has swept us into the complete disregard of doing our jobs properly and timely? Thankfully, many people are immune to this virus! Get the fever; it's much more patriotic and promising!

16. Participate in memorials that honor our fallen heroes. My cousin and I were fortunate enough to be in New York City on 9/11 and participate in the services on that day in 2007. We could write reams on the emotions we felt that day. We spent

hours walking the city on that rainy day going from memorial to memorial. We were there during the reading of the roll of the victims and heroes and were amazed by the never-ending list. As we looked around at the crowds, we saw such solemn faces but we also saw something else; a resolve that this would never happen on American soil again and we witnessed a country united in thought. It was incredible!! We walked to Battery Park where there was a flag for each fallen firefighter (we believe). A family member could remove the flag and with the help of a uniformed escort, march the flag to another area, and place it in the ground. To watch these grieving survivors was almost more than one could bear–their loved ones are lost to them forever over such unnecessary fanatical evil. Also at this memorial were the boots and fire helmets of the fallen firefighters lined up next to the eternal flame, it was a very sobering sight. Another sobering sight is watching a procession for a fallen soldier, a brave man or woman who has given their life for our country. We had the privilege of attending such a procession on April 2, 2008 for the 4000th soldier killed in Iraq. We did not say "so" (like Dick Cheney did), we honored him for his service to our country and shed many tears for his loss and his family's loss. For more on his story, go to www.Stltoday.com. We also praise the Patriot Guard which is a group of motorcyclists that ride proudly during these processions and have also taken on the task of protecting family members and mourners from overzealous protesters against the war (or at least that is what the protestors want us to think). Even though you do not know these fallen heroes personally, they deserve to be honored by all true Americans. After all, these people died for our country. We would like to take this opportunity in this book to thank each and every one of them–they have done their part to "Take Back America". Now it is your turn; attend one of these memorials, honor our fallen, fill your heart with the spirit of patriotism, and feel what it is like to be united as one. It is a very uplifting experience.

17. Show reverence for the Pledge of Allegiance and patriotic songs. Jay Leno said it best on his late night show when he said, "With hurricanes, tornados, fires out of control, mud slides, flooding, severe thunderstorms tearing up the country from one end to another, and with the threat of bird flu and terrorist attacks, are we sure this is a good time to take God out of the Pledge of Allegiance?". Therefore, when you hear some fanatic wanting to ban or change something that has been a time-honored tradition in our country, do what you can to prevent it. The Pledge of Allegiance should remain word for word, the way it has been for more than fifty years. For those of you wanting to change it, what gives you the right to dictate to patriotic citizens who grew up with this custom and honor it as a tradition here in the United States? Many of us would feel bereft if the Pledge were changed; we want our children and grandchildren and their children and grandchildren to feel the same way. Furthermore, when one of our musical stars writes a patriotic song, it should be a number one best seller right off the bat if it contains merit. If they can take the time to write, produce, and record, the least the American public can do is listen and buy. Patriotic songs are a great part of our history dating back to My Country Tis Of Thee to the beautiful words of God Bless America written by Irving Berlin to some more recent ones like This Land Is Your Land by Woody Guthrie, I'm Proud To Be An American by Lee Greenwood and of course, my favorite Our Country by John Mellencamp. This is a very short list, there are hundreds more. When you hear such songs, your heart should swell with pride for this great nation, and you should certainly "Be Proud You Are An American".

18. Visit Washington D.C., our nation's capital. Washington D.C. was built to inspire awe from visiting officials; they did an excellent job. No one could walk down the National Mall without feeling reverence for the Country it represents. The Lincoln Memorial, the Washington Memorial, and the Vietnam War Memorial are just a few of the sites you can

visit that will put a lump in your throat. The National Mall is just the beginning. You can visit The Library of Congress, The Smithsonian Institute, not to mention the Capital of the U.S. You can take a stroll in Lafayette Park and admire the gardens of the White House. If you are lucky enough, you can book a tour through the White House (visits are not always possible because of scheduled government events). Find out more about visiting our capital at www.thedistrict.com. No matter what you see, no matter what you do in this great city, you will feel the history around you. I am sure this will make you "Be Proud You Are An American".

19. Get involved politically. In America, we have the chance and the opportunity to influence our lawmakers or legislators. Between the news, CNN, newspapers, and the internet, it is easy to stay well informed. A well-informed voter will want to protest actions by the lawmakers with which they don't agree. You can attend community meetings and political events in your area, and you may consider being more involved in the decision making. You can write to your congressman, legislators, senators, and even the President himself. I realize your letter may or may not get you a response, but how many issues do we hear about that encourage us to write our leaders? Several!? What if you began writing letters about your opinions and others began doing it, and those who do it already continue to do it, it is very possible that all those voices could have an impact. You never know till you try. All we are saying is give it a chance and in the end you will realize that you are a part of the democratic process.

20. Realize the importance of our elders and treat them with respect. Without our elders having done the work to keep this country going, we would not have as many freedoms as we do. Many generations have made great sacrifices to give us the freedoms we so relish today. Do not disregard them! They are invaluable because they are a part of our history. The stories they can tell will fascinate and astound; we stand to learn a lot from them–listen and you will learn things that may be very

> critical to America's future. Try something different; instead of sitting in front of a television or computer for several hours, trot yourself down to the nearest nursing home or hospital and meet elders from the greatest generation. Befriend an elder and expand your mind. You will learn that we all have so many things for which to be grateful such as the many advantages of our modern world, the everyday things we take for granted. Visits such as this can give you a new perspective on life, and surely it will make you understand how lucky you are to be an American!

A few ideas about the pride you should take in your country, the qualities you need to possess to do so, and the importance of pride in country have been explained in this chapter. There is so much more, but I hope that you have been inspired enough to take this seriously, know the importance of patriotism, and begin a crusade to show all Americans why you should "Be Proud You Are An American". We really have so many reasons to be grateful. Let us count our blessings and do everything in our power to bring our people back to a common bond that will unite this country, so that all generations in the past and definitely generations in the future will be proud to call it home. After all, home is where the heart is.

Chapter 6

Take Pride in Your Work

"You are young and you are the future, So suck it up and tough it out, And be the best you can."

From the album Scarecrow from 1985
Lyrics from the song Minutes to Memories
Written by John Mellencamp and George M. Green

Now, perhaps more than ever in history, you need to "Take Pride In Your Work", if for no other reason than to feel better about your contribution to commerce. In the past, the craftsmen of this country were the best in the world, and the most respected. At some point, many Americans decided that work was someplace to spend time and get paid. When did we stop going to work to work? Pride in one's self is a precious commodity, and can only be earned by doing your best in everything you do. Please try one or two of the following suggestions, make them a part of your work ethic, and bring back our reputation as a Nation who takes pride in their work.

1. Strive to be the best in all you do. Rethink your job performance. Stop screaming foul and do your job! Do you think anyone can do your job? If you do, perhaps it is true. If you are not going that extra mile to do it as well as it can be done, then perhaps anyone can do it as well as you can...think about it. Are you at an entry-level super boring job? Do it better than anyone else because somebody out there is ready to take your job, and besides you may move on to something more interesting and rewarding within the company, or receive a good letter of recommendation if you move on to bigger and better things elsewhere. There are strong political and

economic forces moving jobs around the world; therefore, doing our jobs more efficiently while maintaining quality has never been more important, or more urgent. When workers show the will to do their best, America is more likely to keep jobs for the hard working citizens of the United States. Good for you, good for America.

2. Arrive on time. Do you always arrive on time? If not, you are doing everyone you work with a disservice. If all the late minutes in this country were added up each day, the numbers would be staggering. If you are relieving another person, you are imposing on their time, and needless to say their goodwill. For a company to run smoothly there has to be a certain amount of respect among the workers. Lateness, as a rule, causes hard feelings among fellow workers. There are, of course, certain emergencies. However, if it is just bad work habits, look at the way you manage your time and do better. Go to www.sideroad.com/Self_Help/being-late.html for tips to help you avoid this problem. Being on time makes life better for all involved and makes industry more likely to stay put.

3. Work safely. Perhaps one of the most important things you can do for yourself and your employer is work safely. How does working safely make America stronger? For eight years, I ran a safety program for my crew. During this time, we brought accident rates down by everyone watching out for each other and reporting work place hazards. One of the many reasons companies fold up and leave America is the high cost of workman's compensation insurance. In any industry, there will always be non preventable accidents; these people deserve the best of care. However, there are still those who play the system and they are the ones causing our workman's compensation system to falter. Medical bills will continue to rise so we must see that working safely is a part of everyone's work ethic. If we can lower the cost of doing business in this country, maybe we can keep more jobs on this side of the

Pacific. The most important benefit, however, is that you will stay whole and healthy.

4. Practice good hygiene for health and safety reasons. Food safety is a real problem in this Country. If you are working anywhere in this industry, it is of the utmost importance that you take enough pride in your job to keep the rest of us safe. It does not take much of a slip to make many people very ill, or even worse, dead. Each of you in the food service industry is responsible for our very lives. Please think about what you are doing. Keeping yourself and your work area as clean as possible; it will make America safer when you take that much pride in yourself and your work. All of us will thank you for it!!

5. Respect the rights of the road. All over America, there are men and women driving 18-wheelers down the highway to make sure the products you need are there when you need them. Most of these men and women are hard-working honest people just trying to make a living. To all of you who drink, drive or take intoxicating pills or other drugs, we are tired of you endangering our lives. Remember one accident is one too many. You damage the reputation of the hard-working truckers across the country. Please find another profession that will not have such dire consequences for other drivers. Let these proud men and women do their job so they can get the proper respect they deserve. The highways are made safer by the pride most truckers take in their work. We should all be grateful to those who do this lonely and thankless task. Imagine what the US would be like without our trucking systems, empty shelves and empty gas tanks. America needs our truckers to "Keep on Truckin".

6. Keep our technology in America. Is your job highly technical? And/or scientific? If so, you are in the area of employment that once made America the most powerful Nation in the world. That was then, this is now; we no longer lead the pack. However, we can and will lead the world again. Go to www.

futureofinnovation.org to compare our technology to other countries. We must not let our technologies go overseas to be manufactured by foreign companies who pirate the technology and then sell it back to us at Wal-Mart. Overseas manufacturers can charge cheaper prices because they pay no tariffs or royalties. We must work better and smarter than any country in the world to win back our lead, and make sure our leaders do not give it away again. This is one way to "Take Back America", be smarter than any other country. Smart business is business that remains in this Country.

7. Minimize the effect of health insurance. At one time, this Country led the world in medicine. We are now a joke, and a dirty joke at that. We pay more for less care than any other country in the world. Each American should insist on electronic or computerized medical records because it would save approximately $80 billion a year in labor and paper work, not to mention saving all those trees. Go to www.findarticles.com for more information. Money saved on paper files could help lower insurance rates. We have about the same infant mortality rate as some third world countries and what's even worse; some of our children have no insurance. What is wrong with this picture? Do our doctors and nurses care less? No, I don't think so. Insurance is the real culprit for most of our medical woes. So, I do not address this to our doctors, but to those in the insurance industry. Work better, work smarter, and work with your fellow Americans in mind, because we are the ones who suffer when you spend more for advertising than you spend on your patients who need medical tests that you won't allow. If I were asked what I think is wrong with America, I would have to say private health insurance would rank in the top five. Think about it, do better, or when we "Take Back America", private insurance could become a thing of the past. I don't believe there would be many Americans who would mourn its passing.

8. Nurse with pride. Now that we have vented about those in the insurance industry, we do need to address the rest of

the medical profession. Most people involved in nursing are dedicated professionals who truly desire to give the best health care possible. Even so, most of you are stretched so thin in your work that it has become almost impossible to give the level of care your patients need and deserve. We can only ask for the best you can give and that you treat your patients with dignity and respect. Help to keep infection down by constant attention to sanitation and housekeeping. As health care has been taken over by "for-profit" investment corporations, it becomes ever harder to keep up with the care of those in your charge. Nursing has always been a proud profession for caring people. Please try to keep it up as we are all in this together, so take pride in what you do; we all need you to continue to care.

9. Doctor with pride. Most doctors come to us with a huge debt, mainly college loans. In light of this, the first years of practice are to repay their debt. We all think of an MD license as a license to steal because of the high price of medical care. Wrong. Most doctors make less take home pay now than 50 years ago when adjusted for the cost of living. The cost of everything it takes to have a medical practice has risen to such outrageous heights, it is a wonder that new people get into the field at all. As a patient, however, I will ask you to think about the way some offices schedule up to six patients in the same time slot. A person who is not well should not be asked to sit for two hours in the uncomfortable chairs you provide. Everyone's time is valuable. Not only that, we do pay for your services and time, either by cash or by insurance, or both; so do not make us feel like we are a burden on your time in your chosen field. When we are in your office, we deserve your undivided attention; you need to listen to our health concerns. Keep in mind, we contract your services: same as a plumber, electrician, or anyone else. As a doctor, would you want your electrician to begin his work without knowing the problem? I know this is an old joke, but it is still pertinent today. Do you know the difference between

God and a doctor? God doesn't believe he's a doctor! Think about it! Most of us lead busy lives, and do not find it easy to sit and wait for your services. As you, the doctor, would not want to sit and wait for other services. We do acknowledge that doctors have many demands on their time, but common courtesy also applies to doctors.

10. <u>Take care of our elderly and disabled with pride.</u> Perhaps of all the people in the medical field, no one is as important as those who care for our most vulnerable people, our elderly and disabled in nursing homes. We cannot be there everyday to make sure they are getting proper care and being treated with proper dignity. These are not husks, these are people who lived a useful life and gave care and love to their families. Please give them the care and respect deserved and needed. We know yours is one of the most difficult jobs in this country, so if you are unable to cope with this job, please get counseling or leave the field for something less demanding. Only those who can empathize with the elderly and disabled should do this work. For those of you who have mastered this art, we thank you from the bottom of our hearts, because you are in charge of our family heritage.

11. <u>Realize everyone is valuable.</u> For those CEO's who think your services are worth 10,000 times more than the employees who actually run the company, you are not! If your conscience does not tell you this is wrong...I am. Get over yourself. You are destroying the American dream for everyone else. Realize that your company could not function without the labor of your employees whether they are blue or white collar. How many millions could you make without these employees? And besides, how many millions can one person spend in their lifetime? People who let greed drive their life can never be truly as happy as a person with true compassion and empathy for their fellow man.

12. <u>Worry about quality, not quantity or cost.</u> The building trades in this country were once the place of men who took pride in

their accomplishments and of what they built. Where have you all gone? In days gone by, men drove their families pass the fruits of their labors and made their children understand the pride of accomplishment and the realization of having built something in their community. Imagine the pride of the descendants of those who worked on the Arch, that soaring monument in St. Louis, Missouri that is "The Gateway To The West". Some of the projects worthy of pride are the building of a home for a family to live in, a mighty skyscraper, or a graceful bridge. So before you take that next shortcut or use a cheaper material to save a dab of money, think what your grandfather would have done. Was he someone who took pride in his work? If so, refer to his conscience and follow his thought process so that the quality of your work does not diminish the quality of his. Always remember, "Take Pride In Your Work".

13. Hire fully qualified legal employees. To the contractors who hire illegals to do the job that affect my life, our country needs you to stop immediately because the damage you are doing can not be measured! I want that work to be done by people who work to the job's proper specifications. In order to do this, they must speak English. America will hold you accountable for mistakes made by your cheap labor. We are watching, we will report you to the proper authorities, and advise others to do the same. Go to www.reportillegals.com to help report illegals anonymously. We cannot "Take Back America" if we hire employees that are only interested in a quick dollar and have no interest in quality or the honor of pride in their work.

14. Landscape your community with members of the community. In the past, and the not too distant past at that, high school kids could get summer jobs in landscaping. It was great for the kids and the community; they learned to plant, appreciate those plants, and the beauty they added to life. Not anymore! Now we have a new labor party called The Mexicans, and they send the American money they earn back to Mexico.

America, take these landscape companies to task!! It doesn't help our kids get that first car or save money for college. Those who are not going to see their work as a part of their community have no incentive to do their best. Give the jobs back to the kids, they will take more pride in these jobs, learn the responsibility of earning their own money, and learn the value of being a part of their community. Not only that, the wages will stay here in America.

15. Un-customize customer service. Those who work in customer service in this country are appreciated by most. You have a difficult job. Angry consumers often fire first and think later. I know this for a fact, I was one of them. Customer Service Representatives should be more understanding. Surely you can relate to time issues that make people angry, such as when a customer spends their time on a simple call and an hour later they are talking to the third person that can't, or won't solve the problem. Please try to get your supervisors to set up problem solving meetings so that you, the person directly dealing with the public has a say in how these things are handled. Un-specialize! Get rid of the computer aided circle jerk–you will find that your customer is not as agitated when you begin your part of the service call. In dealing with the public, the first person contacted at your firm should have the knowledge to solve most problems, or direct the customer to the person who can... make sure it doesn't take five transfers. Why do we use computers? Hopefully, we use them so all matters to do with customer service can be in front of you. Think about this, find ways to convince your companies that customers are right a great deal of the time, and in general, pay your wages. A happy customer is what makes your business more successful.

16. Advertise with American morals and values. Now on to my personal pet peeve, the advertising industry. Everyone I speak with is sick to death of your tasteless, offensive and downright sleazy commercials and advertisements. They are sent out for all to see and seethe over. Example, I would rather have

diarrhea than take Pepto Bismol. I will never buy that product again because of their tasteless commercials. We are all sick of blue liquid poured on sanitary napkins; these commercials are on shows that children watch which we find completely unacceptable. For some odd reason, it has become popular to make American men look foolish. Should we buy any product that makes the average American look slovenly stupid, selfish, or infantile? There are tasteful ways to promote your products if you take pride in what you do and pride in the American people. Stop offending the American consumer in front of the whole world, or we will no longer buy the products that you promote. We have a voice in what you do, it is called a boycott. Do you understand this? Shape Up! A return to good taste and respect for all Americans would be appreciated.

17. Serve the way you would like to be served. Here is a note for the wait staff at any and all restaurants. Yours is a sometimes a thankless job, but all of us value good service. Customers pay good money at restaurants for these services, and expect to be waited on in a timely cheerful manner. The word tip means to insure proper and prompt service. If you are not getting good tips, perhaps you should review the way you interact with your customers. Surly servers do not make a lot of tips. If a person asks for something in a certain way, do your best to provide it, and do so cheerfully. Your job is to serve. Make your customers comfortable without hovering. The people you serve will be much happier, and so will you. Take pride in the fact that your good service made someone's day better, and you will be rewarded with loyal customers and better tips.

18. Serve your country with pride. Bureaucrat…it even sounds dirty. Those of you in these mid-range government jobs need to have an attitude adjustment. You all know who you are; some of you have three or four years until retirement, and know your job is pretty secure. Guess what? No job is secure any longer. Take my advice, be nice to the people you deal with because we pay your salary. So the next time you take a personal call and keep us waiting, you will get a complaint lodged against you. Do your job properly with respect and

courtesy; make clients feel more comfortable while doing their necessary business with your department of the government. You work for us, you need to take more pride in your job as a civil servant, and realize we are not your enemy. We are Americans just like you who pay taxes that pay your salary. We rely on you to answer our questions, please do so promptly and politely so that America is a better place to do business.

19. Maximize your integrity in the business world. Are you tired of feeling your job is just a job? To all store managers, we all know the bottom line is what drives your business. Your bottom line is going to get very bad if you don't start providing products "Made In America" and sold to us by pleasant English-speaking customer service representatives. We need to make sure there is incentive for an employee to do better for themselves. Manage your business and employees more efficiently. This was once the greatest country in the world, a place where business managers and owners knew the value of their customers and employees. Our country was well respected in the world for that reason (the French do not have a monopoly on rudeness anymore). Do we want their reputation? We think not! We demand a return to more civil business practices. Maximize your integrity throughout the business world, and by doing so, the integrity of American companies around the world.

20. Make honesty the best policy, and image part of the plan. How many shows and jokes are there about sloppy plumbers and other home-repair folks? I know it is in the thousands. Please, when you come into our homes, make sure you are properly dressed so that your private parts are kept private. Your appearance can instill trust or distrust. Please also realize that women and the elderly are not as vulnerable to padded bills and poor service as you think, we do fight back. Why should fighting back be necessary? Put honesty back in your work ethic. We all need to treat each other with more respect. I hope you will read this and take it to heart, we are all Americans together, let us behave better toward each other.

When others don't take pride in their work, it can have devastating effects. For instance, if an auto worker doesn't go his job, quality is affected; when the qualities of our vehicles are jeopardized, sales diminish. When sales diminish, hard-working people lose their jobs. Cities and towns are often devastated by the effect of so many lost jobs; and their tax base is lost causing programs and projects to be cut. When these programs and projects are cut out of the budget, other people lose their jobs. The trickle down effect affects many not just the auto industry. This situation happens in all aspects of business. Americans can help take back this country just by taking more pride in their jobs; this applies to all career fields from the everyday job to those at the very top of their field. Remember it takes all of us to run this country; the most common job cannot be done without the supervision and coordinating it takes to run that business. And most importantly, the people in top positions need to remember and respect that there is not much that can be accomplished without the working class. Let's all do our best when we are at work to give America back the reputation it so rightly gained as a very productive, respected power in business, one person at a time.

Whether you install windshields on a production line, walk the high steel of skyscrapers, or assist in major surgery in an operating room, it all comes down to the same thing, "Take Pride In Your Work" and give it your best. No man is an island, everything you touch and everything you do effects the world around you. The hours you spend at your job earning your pay to support yourself and your family are not hours to be wasted. Earn your money. Work is not a place to play or conduct your personal affairs, it is a business that needs all of its employees to be the best they can be. When everyone takes pride in their work, companies become well respected and more profitable. You may not see your particular profession or career in these ideas, but ideas from each segment can be used in any field. Pride in job, courtesy to others, and respecting those around you applies to every field everywhere. By applying these ethics in your life, you make the workplace around you a more pleasant place and in doing so, you begin to help "Take Back America".

Chapter 7

Be an American Consumer

"Now Main Streets whitewashed windows and vacant stores, Seems like there ain't nobody wants to come down here no more, They're closing down the textile mill across the railroad tracks, Foreman says these jobs are going boys and they ain't coming back to your hometown."

From the album Born In The U.S.A. in 1984
Lyrics from the song My Hometown
Words and music by Bruce Springsteen

When Springsteen's great song My Hometown came on the scene, PPG Industries was getting ready to close down Works 9 in Crystal City, Missouri. On February 14, I got a pink valentine (a lay-off notice). I was laid-off and I would not be coming back to the plant my father worked at and held so much of our family history. I had to leave my family behind and move to another state. I still had a job but lost the joy of being with my family in our hometown. This had nothing to do with my job going overseas. American jobs are going overseas now and have been for too many years. We must take steps to stop this before it's too late.

1. BOYCOTT ALL CHINESE GOODS. There is no easy way to say that and I am not being biased, it is just a plain fact. So don't shop at Wal-Mart or the dollar stores. Impossible, no way. Go to www.msnbc.msm.com to learn about one mom's quest to boycott China (story from 11/21/2007). Shop on-line where you can find American made goods. Type in "American Made" plus a slash with whatever you are looking for, you should be able to find it. We all know we put ourselves here in this dire situation by depending on cheap foreign goods, now

we have to get ourselves out of it. Taking this into consideration, there is now a resurgence of demand for American-made products, and some companies are even scrambling to fill that void. Do your part to encourage this demand by purchasing American-made products, by only dealing with corporations that keep their manufacturing base in America, or by purchasing the products from new corporations who have started up specifically to make American made products.

2. Educate yourself on the origins of your medicine. A lot of our prescription medicine is now made in China, the same country that sends us poisoned pet food and lead-painted toys. Many people have had problems because of contaminated medications from other countries. When you order your medications, please be aware of its content. Find out where your meds come from before you purchase them. To find out the origin of your medications, go to http://pharmtech.findpharma.com

3. Demand country of origin labels on everything you buy. Complain long and loud to your Representatives, both state and federal, until all products such as toothpaste, mouthwash, shampoo, seafood, and endless other products have country of origin labels. By doing so, we can know where everything is made and make better choices on our purchases. It is a law that the Commerce Department has not enforced. Let's make them accountable for their non-action.

4. Reclaim our manufacturing base. We all know that it is hard to find American-made clothing, just because this is the case, it makes it ever more imperative that we demand just that. There is a scene in "Gone With The Wind" in which Rhett informs the southern aristocrats that the North will win simply because they manufacture and the South doesn't. America is headed that way if we don't reclaim our manufacturing base.

5. Bring jobs back to America. As we have exported good jobs, we have imported cheap labor from Mexico. Is this insane

or what? Think about it, we send our manufacturing jobs overseas and import cheap service labor. They come here, take our jobs, and then send our money back to Mexico!!! America has become the biggest debtor Nation in the world while all of us sat back and let this happen. Demand American-made goods that are made by American citizens.

6. Beware of what your hard-earned dollar funds. Free trade agreements are not free for you and me. Think about it. Is a Barbie doll any cheaper because it is now made by a nine-year old Chinese child who makes 12 cents an hour than it was when it was made by an adult American? No, it is not!! So where does this money go? To CEO's and stockholders and to shipping companies who use enormous amounts of oil to ship back and forth across the Pacific. Has every politician lost their minds? Maybe their wallets are getting so heavy it is affecting the blood flow to their brain or they are just very greedy. Do not allow your dollars to go to these greedy parasites.

7. Shop locally. On the horizon, a few bright lights are starting to appear. In many communities, there are coops starting to promote locally grown foods and hand-crafted products. These coops are being organized all over the U.S. To locate a coop near you or list yours, go to www.localharvest.org. A good example is the Sappington Farmer's Market in St. Louis, MO. Formerly an international market, it was purchased by a coop of farmers to promote locally grown produce, meat, wine and crafts. Some coops have began teaching classes for people who have 10-12 acres to devote to raising organic food and boutique style cheeses. Please check around your area and patronize these folks. Help to make them successful, they have great potential.

8. Go green and create American jobs. THE GREEN REVOLUTION. While it is very late in arriving, it gives us a lot of potential for "green-collar" jobs. Please investigate these opportunities and products by going to www.

environmentalcareer.com or www.greenerchoices.com for needed information. Do what you can and help keep the jobs created by these new technologies in this Country. Somehow, it just would not seem right to buy a solar panel made in China. In St. Louis, the Reverend Larry Rice is busy supporting renewable energy sources and training the homeless to install green tech. He is to be commended and supported by those interested in keeping these jobs here. Kudos to Reverend Rice!!!

9. Decorate with an American flare. It is still relatively easy to find American made products in some categories. Most furniture sold here is made here. Give support and praise to these companies and let them know you appreciate them. When you are decorating a house, while your furniture may come from the U.S., be careful of decor items such as lamps, vases, and pictures that may be made overseas. Check antique and craft stores for your decorations to ensure of American-made products. Your area should have many antique and craft malls, patronize these not just for American made products but a walk down memory lane.

10. Enjoy American wine. One point of commerce that the U.S. excels in the world over is wine. There was a time when it was thought the only really good wines came from Europe. Now our wines are shipped world-wide and known to be among the best. Find American wineries at www.officialwinery.com. Remember, wine is not only for sipping, it is wonderful for cooking, and is healthy when used in moderation. So when you buy wine for an event, remember to take advantage of our products, some of the best wines available.

11. Reinvent gift giving. Necessity is the mother of invention, an old saying that rings so true today. As imported toys grow ever more dangerous, reinventing gift giving for children has become a necessity. More often than not, books are printed and bound in this country. So please consider them ahead of a video game which are all often too violent and made in

China. Reintroducing your children to reading can be very worthwhile not to mention educational. A winning situation all around.

12. Be wise, don't compromise. The snack food industry in this country is out of control. It seems there is a new chip or snack comes out on the market each week. The health of this Nation is in danger. Shop to see what is healthy and what is not, you will find most of these new snacks are not. Don't let commercials run your life, learn to say no to your children, and feed them healthier snacks like fruit and popcorn. The possible result is healthier, wealthier, and wiser Americans.

13. Waste not, want not. Part of being a good American consumer is not being wasteful. It is financially responsible, conserves dwindling supplies of fossil fuel based bottles, and reduces trash in our landfills. How many times have you tried a new shampoo and/or conditioner to find that it just does not work for you? You don't want to throw it away so ask your friends or family if they would like to try it. Turn your bottles upside down to get the most use out of everything. Pass it along, less waste in money and trash (win-win).

14. Give credit where credit is due. If you have merchants in your area who try to stock more American-made products, shop with them and encourage your family and friends to do the same. Always let these businesses know how much you appreciate their efforts to sell American products. Let's hope their competitors emulate them. Giving credit to friends and family for buying American products will also encourage others to do the same.

15. Rebuild with American products at home and abroad. We start a war and destroy a Country. We rebuild same Country using items produced in China. Can we get nothing right? Our own Government constantly works against us!! Demand our Government use products made on our own soil to replace what we destroyed in this worthless war. The least they can do

is to pay Americans to make the replacement items and keep some of the billions here in the United States.

16. Fly the Red, White, and Blue made with pride in the USA. Is that a Chinese-made American flag flying on the flagpole? Did you know most American flags are made in China? I find this obscene, don't you? Demand the symbol of our Country be made in our Country, do not settle for less.

17. Honor the work of Americans as befits an American. As most of us know, a new monument is being added to the National Mall in Washington D.C. It is a monument to the late great Dr. Martin Luther King, Jr. It is most fitting; he should join other great Americans there. What is not fitting is that a tribute to the man dedicated to equality for all is being made in a Country known to have violated all human right ethics. Yes, Dr. King's monument was made in China, shipped to the US, and is being assembled on the National Mall. Dr. King would be appalled and so should all of us who knew what he stood for. I am sure this was not part of his dream.

18. Understand everything we consume cannot come from America. Pens, pencils, papers, and computers, the things it takes to write a book or letter. It is our misfortune so many of these things are made elsewhere. The only good thing I can say about this is we are using these objects to persuade you not to buy things made overseas. Strange world! Not everything we use can be made here, but what we have to buy from other countries should be used for the benefit of our country.

19. Do your homework. Finding products made in this country is just not that easy. Hopefully, it will get better when all goods are marked with country of origin labels. Until that time, read all labels, search for American products on the internet, and patronize businesses that promote American products. We appreciate the difficulty and the time it takes, but the benefits to this nation are endless.

20. <u>Wake up America.</u> Can you tell me why raw ingredients grown or mined in this country are shipped to China, turned into product, and shipped back all the while damaging marine life? Is this some kind of Orwellian nightmare? We are running out of oil, yet we use it to ship things across the Pacific twice to take advantage of lower wages while our unemployment rates skyrocket! Get serious, my great grandsons, ages 6, 5, and 3 can plan better than that. Surely someone in the Department of Commerce has thought of this. If not, do so now. Less shipping, less use of fossil fuels, duh!! And the benefits are more jobs in America.

In order to offset the publishing costs of this book, we printed bumper stickers that say "Take Back America Boycott 'Made In China'". Our colors of course are red, white, and blue. "Made In China" is in red. How does not buying Chinese goods help to "Take Back America"? Simple, it will stop feeding American jobs and American money to a rising super power, a power that has a very bad reputation as a human rights violator. Their Navy also shadows our Pacific fleet during naval maneuvers and has spies buying our military technology. Each one of us can voice our displeasure in only one way, do not purchase Chinese merchandise when at all possible. You may have to shop longer and buy less but we can do this, we must do this, we will do this. How many products in China would have the label "Made In USA"? Buy American; make it be known that you want products made by Americans for Americans. Americans must be ever more vigilant to the loss of industry in our country. Some of the things we ask of you are difficult, but you can find one or two things in this chapter to make your life richer and fuller. There was a time when you could pick up a garment, look at the tag, and it said "Made In USA". This is a rare thing these days, but go on-line and type in clothing made in America and there are things there to buy. It may not be designer labels, because most of it is made in China by children who make next to nothing. Child labor is no longer practiced in our country thanks to the unions. Buy items only necessary when not made in America and let the store manager know why your purchase was so small. When we all work together, we can stop the hemorrhaging of American jobs. Many voices in retail stores nationwide will make a difference.

Chapter 8

Put Americans First

"My affections are first for my own country, and then, generally, for all mankind."

Thomas Jefferson (1743-1826)

In these current hard times, it has become ever more important to put our American citizens first in every way. In the past, our country has always had an extra hand extended to help any country in need. Many times the help is warranted, we don't want to sound like we should not lend a hand where needed. Recently however, it has lent too many hands–at the expense of its own citizens. So, if our government will not put us first, it is time to do so as individuals. Let us step up to the plate, one and all, and "Put Americans First". By doing so, we can all have a hand in making this a great Country once again.

1. Take care of our veterans. A very important matter exists on how our government treats its veterans. Did you know that every night our homeless veterans sleep under bridges and in parks? Veterans are unable to make a living because of mental and physical problems that started in the military and continued into civilian life. Therefore, men who have served our country end up homeless! There is no one to represent them! Nowadays, all you have to do is turn on the TV to see another sad story about a Veteran of the Iraq War being mistreated and abandoned by a Government that won't end this useless war. For a story on an Iraqi vet, go to www.foxnews.com. Let us all write the Veterans Administration and Congress to let them know of our anger over the way these men have just been forgotten after their service to this

nation. A Veteran is an American jewel, a gem full of courage; not a stone to be tossed aside.

2. Be aware of how you can diminish the effect of homelessness in your community. The price of housing has risen as good jobs have moved overseas and to Mexico. The service jobs that have replaced manufacturing jobs often do not pay enough to pay rent or house payments. Section 8 housing is not available to everyone, so if a wage earner in the family misses a few paychecks, families are pushed over the brink into homelessness. Intervention before homelessness can make a big difference. Go to www.nationalhomeless.org for more information. There is no easy solution to this problem, but a way to help would be to organize a group willing to give time to study a way to arrange the resources available in your community into a guide that would easily be available for families in crises. Church organizations such as St Vincent DePaul help families in bad situations. So there are sources available, what you need to do is have all these sources cataloged to guide families to them. Wouldn't that be a time saver worth having for stressed-out families? Does your city have a lot of homes no longer on the tax rolls, sitting empty and falling apart? There are agencies that will help to rehab these homes and put them into the hands of families who need housing. If the homes are not salvageable, try to get the house demolished and perhaps the empty land can be used for a community garden. This is a win-win situation. The house returns to the tax rolls and a family has a home or there is a good place for a community garden. These are just a few ideas to help diminish homelessness in your community. We need your help; find out what you can do, think of some new ideas, and get started!

3. Do your part for mental health. Mental health facilities are not as available as they were before Ronald Reagan's administration. If you travel much in this country, you will find mentally ill people living in rest areas and truck stops all over this land. During the black reign of Ronald Reagan,

the doors to mental institutions that were state supported were thrown open and the patients were let go to make their own way in the world. Today, those with no families able to care for the mentally ill are on the street. The funds that were once used to run these institutions have gone to other areas of Government, as the national debt grows. As citizens of this nation, we need to find a way to help these people, some of our most vulnerable citizens. Currently there is a movement in this nation to make insurance companies treat mental health with equality, enabling families to keep their mental health patients hospitalized longer. Please write your reps to push this idea through Congress.

4. <u>Help create jobs.</u> We need more help for small businesses, in many areas of the U.S., small business accounts for 70% of the job market. Please vote for small business incubators that give tax breaks to businesses that move into often blighted areas in your cities. The tax breaks given in these areas help to grow jobs for your community. Attend City Council meetings and make this your mission to help create jobs for your town. Creating jobs in your area will help "Put Americans First".

5. <u>Invent, innovate, and share.</u> When you have come with a new way to do things or make your own power, share it with others that can use this knowledge to help America towards energy independence. Innovate; you may come with good ways to produce or store food, share with all that can use these ideas to help themselves or others to keep a stock of food. Share all things with your fellow Americans; help us all to get through the coming bad times.

6. <u>Keep American jobs for Americans.</u> Please help stop undocumented and H1B workers from taking good American jobs. Report employers who bring in H1B visa workers without first hiring qualified American workers. It is a violation of the law to not give first chance at employment to Americans. They are required to advertise for workers in the local newspapers and local employment agencies. If they hire H1B workers

without meeting these requirements, they are in violation of Federal, and in some cases, state laws. It is up to us as citizens to make sure these statutes are enforced. Form a group to monitor these companies and turn them in as soon as you see violations. Tech companies are the frequent offenders, Microsoft perhaps the worst. What's more, if you know of companies guilty of these infractions, boycott them whenever possible and let them know why.

7. Don't make American women drive 100 miles to give birth. Our hospitals are overwhelmed by illegal aliens. Do you realize that most gynecologists along the U.S.-Mexican border have closed their clinics? Want to know why? Because Mexicans cross the border just in time to deliver a baby so the baby is a U.S. citizen, however they never pay their bills to the doctors and hospitals. American women living on the border have no place to give birth without traveling a hundred miles in many cases. Approximately 20% of all health care costs are caused by uninsured illegal aliens. Would it be possible to have an American Universal Healthcare System without this problem? Solution: give hospitals the right to refuse service to illegal aliens. Write your state and federal representatives to let them know what you think of the situation. Here is another reason to close the borders tight and "Put Americans First".

8. Help your local food pantries. During the last years of HW's presidency, my sister gave a fund raiser for the Ozark Food Pantry and raised $2800 for them. It was greatly appreciated and a lot of fun. We sold crafts that we made and rented booths to others. A raffle for handmade goods completed the evening. Can everyone do this? Probably not. However, when everyone makes whatever contribution they can, our local food pantries can survive. Go to www.secondharvest.org for more information on how you can help. "Put Americans First" by donating your time, money, or both to your local food pantry.

9. Help stop moronic government policies. Why are there hungry people in this country to begin with? We pay farmers not to grow food to keep the prices artificially inflated. Does this make sense!! But in order to change this, we need more upstanding politicians who do not bow to lobbyists and political action committees. In a Nation that can grow enough food to feed half the world, why do we have children going to sleep hungry when we are paying people not to grow food!? This is another example of a top heavy system where the greed of the rich pays no heed to the needs of those less fortunate. We must make more demands of our government. Thomas Jefferson said, "That in order to maintain a true democracy, there needs to be a revolution every hundred years". While I do not condone a fighting revolution, I believe we need a wakening of the American spirit to take our politicians in hand and create true justice for all because this is just one example of truly moronic policies.

10. Help lower the deficit by buying American products made by Americans. Why is our country broke? When the manufacturing of goods is done in another country, there are no taxes collected for the salaries of the workers or on the profits of that company. Every time you buy a foreign made product you are sending money somewhere else. Even when buying a foreign car that is made in this country, you can assume the profit from that sale is being sent elsewhere. When we allow illegal immigrants to work in our country, our money is sent to their country and so on and so on. A solution is to demand American-made goods made by Americans. It will not be an easy task; but if a nation demands it, there will be no alternative for big businesses but to listen. It's not too late to turn it around and keep American money in America so that we can preserve it for future generations.

11. Realize why driving is so expensive. Why is gas so high?!! Guess what? It is not only a result of mid-eastern problems but it is also a direct result of buying all those cheap Chinese goods. More jobs there add to more financial freedom there.

Da-Duh!!! They have more money for cars, motorcycles, etc. So now we gave them our jobs, and they compete on the international market for oil resulting in higher energy prices here. We did this to ourselves with blinders on. Our policy makers actually paid to ship our jobs overseas; surely they knew the results and did nothing to stop it. Now it is left up to us to turn this around as good American citizens, one boycott at a time.

12. Keep American money in America. So what else has this done? Our infrastructure is for sale to the highest bidders. States are selling our turnpikes and toll bridges to foreign Governments and corporations so they do not have to maintain the structures that the citizens of this country pay to use. What's next? Airports, seaports? If you look into this, this is one of the scarier things going on now. So how do you stop it? Do not buy foreign made merchandise because this allows other countries to become richer enabling them to buy America. There is also the problem with Chinese currency manipulation, making the dollar worth less and the yen worth more. Make due with less and buy American, keep our money here; it is for the sake of your children and generations to come.

13. Be part of "One for All and All for One". The Three Musketeers had the right idea, but they were short by hundreds of millions of people. We Americans have to work together to adapt to the way our country has changed and that means that we need to be open to ideas and suggestions from friends, neighbors, and family. Let's join together to raise food and if possible, market it locally. Create together an organization that can leverage better prices on food and grocery products, this is not an easy thing to do, but with a lot of like-minded individuals, it can be done and the savings can be substantial. Go to www.Angelfoodministries.com for more information on how to start one in your community or learn where the closest one is to you. Give it some thought, talk to everyone, and come up with your own ideas about ways to become one with your

community. You may be able to start a movement that will be useful to one and all, beneficial to you and everyone else.

14. Think of ideas that will enrich American lives. When you wish upon a star, you are wasting valuable time. Time better spent to help your community. Remember that national changes can start at grass root levels and could be the beginning of a national movement created by one of your successful ideas. The thought that you could come up with an idea to change thousands of American lives for the better should spur you on to expand the scope of what you and your community can do. There is gold in dem dar ideas.

15. Keep families together. Homelessness is growing in rural America. For many years, homelessness has largely been an urban problem. With more outsourcing of jobs, families that were once on firm financial footing have begun to stumble. These folks have taken second mortgages trying to stay ahead of the bill collector, until one day, there is no more equity in their homes. Even with both adults working full time at lower paying jobs, they are unable to make the payments, so they slide into homelessness. Right now there are more foreclosures in the paper than ever before; every notice is another family with no home. Some will move in with other family members or friends; these situations rarely work and are hard on everyone involved. We have to find a way to put these people in private accommodations and keep their children in school. Possible solution; use the thousands of mobile homes from natural disasters sitting around and falling apart from disuse. Move some into areas that have a high homeless or unemployment rate and allow people to live there for a small fee until they can get back on their feet. If you agree that this is a good way to use already purchased Government property, write your reps and let them know how you feel. This could be an up side to otherwise wasted Government spending. If you don't agree with this, let's hear your idea.

16. Find a way to reduce child care expense in your community. In a family with two working parents, child care is huge expense. In the past, relatives often helped with this problem, but now everyone in the family works. There are some viable alternatives, start a child care consortium. Example, in a group of ten couples, there are 14 children, six school age, and the rest four or under. You have some working straight days, some on second shift, etc. Make a schedule that can work for everyone and exchange child care hours. If one person is working more in child care than others, they can get a night out in return. This can only be done by setting strict ground rules agreed on by all. So, this should be a group that is close and will understand the problems that can arise. The savings can be enormous and the children generally get a better level of care.

17. Walk when possible to save energy. With the ever emerging fuel shortage and cost associated with this, returning children to neighborhood schools and figuring alternate ways to stop busing children across the country sides and cities is just one example of wasted fossil fuels. By doing this, children would be more likely to walk to school. I have also noticed parents running their cars as they drop off their children or pick them up at bus stops, total waste of fuel (unless it is extreme weather). In days past, Americans adjusted to temperatures too hot or too cold, we dressed appropriately, walked, and guess what? We survived and probably are healthier for it. Please! Walk your children to bus stops, better for you, them, and Mother Earth (one mother we need to take better care of). You can always trade with other parents and walk on different days. This is only one simple suggestion to incorporate walking into fuel savings. We are the most overweight country on earth; WALK, it is good for everyone.

18. Use Government Entitlement Programs only if you need them. We need true Americans to stop taking advantage of Government Entitlement Programs such as Food Stamps, Department of Family Service, Medicaid, and Medicare. If

all Americans stopped taking advantage of these programs meant to help those who cannot help themselves, America could save billions and have people with more self-respect. Just because you can sneak into these programs does not mean that you should. Hard work and self-respect go hand in hand. If you are capable of working, please do so; it is good for the economy and good for the Country. If you are disabled and cannot work, these programs are needed and will only remain solvent if the people needing the help are the only ones using it. For all you hard-working Americans who do not need these programs, you can also help. Turn in any cheaters, there are many who defraud the system and take advantage of you, the taxpayer. Help see that the money is well-spent, evenly distributed, and not wasted. Encourage the Whistle Blowers who report the fraud in these programs, it takes a lot of courage to take the chance on losing your job. They should be commended as any of you should if you help stop this ridiculous waste of money. Make sure our tax money is helping the needy, not the greedy.

19. Help Americans understand the value of strength of character. Family values are not a republican exclusive. Things I learned at my father's knee are still with me today. My father was raised in the Odd Fellows Orphanage in Liberty, Missouri. Orphanages ruined many men and women, but Dad had an amazing strength of character that enabled him to overcome his past and raise a family with a sense of security and value of a man raised in a large, loving home. Strength of character is a phrase I cannot apply to many people and this is a shame of modern life. When this particular trait is needed the most, it seems to be lost in so many of our citizens. I would not apply it to many of our public figures and fewer politicians. There is one sports figure I will always admire, and though he is no longer on the cover of every sports magazine, Kurt Warner is a person I respect. I wish more sport stars would follow his example and use their celebrity to make our world a better place for everyone, especially our children. Kurt Warner is a

man with strength of character–he puts his ethics above all else, he gave many of us hope for public figures and that is putting Americans first. More information about Kurt can be found at www.snopes.com. Yeah, Kurt!!!

20. Look to the past for good ideas. History books are created for a reason, those who do not study history are doomed to repeat its mistakes, but we can also triumph from the study of their successes. Volunteers drove the American Revolution. Volunteering to keep things going well has always been part of being an American. Every hour you give to a cause close to you, you are putting Americans first. In the dark days of World War 2, everyone worked to make sure of our nations victory. Many things were rationed for civilians to help in the war effort. People of this era had just gone through the Great Depression of the 1930's; they learned to make due with very little and brought that spirit into the war. They sacrificed with grace and humor. Sugarless and no egg cakes were invented to make use of what they had. Let us take advantage of their leadership, learn to make due with less, and keep more money in the country.

With American ingenuity we can take our country back to the way it should be, a Country full of hope, opportunity, and respect for our fellow Americans. By putting Americans first, we will encourage our future generations to do the same so that we have hope as we all begin to age. The Baby Boomers are going to require our American strengths in large quantities: compassion, sympathy, consideration, and the will to "Put Americans First". The current system has betrayed us all; therefore, we need to be the best Americans we can be. Let us put the needs of our people first, and in doing so, "Take Back America".

Chapter 9

Respect American Culture and Language

"In the first place, we should insist that if the immigrant comes here in good faith becomes an American and assimilates himself to us, he shall be treated on an exact equality with everyone else, for it is an outrage to discriminate against any such man because of creed, or birthplace, or origin. But this is predicated upon the person's becoming in every facet an American, and nothing but an American....There can be no divided allegiance here. Any man who says he is an American, but something else also, isn't an American at all. We have room for but one flag, the American flag...We have room for but one language here, and that is the English language...And we have room for but one sole loyalty and that is a loyalty to the American people."

Theodore Roosevelt (1882-1945)

Here I am again climbing on my soap box. It's so bad, I have had to have one especially built to accommodate my bad knees. I have had to think long and hard in order to keep this chapter from sounding like I'm racist because I'm not; I just believe strongly with the quote from above. We need to find a way to pass on the best of the American Dream to the coming generations. For decades now, there has been an active war on the American middle class; our culture, our language, and the American family unit is at risk. Illegal immigration has taken its toll on our way of life; too many ethnic groups want us to live their way of life while they are living in America. It is time to fight back. We are willing, are you?

1. Insist on English in America. Isn't that the logical thing to do? You are in America; our language is English, PERIOD!!! Americans should not compromise this principle. When you get calls or make calls and end up with a person you cannot understand, hang up or insist on an English-speaking supervisor. Lodge a complaint immediately to let them know you will not do business with them if they do not change this bazaar method of business or if they do not employ staff with at least understandable English skills. Use this practice in all aspects of your life when at all possible. Whenever you are in America and find you cannot understand the person you are doing business with, use the same procedure. At times, you may have to use rudeness to get your point across, but we must do whatever it takes to keep our language in tact in our country. Until we all stand up and insist on the exclusive use of English, we will continue to have this language barrier. We are more than happy to share our great nation with foreign tourists and by no means expect them to learn our language for such a short visit. However, for those who have come here to work and live, it is necessary for you to learn our language. It is not too much to ask. You want to share our freedoms, learn to share our language.

2. Respect family traditions. As I write this, the holidays are looming large. Thanksgiving is predominately an American holiday. Use this chance to hold your family close and be thankful for all God has given us in this beautiful land. In some families, the tradition is for each family member to give a reason why they are thankful. I like this tradition, but would add one more...everyone needs to think of a way to keep these traditions sacred in your family. Learn more about family traditions at www.americanfamilytraditions.com. Remember, your family traditions are a part of our American culture.

3. Learn the value of age and wisdom. We are nation who has come to value youth above all else. Staying young in mind and body is good for the health, but we do not value our elderly as

we should. The last two generations of Americans technically advanced us further in less time than any other generation. They survived the depression that took over the world and a war that killed many millions of people. They did this while keeping tradition and hope alive. We must learn from them and value their courage.

4. Respect our forefathers. When our forefathers arrived on these beautiful shores, this land was already occupied by various American Native tribes. We took this land and then we took our freedom from England. We all need to remember and revere the Native Americans and their cultures. We can learn from the good stewardship they gave to Mother Earth. Go to www.whatwouldourforefathersdo.com for more information on this subject. During World War 2, the Navajo code talkers provided an unbreakable code that helped us win the war in the Pacific. By having a good relationship with the natives of this country, more lines of communication can be opened to help keep this country strong and in doing so, "Take Back America".

5. Keep family history alive. Among my biggest regrets in life is not writing down the stories my parents told. They were both great storytellers; their stories, while sometimes tragic, were always told with humor and compassion. Please keep your family stories alive for this is the good stuff of life, better than Shakespeare. It is your own family's history! You should read these stories aloud at family gatherings for a touch of your very own culture. Go to www.learner.org/interactives/history/map/index/html for a fun web-site that will help learn history.

6. Get involved in the labor movement. The labor movement in this country gave us a better life. It is time to get back to making life better for the working men and women of this country. We lost so much ground from the beginning of Ronald Reagan's Administration. One of his first acts was to dissolve PATCO, the air traffic controller's union. Study

union organizations to learn how you can bring back the labor movement. I recommend two movies to watch, <u>Norma Rae</u> with Sally Fields and <u>Mattawan</u> with James Earl Jones. Both of these movies are guaranteed to get your blood stirring. Keep in mind, that before the unions, we had children working 12 and 14 hours a day in sweat shops (doesn't that remind you of other countries that Americans now find abhorrent). We must remember what this country was like before there were unions and vow never to return to those dark days with unacceptable working conditions. As Americans, we have come to expect better than this! We must "Take Back America" for the sake of our children and all future American generations.

7. <u>Fight to keep your Country American.</u> America has always stood for courage and a "can-do" attitude. We must not waiver when things go wrong. Remember what our ancestors went through: war, poverty, famine, disease, and the fight it took to make America, American. We are stronger, healthier, and better able to take on those who would make America into an extension of Central and South America or any other country. After all, America is the land of the free and home of the brave. It is our job to keep it that way.

8. <u>Realize what illegal immigrants are doing to our country.</u> As a sovereign nation, we have the absolute right to have a say in how our borders are controlled. We must hound our leaders into closing our borders before our culture is either absorbed or diluted beyond recognition by our southern neighbors. We must realize the effect of 12 million illegal aliens, not to mention the legal Latinos, are having on our country and the way other nations perceive this effect as a weakness. Mexico has one of the most corrupt governments on the face of the earth. Do we want our country to be the same? I think not! By allowing our country to be overrun by illegals and granting them amnesty, we could eventually become an extension of Mexico. In our fight to "Take Back America", every American needs to stand up, talk loud, and demand our culture be respected by those who come here, illegal or not.

9. Educate the ones who litter. Keeping America beautiful is the job and responsibility of all Americans and those who visit America. It is a long-standing tenet of American culture that we try to keep our land free from litter. Find out more at www.litteritcostsyou.org. Unfortunately, those who come to our country do not feel the same and tend to use our nation as a trash can. How would you like it if Americans did the same to your country? Respect our beautiful land the way you would want us to respect yours. A message to all litterbugs...littering is juvenile, immature, and downright lazy. A beautiful country is a big part of the great American culture.

10. Educate yourself on the use of guns. America is also a gun culture. The right to bear arms is in our Constitution. Boy, am I starting to sound like a redneck Mother or what!? Oh well, this right was originated so governors could call up an armed militia (early National Guard). We may need to have our own militia one of these days. Make the art of target practice (no I don't mean shopping at the store of that same name) a part of family tradition. Remember, education is the best policy when it comes to guns. For more information of gun safety, go to www.nrahq.org/education/guide.asp. Buy and maintain fire arms in your home and keep a good stock of ammunition. Keep these things locked away from children and in an area of easy access for the adults in your home. Hopefully you will never need them, but it doesn't hurt to be prepared. We need to protect our families and our country at all costs.

11. Value your family heritage. A part of family traditions is family recipes. Create a family cookbook to pass onto future generations. Food is a large part of everyone's heritage. What family recipes have been passed down to you? The way your family makes the stuffing for your Thanksgiving turkey, for example, is a part of your culture. Keep these things with you always because family heritage can help keep America strong. If your family has always been patriotic Americans, passing family recipes along will keep it that way by the continuity of

strong unbroken traditions. We must keep these bonds and traditions alive to preserve our culture.

12. Return to past traditions that enable Americans to be self-sufficient. As a child some of my fondest memories were on gathering trips. We would pick blackberries for jelly and jam in the summer, and walnuts and hickory nuts for baking in the fall. I know this may sound really down country, but these were fun family times we all enjoyed. We still speak fondly about those trips today. We also gardened and canned in the summer. Although you may think this doesn't belong in the cultural section, it does, because it teaches you another way to be self-sufficient as our ancestors had to be. Plant fruit trees instead of shade trees and gardens instead of grass. Start these traditions so that your family knows the joy of home food production to prepare them should the need arise.

13. Learn and teach the true meaning of Independence Day. Independence Day is a double holiday in our family as my dad was born on the Fourth of July. A truer patriot never existed. Begin the celebration with the Pledge of Allegiance and continue the holiday with parades, fireworks, BBQ's, family, friends, and fun. Fly the red, white, and blue. Celebrate America and who we are. We are "We the People of the United States". Because it was a great venture by men of courage, it is imperative that we all understand that Independence Day is a momentous event to be celebrated by showing your patriotism for all to see. Go to www.holidays.net/independence/story.htm for all the information you need on this wonderful American holiday. Be proud and hold this dear, for much has been sacrificed so that the United States of America could exist.

14. Understand the value of family patriotism. Start teaching your children when they are young about love of country, family, and friends. Teach by word and example that a life lived in the warmth of family, friends, and country is just as important as material things. In the days of consumerism,

we realize this is a difficult thing for children to understand. Their friends all have new running shoes, expensive clothing, and tech gadgets. They must learn that the experience of a life of love and devoted family is worth more than any iPod or Xbox. After all, love makes the world go round and is definitely more fulfilling. A person fulfilled is a better, patriotic citizen.

15. See and learn about the USA. As the world turns into a more dangerous place, family vacations are still very important. At this time, we feel vacationing in the U.S. is the best choice for Americans. Ours is a beautiful land and the more of it we see, the more we are able to appreciate the responsibility of caring for it and keeping it safe. Everyone should try to see all areas of this country: mountains, desert, sea coasts, and cities. We have everything here in vast abundance. See as much of it as you can, you will never be sorry; the beauty is incredible. And besides, it keeps your vacation dollars at home which we so desperately need.

16. Know your genealogy. The Mormon Church has a great tradition of researching the genealogy of all their families. The importance of knowing your family history and where you came from will help you better understand yourself and your place in history. Home computers have made researching your ancestors so much easier. One web-site you can use is www.familysearch.org. Working on this hobby with the whole family is a way to keep yourself and your family well-grounded in the history of your ancestors. Your family chronicles will seem more interesting as your children relate family history to past events and individuals. Regardless of the way we teach, learning always has a benefit.

17. Honor those who served our country. Did you realize that 1000 World War 2 vets die each day? With them go stories of incredible courage and strength. Rarely would I ever approve of war, but their war was a just war and they fought it with rare courage. We all need to honor them on Memorial Day and

Veterans Day. As we stop to honor them, our children learn from us that courage will always be honored over artifice. Stop long enough on these days to remember what the veterans gave up for us. They earned our continued freedom and they definitely earned our respect.

18. Make Christmas about family, not material items. Ahh, home for the holidays. Yes, it can be all it implies as long as you leave the commercialism at the store. My family has decided to give gifts only to the children this year and nothing from China. There are toys made in this country. Shopping for them will give you more satisfaction than giving in to the urge to shop at Wal-Mart for the latest plastic and lead-coated toys now advertised on TV. If your children nag for these things, maybe they are watching too much television. Make the joy of being with family and friends and the sharing of a good meal the main part of your holiday. The stress of shopping can be a thing of the past, just learn to enjoy the simple things more. Remembering the reason for the season should become your family's culture.

19. Enjoy the simple things in life. Fall is my favorite time of year for many reasons. Fall gives you the feeling that you can slow down and go see the beautiful countryside in its coat of many colors. During this wonderful season, all families should try to take a long ramble in the country. Potluck for lunch in small town cafes and a walk in the park is a wonderful family tradition. Fall is a time to make homemade soups and stews, and revel in the fact that as winter moves in, you are warm, dry, and prepared. See what nature is doing to close shop for the winter, it is so relaxing. It is also time to attend church bazaars and fall festivals where you can find American made gifts from local craftsmen. By patronizing these folks, you encourage small business and "Made in America" products. In a complicated world, learning to enjoy the simple things in life will help us appreciate and respect American culture.

20. Be patriotic. Do you fly the American flag at your home? Sometimes it is hard to feel patriotic when you hear nothing but war, recession, and political corruption. Because of this, it is the very most important time to be a patriot (no I certainly do not mean the football team, we are Rams fans around here, and we are firmly seated in football hell). Back to the more important subject, love of country, we must love and protect this beautiful land from the very people who run it as if they own it. We must not allow this; we must pay attention to our leaders and make our feelings known at the polls. Our country is in great need of true patriots to help "Take Back America".

You will find the same thoughts strung throughout this chapter and this book. For those of you who have already come to the same conclusions that this book expounds, this is good. Please spread the word to those individuals who have no idea what is happening in this country. Love this country and protect her from harm plotted by evil men and women who want to destroy our American Culture. Help to keep her safe through the difficult times. It is our tradition, it is our culture, and it is our lives that are in peril. To sum this all up, listen to your heart and your conscience. Keep America the greatest Nation on earth by keeping our traditions and culture in your mind at all times. Do the things you know will help to preserve your family, your home, and the coming generations. We are a great people, we just have to return to our core culture and look out for each other. We can "Take Back America" by being citizens of this country and of the world. John Prine wrote a song in the sixties called Your Flag Decal Won't Get You Into Heaven Anymore. But then again, it can't hurt! God says love your neighbor as yourself. After all, aren't all Americans neighbors?

Chapter 10

Help Secure Our Borders

"In these days of uncertain futures, Who knows what the masters might do, They got their big deals goin' on, goin' on. Got nothing to do with me & you."

From the album Uh-Huh from 1983
Lyrics from the song Golden Gates
Written by John Mellencamp

There is a need to stop illegal immigration because of crime and terrorism, but also because our country's schools and hospitals are overwhelmed by uninsured, undocumented illegal aliens. Illegal immigration is one of the most important and controversial problems in the U.S. today. In the 1980's, Ronald Reagan's Administration granted amnesty to millions of illegals in this country. The border was to be watched closer and employers fined to keep illegals out of this country, and off our welfare roles. Of course, this did not happen, and we currently have somewhere between 12 and 20 million illegal immigrants in the country. Do not ever believe that they take only the jobs no American wants, 33% of all construction workers in this country are now illegal immigrants which has driven down the wages all across this land. Many true Americans have been left without jobs. Here's what we need to do.

1. Do not hire undocumented workers. In the rush to get ever richer, construction companies and many larger corporations have begun to hire illegal immigrants because they work for so much less and do not demand insurance (you and I end up paying their medical bills, so why do they need this benefit?). We must boycott businesses that hire undocumented

workers so that these companies feel the same pinch that true Americans are feeling. Illegal immigrants do not recognize the laws of this country and feel they have a right to cross our borders as they please. Month after month lately, we lose thousands of jobs; I would bet most of those jobs were held by hard-working American citizens. I am almost certain that when these companies hire again, it will be illegals who will work for less money and no benefits. We cannot allow this to happen! Boycott any company you know that hires illegal immigrants. Protest to your union representatives when they defend illegal immigrants over the men and women of this country who pay union dues! Many Americans together can make a difference, but we must stand together!

2. Stop renting to illegal immigrants. If you are a property owner, please refrain from renting to the undocumented. In general, they are not good neighbors because while one family might rent an apartment, often three to four families will live in that one apartment so that they can provide money to relatives at home. While landlords often profit from them as renters, the taxpayers foot the bill for their children to go to school, the food they can't afford to buy, and the medical bills that they can't pay. We know they do not insist on benefits so that they can take our jobs. The rest of the Country is sick and tired of picking up the tab for these people in our communities. If they can't find a place to live, maybe they will move on or go home.

3. Report employers who hire undocumented immigrants. It is the duty of all Americans to report a crime in progress. Since it is illegal to hire undocumented workers, it is a crime. Report it every time you see this crime in progress at www.reportillegals.com, your call is anonymous. Sooner or later someone will act on your report if you call the police often enough or continually report it through the above named web-site. You could be the key to reversing the trend of hiring undocumented workers.

4. Keep track of falling wages. If you have been watching the wages fall in your area as prices rise, it is very likely that the reason is undocumented workers hired for less than minimum wage. One reason prices are rising is higher demand for products; the more people, the more demand, prices rise. Remember every illegal immigrant who works in our country drives down the hourly wage of real Americans. Just ask Lou Dobbs.

5. Do not patronize ethnic restaurants owned by illegal immigrants. Check ownership before eating at ethnic restaurants. The way many areas gain large populations of illegal immigrants is that a few arrive, pool their money, and open a restaurant. Their families soon follow. They all work in the business and learn the trade. Some will then splinter off and open another restaurant. It is like dominoes falling or rabbits multiplying, you soon have a large group living in your area. In some cases, these restaurants are a front for drug operations, so lawlessness soon follows. As lawlessness grows, gangs form. The best thing is to starve these places out and avoid the problem from the very beginning.

6. Write your representatives and make your feelings known. One weapon we still have is to flood our elected government representatives with complaints and reports. Do this by phone, letters and e-mail. When the Senate and House were trying to pass the Kennedy and McCain Comprehensive Immigration Bill, they received so many calls and letters, it was defeated. Shortly thereafter, they tried to revive it and were again bombarded with protests and it failed again. Thanks to all of you who exercised your right to protest. Another example of voter protest bringing justice is when President Bush wanted to sell the management of our ports to mid-eastern governments. The people were heard...our ports are still our ports. Your voice can make a difference. You can find forms to print out for mailing at www.forms.house.gov/wyr/welcome.shtml. Use your voice for all the right reasons, especially to help "Take Back America".

7. Remember other countries believe that what is good for the goose is not always good for the gander. You can not move out of this country to another, take a job, and buy a house without legal papers. Many countries have very strict immigration policies and do not allow the working poor from other countries into their nation without proper papers while the U.S. has some of the most liberal immigration laws on Earth. The penalties for entering without papers in Mexico are immediate deportation or jail. I believe in quid pro quo, I really don't want to support them in jail; I just want them to go home. They should build a country that they are not so anxious to leave. Mexico is very wealthy in natural resources; they should use these resources to build a great nation of their own.

8. Make your vote count. The states of Texas, California, Arizona, and New Mexico are almost at the point of being run by illegal immigrants. They have positioned themselves so that if they are granted amnesty, they will have the numbers to be able to take over politics in these states. Please vote every pro-amnesty Representative and Senator out of office. Get involved in politics at local and state levels so your voice can be heard. Convince others to do the same. If Mexico wasn't such a mess, they would not want to come to our country so much. Do not allow our country to be run like Mexico. Your vote can and will make a difference when all Americans take a stand against this foolishness.

9. Speak English in American businesses. When the Cuban crisis occurred, South Florida became overrun with Spanish-speaking immigrants. It did not take long before Spanish was spoken in more places of business than English, and Florida declared itself a bi-lingual state. While I can speak and understand rudimentary Spanish, it outrages me to have to do so in the U.S. We have spoken English in this country for well over 300 years. Refuse to speak to anyone in an American business that does not speak comprehensible English. For me, I am never more offended by a business than

when I can not understand one of its employees who works in the U.S. Learn to speak English, or go home.

10. Answer calls in English only. There is nothing more infuriating than to pick up the phone and have a heavily accented voice butcher my name! Have these businesses no sense? Americans hate to be bothered by unnecessary calls in the first place, but to add insult to injury, you can not comprehend what they are saying. From now on, Americans must insist on talking with their supervisor to complain or just hang up. All Americans should make this a habit so that the companies who hire these non-English speaking people will have no choice but to review their hiring processes.

11. Make sure your community does not go bi-lingual. Work to keep English the only official language in the U.S. As stated earlier, Florida declared itself to be bi-lingual. When this happened, it became very difficult for Americans who did not speak Spanish to keep and find jobs. Do not let this happen in your area. Attend community meetings, write letters, and let your voice be heard, in English only please.

12. Do not use the products or services of those who hire illegal immigrants. It has been said that if Wal-Mart had to pay the fines currently in force for the illegal immigrants that work at their stores and warehouses, the company would be bankrupt in a month. Whether this is true or not, we all know they do hire many. Hmmmm! Let's see now, most of the merchandise comes from China, many of the workers are undocumented, maybe we shouldn't shop there. You think?!!

13. Watch out for unlicensed drivers. Some states (Illinois) give driver's license to illegal immigrants, but most don't. No license, no insurance! If you are hit by one of these people, you are "up a creek". You should make sure they do not leave the scene before the police arrive. You still won't get the accident paid for if you do not have uninsured motorist protection, but maybe you can put them in jail, or better yet, have them

deported. Does this seem fair? Wouldn't it be nice if we all followed the suggestions in this chapter, and we didn't have to worry about this problem any longer? Now, that would be fair!

14. Make your opinions known. Illegal immigration is now a problem in many communities. Write letters to the editor of your local papers voicing your opinions on illegal aliens. Keep your facts straight because many people read the letters to the editor. You may be able to inform people of facts they do not know and win more people to the cause of enforcing immigration laws. Anything we can do to stop the bleeding and "Help Secure Our Borders" is one step closer to "Take Back America".

15. Watch Lou Dobbs on CNN, take part in his polls. Lou Dobbs is very vocal about the devastation caused by illegal immigration in the U.S. His program will teach you many of the facts regarding this unpopular issue. He is very aware of the harm done to the middle-class by employers that hire illegal immigrants unlike many other newscasters. He is also aware of the falling paychecks in this country from the same problem. Taking part in his polls will let many others know where Americans stand on this issue; you can do this at www.loudobbs.tv.cnn.com. Americans need to keep his voice heard because he truly represents and understands the true concerns of the middle-class.

16. Write or e-mail Jack Cafferty on CNN to voice your opinions. Jack Cafferty does segments on The Situation Room with Wolf Blitzer on CNN. Fortunately, his views do not usually coincide with that of Wolf Blitzer, and his interests lie in what is good for the middle-class, another voice speaking out to help those of us who have been disenfranchised by the current Administration. For more information, go to www.cnn.com/CNN/anchors_reporters/cafferty.jack.html. Write or e-mail Jack, and hopefully, you will hear your opinion

live on TV. Maybe you can inspire others to let their voice be heard.

17. Educate yourself on voting records. Go to www.govtracks.us to find which Senators and Representatives have been involved in easing immigration laws. Campaign against them; let your friends and families know about their voting records. Numerous lawmakers who have spent many years in their current position have built up debts to campaign contributors. These debts often involve the contributors wish to ease immigration laws to help their bottom line. More immigrants, lower wages, more profits! Be a part of a movement in your area to make sure this does not happen!

18. Support what works to "Help Secure Our Borders". September 11, 2001, need I say more!? Close our borders for the security of all Americans. Sadly enough, we have become a Country that is hated by most of the world (in the past, most countries were jealous of our freedoms, now we are hated for our egotistical belief that we know everything). Because of the hate that has become endemic by most of the world, it is now more important than ever before to know who is entering and leaving our country. We cannot say our border is secure when we have hundreds of thousands of illegal immigrants entering our country yearly. America needs to find out what works in order to keep these thousands out of our country because any one of them could be a terrorist. The new double-walled security fence can be looked at from many points of view. Many think it is the only solution while others believe it's an insult to freedom, while still others are torn between the problems that face this nation caused by unfettered immigration and the freedoms we all cherish. It has been proven that the virtual fence does not work, so we have to open our minds to the fact that this may be the only solution. What is more important, our security or a scenic view of the Rio Grande? The decision is difficult, but must be made on the side of security in our newly threatened Nation…a Nation

that is not only threatened by terrorists, but by economic disaster caused by illegal immigrants.

19. Form neighborhood watches and patrols to watch for illegal immigrants. MS13 is known to be the most dangerous gang in the world. They cross the border like it is not there, because even when they are deported, they return easily. The initiation ceremony into MS13 requires each initiate to kill one person. There have been many programs on TV in the last few years about this imminent threat to our society. So we must all be vigilant and report any sign of gang activities in your area to the police immediately. Some of these gangs are better armed than our police forces and SWAT teams. Imagine how our police force feels being outgunned by Latin gang members because our government dropped the program that provided grants for extra police personnel entered into law by the former President Bill Clinton. The danger of these gangs will only multiply if we do not act decisively to permanently deport all those involved. Please get involved in your neighborhood watch or form one of your own so that you can report any gang activities to the authorities. For ideas on how to form your own neighborhood watch, go to www.oag.state.ny.us. Be persistent and vocal, they can't ignore you forever.

20. Fight against school boards that want to teach English as a second language. Our school systems can barely teach the children whose parents pay school taxes. Now we want them to teach English to the children of illegal immigrants. In order to do so, we have to hire bi-lingual teachers that teach only Spanish children. Is this fair to American children? No Way! We have to drop other programs in our schools that our children need in order to teach English to Spanish-speaking children. This is outrageous!!! Our money should teach our children the necessary things to thrive in American life. The taxpayers of this country should have the right to decide what courses are taught in our schools. After all, we pay for them. It is unacceptable that our children's education is in jeopardy

because our government won't enforce immigration laws. Let your school board know your thoughts!!

Here are some final words on this subject. It will cost approximately 50 billion dollars to forcibly deport all illegal immigrants; on the other hand, it will cost over one trillion to allow them to stay. I've heard all the arguments for and against enforcing our laws, but they are the laws of this country. Let's make our government enforce them. Mexico is a very rich country, the problem is poor Government. Instead of invading our country, they should work harder to set up a just Government of their own and give America back to us. Americans have always accepted immigrants when they are hard-working productive citizens that do not undermine the working conditions that Americans have worked so hard to gain. One of the worst parts of this illegal immigration problem is the crime factor–many Americans are victims to this crime. It is not fair! Oklahoma has done marvelous work stopping employers from hiring illegal aliens and as a result they are leaving. There are 44 states with Pro-American Association Employers who absolutely refuse to hire illegal aliens. Before you hire contractors, make sure they belong to the Pro-American Association. When Americans follow some of the suggestions in this chapter, we make it harder and harder for the illegal immigrant to prosper in the United States. This can make a huge difference, because if they can't work here, they will have no choice but to go home and rebuild their own country. And when this happens, it will be easier to "Help Secure Our Borders".

Chapter 11

Don't Be Bitter, Be Pro-active

"And so, my fellow Americans; ask not what your country can do for you, ask what you can do for your country."
John F. Kennedy (1917-1963)

Have you ever seen something that makes you very angry? But...you don't know what to do about it! "Don't Be Bitter, Be Pro-Active". Take a stance to right the things you know are wrong. For me, this is a good topic because it reflects some parts of my life when I should have done the same. My daughter could write reams on the years of my life when I worked swing shift and my smiles were somewhat rarer than hen's teeth. Since retiring, I have been looking for ways to be more pro-active, to help the American people rise above the dilemmas our country faces because our leaders chose to ignore the uncertainties the middle-class is about to encounter. Here are some of my ideas.

1. <u>Be prepared for hard times.</u> Times are liable to get rough in the near future, I advise everyone to have a store of vegetable seeds put aside. Keep a garden area tilled and ready. If you are able, build a small greenhouse so you can start seeds. Help your neighbors to do the same. It may take the cooperation of a group of friends and neighbors to keep things going. Try to build a group close to you. The Mormons keep a two-year supply of food for the possible bad times. I know most people cannot afford that, but if you buy a few things to put back, you will be better off if something should go wrong. Rice, beans, sugar, salt, water, flour, vegetable oil, canned vegetables, canned meat, coffee, and tea are all items that store well and have a long shelf life. Things like pepper, cinnamon,

and garlic powder last a long time and could be worth their weight in gold. Remember, there is nothing wrong with being prepared and thinking ahead, it is called being pro-active.

2. Volunteer for "The American Literacy Project". Unfortunately, there are many people in all areas of the United States who cannot read. They suffer many consequences in their daily life because of this problem and often have a difficult time finding gainful employment. Teaching a person to read opens doors for them and also for you. It is a joyful experience to teach an adult new things. It is much more difficult to fool those who cannot read. Those that are able to keep current through newspapers and books are more likely to be involved in helping "Take Back America".

3. Leave the world cleaner than you found it. When you are at a park, each person should at least pick up one piece of trash that was left by others. Convince others not to litter. Instead of complaining about litter, do something about it. Adopt a mile of road for your group to keep clean (you can learn about this at www.adoptahighway.com). Recycle the trash. Go to www.litteritcostsyou.org for more information. Make America a prettier place. "America the Beautiful" does not ring quite so true when you are driving down a highway littered with trash. A beautiful America is a proud America, do your part for your country.

4. Grow part of your own food. Grow patio plants, or have a small garden so you can eat healthier and have fewer pesticides in your food. Grow herbs year round on a sunny window sill. Freeze or can produce from your garden for year round healthy foods. It saves energy and also gives you something to do besides watching TV or shopping. For more advantages on growing your own food, go to www.ezinearticles.com.

5. Recycle everything possible. Recycling can be difficult, but it is very important. Find ways to help by going to www.obviously.com/recycle/. It takes much less energy to recycle

aluminum than to mine the ore, transport it to a smelter, and melt it into product. Every bit of energy saved, makes the world cleaner. Your children will thank you for it when they are old enough to realize why you made them pack all those cans to the car to take to the recycling center. A pro-active stance on recycling has so many benefits, not just for America, but for the whole world!

6. Be a smart home investor. When buying a home, stop and think!! How big a house do you really need? And how much energy will that home consume? These are two questions to ask because of the rising cost of energy. Be aware of the fact that the more square feet of the home, the more damage to the earth unless it is built "green". Make your choice based on the effect of the earth, you may find a smaller home may be more suitable. As the so-called McMansions fill the landscape, I can only think of the poor thought and lack of imagination on the part of the owners. Why in the world do people need such big homes? A smart pro-active person realizes the need for more energy efficient homes that will help lower the consumption of energy in a Nation trapped by the high demand for such energy!

7. Make sure your donated clothes go to charity. You have probably noticed the yellow clothing recycling huts that suddenly dot the cities. These are not charity collections. These collections go to for-profit companies that sell the clothing overseas. Please take time to give your used clothing to charity, church, or local resale shops where American needy get the benefit. For some ideas on where to donate unwanted clothes, you can get information at www.realsimple.com. Take a pro-active stance for Americans.

8. Always donate useful items to the needy. When you buy a new appliance because the old one no longer suits the needs of your family but still works, find a home for it with the needy instead of having the appliance company haul it off and possibly put into a landfill. Ask around and see if anyone

you know needs it. Call the churches in your area. Most church offices will know of families in need. There are so many benefits to be realized from a donation and a little bit of investigating. Getting involved in these aspects can make such a difference to the less fortunate, giving them a push in the right direction, helping them to believe in the American Dream. When we all believe, we are stronger!

9. Realize little things can help the less fortunate. Ever get a Christmas present you have no use for? Sure you have, because almost everyone has. Are you going to re-gift it? May I suggest you donate it to a shelter for abused women. Also, the shampoos and conditioners that you pick up traveling can be helpful to the homeless or abused. You know who you are; some of us have drawers full of this stuff. We never use it! It saves you space and they will love you for it. Little things can make a big difference in so many ways. When you think of your own little things to help the less fortunate, you are being pro-active.

10. Be helpful when you see someone in need. Have you ever been in a supermarket parking lot and seen an elderly or handicapped person struggling to load things into their vehicle? Ask if you can help, and do so if they agree. Not all will accept because many people take advantage of the elderly. If they accept, you are only taking two to three minutes of your time to make a huge difference in the way they feel about the world. You can also open another line of communication with someone who may turn into a friend. Who doesn't need more friends? Remember, what goes around, comes around. Someday, you may need help and some courteous, pro-active person will stop and do the same for you. That is the picture of America to which we should aspire.

11. Pay more attention to what you hear and watch. Have you ever listened to the lyrics of the music you play? Listen carefully; some of these words are demeaning to the American way. Hos, bitches, and unmentionables, do you really want to

give your money to people whose ideas are so different than yours? It may have a good beat and be great to dance to, but if it is profane, please refrain. Of course, this is just an example, there are other media that degrades Americans and do not deserve our attention. When we ignore and explain to others why they should ignore these degrading caricatures of America, you are taking a pro-active stance to ensure a better reputation for all Americans.

12. Make Christmas more fulfilling. Try this, the day after Christmas, put back one dollar a week for each family member. Watch all year to find a family that is basically self-sufficient, but could more easily "get by with a little help from my friends". Two weeks before Christmas, put the money in a nice card and put it in their mailbox. Watch to make sure a parent picks it up. Never tell anyone besides your family who was involved in what you did. Be a real secret Santa, the rewards are great.

13. Start a compost pile in the back of your yard. Put all vegetable waste from home and all clippings from yard and garden in this. Turn once a week and keep it moist. For more information on composting, go to www.nature.org. Free fertilizer and compost are great stuff for the garden you are going to plant in the spring and the waste is out of the landfill, another pro-active stance for the environment.

14. Mentor a child. We all have areas in which we are proficient, share this with a child in need. Two hours a week can help enormously. A better educated community is more able to make intelligent life choices. Love the earth and her people, one person at a time. Your contribution could be priceless.

15. Organize a neighborhood labor exchange. You like to weed but hate to mow. Exchange jobs with a neighbor and make life easier for several. It is also another chance to communicate with people and keep everyone thinking. There are so many areas in which this idea could work. Think of some ideas in

your neighborhood and see if you can find some pro-active neighbors that will get involved. It could help many without taking much of your extra time.

16. Be involved with positive people. Have cook-offs with families and friends, it's a great time around people who are positive about their cooking. Discussion among family and friends can lead to solutions for local problems. Go to local functions, get involved; it is a great way to spread the word of being a pro-active person.

17. Show interest in other people's life. When you are checking out at the supermarket, say "hi" to the clerk and ask how their day is going. This is a small thing, a few words of interest in their day. It works. If you can make that little bit of difference, why would you not want to do this? When you show interest, you are being pro-active. You have made someone's day a little better.

18. Be a responsible pet owner. When you want a pet, don't go to a pet shop. The puppies there are almost always from puppy mills, raised in very bad condition from mothers that are over bred. Go on line and find a pet that needs rescued. If you are patient, you will find the breed you want. And take my word for it, they are most wonderfully grateful. My last dog, Buttons, was a rescue and was the best pet we ever owned. Another thing, please spay or neuter your pet, it is simply the responsible thing to do. If money is the question, look for spay and neuter clinics which can save you a lot of money. Please do not get a pet if you cannot afford one. A pet is a lifetime commitment, if you do not have the money or the time to properly care for one, please enjoy those of others until you can.

19. Volunteer your time for Meals on Wheels. Most volunteer positions are for 2-3 hours a week. A good meal and some cheerful words of comfort make the life of the elderly more bearable. Find out more at www.mowaa.org. If you become

friends with some of these folks and visit them away from the organization, so much the better, you will have a new companion and so will they. You can learn a lot about practical life from our seniors. Win-win situation.

20. Be a good neighbor. Look around your neighborhood. We all are smart enough to know if there is a lonely older or handicapped person who needs a little cheer; a bouquet of flowers from your yard or the supermarket can make a persons day. You are able to make someone's life better for very little money and very little time. Think about it, opening more lines of communication, the stronger our nation can become.

Pro-active basically means you are prepared for difficult circumstances before they arise. Constantly I hope that if we all work together we can stop the storms that are brewing. Let's all try to stop our leaders from putting us in further jeopardy. But if we can't stop them, let us all be prepared for the bad times ahead. A few words in closing, yesterday I heard the words I have been dreading, the fool in the oval office talking about World War 3. In his later years, Einstein said that he did not know how World War 3 would be fought, but he knew how World War 4 would be fought, with sticks and stones. History has shown us how difficult war can be; take a pro-active stance now before it is too late. When Americans take a pro-active stance, it will be easy to "Take Back America".

Chapter 12

Commit to Family Integrity

"The ultimate measure of a man is not where he stands in moments of comfort and convenience, but where he stands at times of challenge and controversy."

Martin Luther King, Jr. (1929-1968)

The definition of integrity is moral or ethical strength, the quality of being honest and the state of being whole. The point of giving you the definition is to convey to you it is not as simple as it may sound. To really have an idea of your integrity, you really need to know what you stand for and believe in. What is important to you? Integrity exists when you think it, say it, and then do it. In order to show others we are a people with integrity, we, as Americans, must not just say we want to "Take Back America", we have to believe it, and then we must do it. We should all say it, and do something about it. Don't be shy. Tell your children, family, friends and those we interact with throughout the day. The time is now, find out what you believe in, and act on it with conviction.

1. <u>Preserve the family–young and old.</u> For years we have all heard that the family unit is breaking down. We are losing the battle to keep the ties that bind us together once we become adults. Well, this attitude needs to change. Many resources are available to help us. A book at the library could be a valuable resource, Google the topic for additional info and recommended readings, and perhaps the most valuable place to go for information is your own family. Take that first baby step and open your mouth. Begin a conversation, ask questions. You have to take the chance, because nothing

is more important than our loved ones. Find out what you need to do to bring your family closer together. Give some thought to the changes needed and make it happen. Nothing will change overnight, but if you stay the course, it will pay off; this is worth any fight or resistance you may encounter. Remember, small actions have big messages.

2. Expect more of yourself and others. It is so easy to say I don't know what to say or do. When dealing with financial problems, phone calls that need to be made, or friends and family matters, doing nothing only multiplies the problem. Our actions may not always be correct or totally solve the situation, but taking action is a step in the right direction, which can be very difficult. Quit letting yourself off so easily. Start asking yourself the hard questions. Have I tried? Did I suggest something? Did I make a phone call? Did any action occur? Anything you do is an effort, and that speaks volumes. You can't ignore responsibility, it doesn't go away. The old saying is still true today, "You never know until you try". Give some thought to these ideas. You can't wish for changes; you have to take the necessary steps to make change happen and allow them to become habits.

3. Respect others. Respect is not old school. My teenage son and I had a disagreement and I told him, "I would never talk to my mother like that. Not when I was a kid and not even now as a 44 year old woman". His reply was, "Times have changed". I beg to differ. Since when has respect been something we used to do? To say the least, we talked more on that topic. Seriously, respect is something you carry with you always. If you want respect, you must give it. Respect must be taught from the earliest ages until the time they become responsible for their own actions. Go to www.teach-nology.com/tutorials to lean how to teach respect to your children. At our jobs, we earn the respect of co-workers by doing a good job, and in turn, give respect to those around us for the same reason. In marriage, a husband and wife must have a healthy respect for each other; otherwise it is hard to have a really strong relationship. Could

this be why over half the marriages in the U.S. fail? Disrespect has become endemic which is completely unacceptable if we want to "Take Back America". Respect is lacking in America, let's revive this value and really drive it home.

4. Lead by example. Hold true to your principals. Teach a good work ethic and show it by example. Go to www.helium.com and type in lead by example for more information on how to teach this to your children. We all want the reputation of a good dependable worker, and even more so, we want that for our children. This ethic starts early with chores around your own home. When you assume responsibility for a task, take your duty seriously. When we hold ourselves accountable, we should also hold our children accountable. Commitment is a family value that is taught by a parent's example. The importance of studying is a work ethic as well. Studying is a skill that needs to be taught early in life as a sound work discipline; as school work becomes more difficult in later years, it will have a huge impact on their learning process. Success is not mandatory, but trying should be. Don't make excuses for not succeeding, instead show pride in how hard you tried. Keeping one's word and agreements in business and family is so important. If you promise your child you are going to do something, then you had better do it or try very hard. Things come up and adjustments need to be made, but a promise is a promise. Do not throw around the word "promise" without realizing what it means and how it can affect others. The safe thing would be to say "I will try" and then make an all out effort. You need to make it a golden rule to do all in your power to keep your word. Life is difficult and sometimes it is really hard to get it all straight; remember doing your best gives you a sense of pride. No one should expect more than a sincere effort and the appreciation you will receive will make it worthwhile.

5. Strive to do it right the first time. It is not enough just to do the job so it is finished, but to do it properly. Half-way efforts are not acceptable. By not accepting a job poorly done, the

message to do it right the first time have been learned first hand. I am certain every parent has faced this repeatedly. I personally wish I had begun this practice earlier with my own children. As they get older, the more difficult it becomes because you can't teach an old dog new tricks (or so they say). So don't be tempted to take the easy way out and redo it for them (as I did), but be firm and follow through. Show them the benefits of getting the job done right the first time.

6. Keep family traditions. Traditions keep family bonds alive. I grew up with certain holiday traditions. Some of my fondest memories are of those gatherings. I know everyone was not as fortunate to have that privilege, but it is never too late. Give it some thought, decide what you and your family like, and begin one of your own. It doesn't necessarily have to be holidays; for example, plan a family reunion at a specific location every year. Another idea is an annual cookout at your house or rotate locations with other family members. Being a part of a family and keeping it as close as possible is a valuable precious gift in our extremely stressful lives. Face it, keeping a family close is difficult, especially when we all have jobs, families, and other obligations. It is critical to make a strong effort to establish and maintain family traditions. It is imperative to build these bonds in order to "Take Back America".

7. Respect our differences. Honor, honesty, and fairness are qualities developed in a relationship over a period of time. There are simply no free gifts in these areas. Such qualities are time honored and reflect who we are and how we think. This can be applied to personal relationships, at work or play, and in the politics that influence our ideas. Comparing one person's ideas to another is like comparing apples and oranges, no two people think exactly alike. We are all individuals with many facets to our personalities. Just like twins, although identical in looks, they are two very different people. We tend to assume our children have the same opinions as their brothers, sisters, or parents sometimes when this is often not

the case. Respect each other as individuals by accepting other beliefs and valuing the fact that we can all be different. After all, one of our greatest rights as Americans is that each person has the right to individuality. Besides, wouldn't it be boring if we all thought alike?

8. Share in the belief that one voice does make a difference. Encourage your children to be confident in all they do. Positive reinforcement teaches them that they can accomplish whatever they set out to do. Our young need to grow into strong, well-rounded adults willing to let their voice be heard. One such person with these praise-worthy qualities is Oprah Winfrey. She overcame so many hardships as a child and young adult to become one of the most powerful women in the world. One of the most defining aspects of her career is her ability to give back to those in need. The courage it took her to get where she is at came from the belief that one voice does make a difference. Hers has certainly been heard. Kudos Oprah! Honesty and a sense of fairness are admirable qualities that can help make your voice be heard.

9. Make integrity your choice. Integrity does not happen by accident; it is a choice. Many people choose not to have integrity, we all know someone like this. Most of the time we can't depend on these people, they seldom keep their word, and we certainly can't confide in them. Don't misunderstand me; any one of these people could make the choice to change, which would give them better principles and higher moral values. The decision is theirs to achieve the integrity every American will need to "Take Back America". Change for people without integrity is not easily accomplished, due to the reputation they have earned, but it can definitely happen. In a perfect world, we would never have to worry about changing as we mature and become an adult, we would already be a person of integrity. Communicate with your children. Let them know life is full of choices. Teach them how to reason, this skill is not necessarily inherited, it is a learned skill and a skill that improves with practice. It will save them a lot of

trouble throughout their life if they know how to make the correct choices. The skill of reasoning and being a problem solver is invaluable because the person with integrity takes the higher, moral ground. Your integrity is sacred, and a moral no one can take from you unless you give it away.

10. <u>Get out of your safe zone.</u> You cannot make a difference by sitting on your couch and letting life just pass you by. Do you know of anyone that doesn't have an opinion or a belief in something? There are so many areas where you could become involved. You do not have to begin by running for office, but start with some something in your comfort zone. Make it something that interests you; not only will that make it more enjoyable, it will be something you will be more inclined to continue. Most of us are not superstars, but we all have something in common because of the fact that we are normal everyday Americans that have strong beliefs. We may get aggravated with our government or country, but I firmly believe we are proud to be Americans and it is time to let some of that excitement show. The example we show our children and peers could be the beginning of repeat behavior. Who knows, maybe one of our children will be a future president.

11. <u>Show interest in your children, family, friends and coworkers.</u> Ask your child about their school day and listen intently to their answer. Let them know you are not asking because it is your duty to do so, but that you really are interested. The same goes true for others in our lives. If you ask someone "How are you doing?", listen to the answer and participate in the conversation. Sometimes we do these things to be polite, but other times we need to be better listeners. Let these people in our lives know that you really do care. We are all guilty of taking our loved ones or friends for granted, as if they will always be there, and that is just not reality. We all have said things like, "I wish I had done more", "I should have called more often", or "if I had only known". Don't put yourself in that position, do more now, call more now, and put yourself

in the position to know what's going on now. As your children go out into the world, they will share with others that which they have learned at home and wonder why all people don't do the same. When it was such a natural part of their lives, it will be assumed that it is the right thing to do. Wouldn't that be a true compliment to the parents?

12. Have principles. It is easy to say you have principles, but living those principles is altogether another matter. We should all strive to live those principles on a daily basis. Share your principles with your family. Let them know how you feel and why. Standing together as a family unit is a very powerful statement. You will be encouraging your children and family to think and define themselves and what they believe in. Moral values are the core of who we are. Moral is defined by knowing what is right or wrong. Value is defined by standards held or accepted by an individual, class or society. Our conduct reflects our moral values. Far too often we tend to take the easy route to accomplish something even though we know it is the wrong thing to do. What message do we send out? If we know right from wrong and know we should not take the easy way, don't be tempted to deviate from your belief. As a parent, realize your children learn from your example and somewhere they will repeat your actions. Ethical and honorable ways in which we relate to others is how reputations are formed. Don't we all want to have a good reputation? Our conduct not only reflects on us, it reflects on our family. When we all hold true to our principles, we will "Take Back America".

13. Choose the company you keep with care. The company we keep may influence the type of company our children keep. The people we choose to spend time with are a reflection on ourselves and too many people are too quick to judge before investigating (shame on those of you who make snap judgments before you know the facts). This is something we need to teach our youth. While your child was in junior high spending time with someone who knowingly and obviously broke rules, it would not be a far stretch for other people,

such as teachers, parents and students, to assume your child finds that behavior acceptable. As unfair as it may seem, it is how things work. Although your child broke no rules, their reputation was effected and possibly that of your entire family. It is a harsh reality to be judged and labeled in this fashion, but it is something we all know happens and occurs. Remember that old saying that is still true today, "birds of a feather flock together". Wouldn't your family rather be known as a gathering of swans than a gaggle of geese?

14. Be a true loyal friend. Friends, we all have them, or wish we had more of them; but are we being a good friend to those we have? I believe we all have room to improve in many areas of our lives and this is no exception. For help in this area, go to www.ehow.com/how_2108829_be-good-friend.html. A simple phone call can make all the difference, especially when we know our friend is going through something difficult. Return a good deed when one is done for us. If we haven't had a good deed done for us, then do one for someone else and begin a support system. You scratch my back, I'll scratch yours! I want to know I can trust the person with whom I'm spending time, and I really want them to feel that way about me. I doubt I am alone in this concept. Loyalty is the same way. I don't need a fair-weathered friend who only wants to be around me to have fun. We all need and deserve to have friends around us that care in the good times as well as the bad. Basically all you have to do is remember the golden rule, "Do unto others as you would have done unto you".

15. Obey the law. If adults obey the law, children will do the same. Children and young adults learn from example. If we knowingly break the law, the message we send our children is pretty clear. This can be anything from driving and obeying the traffic laws to paying taxes. Our children are pretty smart, we may think we do things that they don't pick up on, but we are wrong. We are their teachers and although we find it sometimes hard not to take the short cut or tell a little lie, we need to refrain from doing so. "Elephants never forget" is a

popular saying, and trust me, children never forget and will bring these facts up at the most inopportune moment. I'm sure we all have funny stories we could tell about that.

16. Take charge of your surroundings. Whether you own or rent your home, it is essential to maintain it. How does this make a difference? While maintaining your home is also gratifying and gives you peace of mind, it also instills work ethic, responsibility (not only to the home but to the neighbors), and pride in your community. It helps with the value of your home and inspires your neighbor to do their part in keeping up the neighborhood. Take part in community activities to beautify your town, because the community is also a part of our surroundings. These values are taught while your children are growing up and the way you keep your property will in all likelihood be the way they keep theirs. Keep each other accountable. The possibilities are endless and hopefully will spur a chain reaction of beautiful benefits.

17. Do not violate or compromise your own identity. No one has ever said standing by our values is easy. There will be opposition. Everyone is entitled to their opinion and everyone is entitled to stick by their beliefs. Just because your best friend has an opposing opinion perhaps, doesn't mean you can't be their friend. You should be able to discuss your differences as adults without war. If that is not possible, agree to disagree and move on. "I may not agree with what you have to say, but I will defend to my death, your right to say it" is a famous quote by Patrick Henry who was a hero of the American Revolution. This idealism allowed us to believe every person has the right to voice their opinion. Many countries do not enjoy this luxury. We have always and will always be the greatest country on earth even though we do have many issues to deal with. Regardless of our faults, ask anyone who has been in another country and come back home, where they would rather live. When you are proud of whom you are and where you live, it gives you a very empowering confidence.

18. Realize that chores teach responsibility. Most parents don't want their children to have to do chores like they did as children and sometimes it is just easier to do it ourselves than fight with our children to get it done. These attitudes are wrong. As parents, it is our responsibility to teach them how to work and we should begin these lessons at a very early age. It instills responsibility, values, and a work ethic that could carry them far into the future. Remember a good work ethic can be passed from generation to generation.

19. Be sincere and gracious at all times. Sincerity cannot be faked, nor should anyone try. Be polite, but never be false. Believe it or not, most of us can tell when someone is not being really sincere. It is not a favorable impression. When you find yourself in a position that makes you uncomfortable, it would be so much better to be honest about it. You can still be honest without flat out being rude. We always worry so much about hurting each other's feelings that we tend to make false impressions. I simply suggest we try to look for the polite way to be honest and begin to address these issues as they arise. Go to www.selfgrowth.com and type in sincere personality for more advice. After all, we do teach our children to stand up to peer pressure and be honest, don't we?

20. Have family meetings. All families should have weekly meetings to integrate many of the ideas in this chapter into their lives. Go to www.childparenting.about.com for more input on family meetings. Families could accomplish this after dinner one night a week; clear away the dishes and begin. Make them fun, not something to dread. Family meetings have a reputation that everyone is going to get griped at about their poor school grades, skipping of chores, or what ever transgression is current. Family meetings do not have to be this way; they can be productive positive fun times. These meetings can be for planning your next family-fun vacation, volunteering in the community as a family activity, or something as simple as establishing a new family tradition. Along with this, the family meetings should be a time to bond

> and discuss current issues that involve your family and your place in the community. During family meetings, members can discuss any fear or misunderstanding of current events that makes them apprehensive. Having an opportunity to talk about these bothersome subjects can open up lines of communication that will help both parents and children. Family meetings also give parents the chance to instill the values and morals they want their children to have. The first meetings may be awkward…be persistent, it will pay off in the end!

Defining yourself is what most of these ideas refer to in this chapter. If you don't know exactly how you feel, spend some time figuring it out. It is not always easy to know how to feel in our complicated world. Deciding what you want to be when you grow up doesn't just apply to our children. Some of us adults (including me) need to decide what we want to be when we grow up too. Some things just take time. We do luckily live in a land with tremendous choices. It can be overwhelming, but in a good way. It would be horrible to live somewhere and be told what we had to do with our life. Can you imagine what it would feel like to not be able to make your own choices? Many times during our lifetime our opinions may change. Circumstances, maturity, and just being better informed can make us change our minds on issues. That does not make us wishy-washy, it makes us human. Do not get caught up in what others may think, take the time to learn what you think; every one of us is a valuable human being. Let's try to be the best ancestors we can possibly be and "Commit To Family Integrity".

CHAPTER 13

BE INVOLVED IN YOUR COMMUNITY

"There is an idea abroad among moral people that they should make their neighbors good. One person I have to make good: myself. But my duty to my neighbor is much more nearly expressed by saying that I have to make him happy–if I may."

R. L. Stevenson (1850-1894)

How can being involved in your community help "Take Back America"? Well...anything we do to make ourselves stronger as a family or as a community makes us stronger as a nation. Each action has a ripple effect. The actions we take may very well help our community, but it may benefit another cause. We become so busy in our personal lives that it is difficult to change our habits; that's what it will take though. You have to decide what you feel strongly about and let your voice be heard. If you are the quiet type, then let your actions be seen. You are not only doing the right thing, you are leading by example for your children and sending a strong message to them. Remember, our children are our future, and we will need them to step up and do these things as adults.

1. Build a neighborhood watch group. It seems to me that lately the laws are made to protect the criminals while keeping law-abiding citizens under control. It seems the police find it easier to go after law-abiding citizens because they know they will pay their fines. Maybe the police could actually convict the criminals if more citizens in our communities got involved. Does your community have a neighborhood watch? If not, contact your local police department to find out how you report your findings to the police or go to www.nnwi.

org for help forming your own neighborhood watch from the National Neighborhood Watch Institute. You could be the key that keeps illegal aliens from taking over your neighborhood if you are aware of what goes on in your community. You could also be the key in stopping a robbery, or preventing an injury. Actions speak louder than words; have courage, be bold, and let's stop the increasing crime rate. If we want to stop crime from taking over our communities, we must all stand together to "Take Back America".

2. Bring back Main Street USA. Mom and pop stores and restaurants are going out of business all across our nation. Certainly this is no big surprise with all the super centers (we all know who this is), chain stores, and restaurants springing up like mushrooms, forcing small businesses into bankruptcy or using eminent domain to push them out. We all want the most value for our money and many times these mega buyers are the only way to get it; however, we need to start spreading the wealth around. Some people boycott these super centers, others only shop there when absolutely necessary, and unfortunately, an even greater number of people shop there exclusively. Does your main street look like a ghost town? If it doesn't, you are lucky. Do you remember the old dime stores? I do, they were a much cherished part of my childhood, and something I always looked forward to when visiting my grandparents. They're all gone; perhaps if we had spread our patronage around, some of these great American icons would still exist. It would be great if we gave them all our business, but this could be an unrealistic expectation. Let's all do the best we can to help keep small business and main street alive. Many family stores and restaurants have been around for decades, generation after generation stepping up to run the family business. These places are struggling and need our support. We do not mean to stand in the way of progress, but do you consider it progress to give all of our money to foreign-based mega chains? We need to be aware of whose pockets we are lining with our patronage.

3. Offer the gift of time. Time is a gift that can keep on giving. During this chapter, we have talked about time and the monetary gift. I would like to take this opportunity to talk about time only. When it is not possible to contribute money, volunteer your time; don't feel like you can't participate. One of the greatest gifts of all is the gift of time. To the bedridden person in a nursing home having someone come in and talk with them is priceless. To those persons who volunteer every time without fail, we thank you (you are angels sent from above). Can you imagine how special it would be for those angels to get a night off by someone else stepping up to plate? Time is precious to us all and none of us seem to have enough of it. Maybe if we managed our time a little wiser, we could find a way to include volunteering in our busy lives. It could mean so much to someone else. The choices of how to do this are endless; so please find time to give something back. Remember, you could be in the same boat someday.

4. Give Blood. Giving blood is truly the gift of life. Visit the website www.givelife.org or call 1-800 GIVE LIFE for more information on locations and times to donate blood; the volunteers will answer any questions you may have. If you're not sure if you are a good candidate, check with your doctor or call the Red Cross, a volunteer will tell you the guidelines. Many of us will find that loved ones or maybe even ourselves will unexpectedly be in need of a donation one day and because someone already donated blood, you can receive needed blood products in a timely manner. Wouldn't it be nice for us to return the favor? Red Cross is also another place needing volunteers. Call to find out if that is something you could or would be able to do. The American Red Cross has formed a community of service from which we all benefit. Don't drop the ball, donate and save someone's life.

5. Know the history of your hometown and surrounding area. Our United States has some amazing history and facts. We always want to go somewhere else more exciting for vacation, and that's normal, but how about a day on the weekend

to explore our own backyard. Discovering your backyard could be as easy as a phone call to your local Chamber of Commerce. When calling for this information, let them know your interests so they have a place to begin. Of course, the internet is a wonderful place to find out what's going on in your area or call the Department of Tourism for your state. Depending on where you live, you could find such things to do as rock climbing, cave dwelling, Civil War history, bird watching, Indian history, or local celebrity homes. You never know, but there is sure to be something for everyone; heck, who knows, maybe you will learn something about your area you didn't know before.

6. Become a companion to those without family. Unfortunately, many people do not have the gift of family. People like this need people to reach out to them and make them a part of an extended family. There are many programs that can help you do this such as Big Brothers, Big Sisters, and organizations that help with the elderly. Also, a good thing to check is senior centers, nursing homes, and homeless shelters. All these people need your kindness and a helping hand. When you do this, you must pledge to be there year around not just during holiday times. Lend your ears, heart, and sometimes your pocketbook to help those in need; in the end, the rewards will be yours.

7. Leave it cleaner than you found it. Do you remember the Indian with a tear running down his face? Many times when you go to your local park, this should be the emotion we all feel. It is a disgrace to see our beautiful land so abused. So, you should remember the commercial that said "you should never make Mother Nature angry"? When you go to the park for a picnic, make sure you pick up all your belongings, throw away your trash, and don't forget to recycle what you can. Don't stop there. Make it a practice that you pick up what was there before you. I am not saying clean up the whole park, but if each of us took some of the trash each time we had the opportunity, it would go a long way to cleaning up our areas.

Use this practice anywhere you go. If you are at the mall and a drink is left, put it in a trash can. You could also form an organization to Adopt a Highway in your community. Others may see you and who knows it could become a trend. The concept is sound, although we shouldn't have to clean up after Neanderthals (people who have no common courtesy); someone has to take the first step.

8. Take pride in your town and home. As a society we have become more concerned about our own lives. We need to get outside our safe zone and take a look around us. Our surroundings and our communities are always in need of upkeep. I do realize how busy everyone is raising families and working to meet their obligations, but we need to build time into our schedules to properly maintain our property. The little things we do around our homes such as landscaping, mulching, weeding, and general maintenance make it look pleasant, clean, and increases the value of your home and the homes in your neighborhood. Some communities have clean up days, participate when possible and form one if none presently exists. Share work with one of your neighbors because many hands make light work. Help them with a job and in turn they can help you; in the past, exchanging labor was common and neighborly. Showing pride in our home and our town can really make a favorable impression to those passing through or possibly deciding to move there.

9. Know your neighbors. Not so many years ago, it seemed everyone knew their neighbors. When you moved into a new area, your neighbors invariably greeted you with some kind of baked goods to make you feel welcome. In this day and time, you are not greeted that way and if you were, more than likely, you would want it to be an unopened sealed package (at least until you got to know them). You may not have always liked your neighbor, but if you had an emergency or needed someone to keep an eye on your home while you were away, you could depend on your neighbor. We have relocated a few times over a period of years, and I have noticed that

becoming friends with your neighbor has taken a turn for the worse. Nowadays, people don't seem to think it's worthwhile whether in the city or the country. If my dog gets out by accident, I want to know my neighbor would let me know. Today, people don't want that kind of friendship and frankly I don't understand why! Shouldn't we all care about our fellow neighbors? Do we want our children growing up thinking that neighbors aren't important? I think we should all start making an effort to say hello, introduce ourselves, and form some kind of relationship even if it's only for common courtesy. Teach our children this is part of taking charge of our surroundings and being a responsible neighbor.

10. <u>Learn CPR.</u> Cardiopulmonary resuscitation is a combination of chest compressions and rescue breathing (mouth to mouth). Local American Heart Associations are a great source to find CPR courses in your area; you can do this at <u>www.RedCross.org.</u> Since this is a skill that is better to practice, it is best to repeat this course every two years. This also allows us to learn any new techniques available or any changes that have been made. We all pray that we never need or have to use this skill; but as in the case of any emergency, preparation is always the best policy and will help you be mentally prepared so you don't panic. Remember, it is how we react in times of emergencies that define who we are. Think of all the people whose life has been saved by a stranger or a loved one because someone took the time to get certified. It takes very little time and is generally inexpensive, but the outcome could be priceless. For your family's sake, locate a class today and make the commitment to learn this life-saving skill.

11. <u>Participate in local functions.</u> Big town, small towns, all towns seem to have their fair share of fund raisers. It may seem never ending; however, these functions accomplish many purposes other than raising money and are always for a good cause. Being involved and building relationships with those who work together for the same cause can be a truly rewarding experience. City or town activities are offered in

many communities. Other functions can be found at local churches, schools, and community colleges which promote projects and festivals. These festivities are a lot of fun to attend. I used to think (when I was younger) these things seemed tedious. I was wrong. Choosing to look at things in a negative way makes them seem like going to the dentist. Most of the time, you will find something to laugh about, get a good meal, or you may even find people to talk to you know. Promote these functions with people you run into during the course of a day. You'll find that a lot of these events are cheaper than going to eat at a chain restaurant or attending the movies. The money goes for a better cause and I truly believe you will surprise yourself and have fun.

12. <u>Change the way we think.</u> Most of us have the attitude that lil ol me cannot make a difference. Think of all the great people in our history that has made a difference, what if all of them thought the same way. Would we have light bulbs, telephones, or sliced bread? Therefore, we need to change the way we think. Increasing our confidence in ourselves can make a difference in our community. Taking back America is a campaign that begins in your hometown; it will require dedication, enthusiasm, consistency, and deep thought. A key component is to protect our own. America needs more people to step up with new ideas and youthful energy to take on some of the responsibility of improving our communities; if not, we will simply remain a stagnant society. Our goal as a collective nation should be to take a look at home and in our communities to find a way we can all make a difference.

13. <u>Help your local food pantry.</u> If your church does not offer one, do not be afraid to contact someone outside your own religion. Just because you do not attend that particular church doesn't mean they would reject your offer to help or your donation of food. Some towns do this as a community and are in great need of your help. The same is true for food delivery, Meals on Wheels is a great organization that delivers meals to the elderly and shut-ins, they are always in need of an extra

hand and most volunteer positions are for 2-3 hours per week. Something else of importance is for someone who has great organizational skills to help put Second Harvest concepts to use in your area. Second Harvest is an organization that helps bring together food items that are outdated and would otherwise go to waste. Just think how much help your local pantry would get if bakeries always gave their outdated bread, if the local grocery store donated their tired produce, or if all the dented cans from the local box store were donated. I encourage you to take the time, explore your options, and get your family involved.

14. Be prepared for emergencies. Everyone knows you need to be prepared for emergencies, but after 9/11, the reality of the need to step up and do this has increased. Most of us just assume we will get prepared eventually, but procrastination is not an option when your family's life hangs in the balance. Better preparation by many before Hurricane Katrina could have prevented many of the tragic results we know as history. For instance, how would it have changed the outcome if the school buses had been used to evacuate those with minimal resources instead of being left to the flood? A wealth of valuable information about planning for emergencies can be found at www.ready.gov. Clothes, water, food, medications, important documents, turning off utilities, and pet care are a few of the topics discussed on this site. Don't put it off. Do it now before the need arises and it is too late. Preparing an escape plan in case of fire is another important aspect of being prepared. You have to make sure all family knows the routine such as where to meet, how to get out of the house if various doors are blocked, and a plan to summon the fire department. Fire alarms need to be checked regularly and everyone should know how to use the fire extinguisher. Take the time to go over these things before it is too late and you have to live with the regret. Keep in mind, an ounce of prevention is worth a pound of cure.

15. Give special help during holidays. At certain times of the year, the need is even greater for community involvement. An obvious holiday is Christmas. All good-hearted people want every child to have a joyous Christmas. Consider giving one less gift to your own family and make a special Christmas for a child in need. In almost every store you will see some kind of donation box available. Organizations promote giving in the media, on the radio, in the newspaper, and on television. Many people take the time to drop off items to these worthwhile causes, but many more folks need to do the same. During the winter, used coats, jackets, gloves, and hats can save the health of those in need. If you don't have extra money, donating unwanted or unneeded items can be your way of being involved. For families in need, the value of that gift is just as important as something wrapped in plastic. Be aware that the need is always there, but at the holidays and bitterly cold times of the year, make the extra effort to do what you can.

16. Donate unwanted items to local charities. I know we have all heard phrases that talk about life being a constant circle. Well...donating is like that. Every day, every week, and every year we find things that we have purchased which we no longer want or can use. Some of us have a tendency to only do this once or twice a year to get rid of our unwanted items. Why wait? As we come across items we no longer need, set them aside. Once a few things have been accumulated, put them in your car and the next time you are near a donation center, drop them off. You will have more room at your home and most importantly you will be giving throughout the year. We have people in our country that are in desperate need now and we need to make our needy come first. If you cannot find a donation center, many churches know of needy families who could benefit from your donation. Make it a habit to take the items you or your family no longer need to a charity or donation center and complete the circle.

17. <u>Be involved in local school systems.</u> If you are a parent, of course you should be involved in your child's school. Your involvement in your child's educational activities sends a great message to many about your commitment. Being part of the learning process is just as important as attending little league games, plays, or dance recitals. If you are grandparent, help your children with their children; any help can go a long way in helping our children succeed. If you are not a parent or grandparent, that does not mean you cannot be involved in the education of our young, become a mentor. What are your best qualities? Do you have exceptional math skills? Or can you read and comprehend better than most? Some children just need an extra mind to help them accomplish their goals. Put these skills to good use!!

18. <u>Ask questions.</u> One of my personal pet peeves with my own family is they never seem to ask enough questions. Maybe some of you can relate to this. Ask questions when you don't know the details of a situation to accomplish the task at hand. It is not a matter of seeming stupid; it is simply a matter of learning something you don't already know. Running errands, applying for jobs, going to the doctor, and contending with bills and paperwork can be simplified by asking questions. Remember, no one knows everything. Many companies, schools, and doctors have certain routines and formats; most of them are different, inquire specifically what you need to bring and exactly where you need to go. Taking the guess work out of our everyday lives makes us feel more confident in what we have to accomplish. When in doubt, always ask questions so you can "git r done".

19. <u>Volunteer in your community.</u> The first thing you need to do is find out what appeals to you. Maybe it's your church or your child's school, but there are so many choices available to you. To determine exactly what is available, research your area and those close to you. Many local papers have a section that can help you find where help is needed and like me, you could learn about groups you didn't know existed. Making a few phone

calls to your local Chamber of Commerce or town hall may give you ideas as well, most of the time these people are happy to give you information or at least direct you to the appropriate place to call. Whether you choose to work with the elderly or disabled, preschool children, or your local humane society does not matter, the important thing is to get involved; your services will be greatly appreciated. Check in to what would appeal to you and give whatever time you have. I realize this is hard to do; maybe it can be something you and your family do together. Wouldn't that be a nice tradition to start?

20. Support those who give in your community. A lot of local businesses are instrumental in helping schools, churches, and other various organizations. Some may sponsor little league teams by paying all fees, buying uniforms, and even trophies. Grocery stores give discounts to many organizations having dinners or needing to provide concession stands. Without that discount, the profit made from these endeavors would be less. Many people with a specific talent or skill donate their time at no charge. Showing our gratitude to these businesses and people by voicing our thanks can be done by patronizing their establishments. Another way to show your gratitude is by word of mouth let all friends and family know about the great work these sponsors are doing in your community. At this time, we would personally like to thank all the generous individuals who give so willingly.

We have heard a lot about this topic since we were kids. Some of us are probably tired of hearing it, however the world has changed and it is time to rethink our involvement in our communities. No one likes change, but change can be a positive stepping stone. I really don't know why we have always connected change with negative feelings. We desire things to be different. Now is the time to look at what we can accomplish and make some adjustments because we all desire to have everyone fed, happy, and sheltered to lessen suffering in our community. While all these ideas are common sense ideas with which all of us are familiar, perhaps hearing it in this context will inspire you to get the family together and get involved in your community.

CHAPTER 14

COMMIT TO PERSONAL FINANCIAL SECURITY

"Before you speak, listen. Before you write, think. Before you spend, earn. Before you invest, investigate. Before you criticize, wait. Before you pray, forgive. Before you quit, try. Before you retire, save. Before you die, give."

William A Ward (1921-1994)

My sister expressed concern about me writing this chapter, as well she should. So right off the bat, I am going to tell you that I have made every mistake there is to make in my personal finances. I have learned from my mistakes, I hope you can learn from them also. Every individual in this country needs to save money and be fiscally responsible. Unfortunately, it seems we are a country of people with maxed-out credit cards, and most of us live from paycheck to paycheck. You should realize that having money in the bank helps not only you, but helps to keep the economy of this country stable. So by being financially responsible you can help "Take Back America".

1. Save money. There is a cousin of mine that saved 10% of every dollar she ever made, starting as a child's allowance and babysitting as a teenager. Oh, how I wish I had done the same. I did not though, so I shall have to suffer the consequences. You, however, won't have to if you start saving a portion of all the money you make now. If you wish to have the good things later in life, make good decisions now and get help at www.smartaboutmoney.org. It is so important for all of us to be financially responsible for the sake of our country.

2. Plan for your retirement. Starting now, think of how you want your retirement to be. Don't ever think you can think about it tomorrow or next week. Now is the time, the very minute you read this. Go to www.ssa.gov/retire2 for help planning your retirement. There are many things to read and practice in order to get the idea of how to plan your future, read them all and PLAN, PLAN, PLAN.

3. Prepare for your career. If you have not completed your education, please do so! Plan a career that will be satisfying and pay enough to make a good living for you and your future family. Hopefully you will find a job with a company or organization that you can stay with throughout your working life. Changing jobs is expensive and often counterproductive for your life plan. It will be harder to retire if you are constantly changing jobs. Many of us have a hard time determining exactly what we want to do in our careers, but once you figure it out, go for it with conviction, and don't let anyone stop you once you set your goals.

4. Join your 401K the first day you are eligible! Study the books and pamphlets you receive from your company's plan or go to www.401khelpcenter.com. At this place in time, I would recommend a guaranteed earnings plan. The stock market is very volatile right now, so I would tend toward long-term earnings at a smaller percentage rate but with more stability. As you know, many companies have invested in the sub-prime mortgage market and they are losing money hand over fist. It is in your best interest to know where your money is being invested and choose the less volatile route. The sooner you get involved with your 401K, the sooner you will be able to retire and achieve your part of the American dream.

5. Keep an emergency account. Create an emergency fund with 10% of everything you take home in a credit union or a savings account at your bank. Emergencies happen all the time and come in all shapes and expenses. You never know when something will turn your life upside down. So if you

have an emergency fund that is earning interest, you can use that money instead of paying interest on credit cards if you have to charge it. If no emergencies arise, this can be the start of saving for your own home. Never mistake this; you need to plan for owning a home from the first day you start to work. Your home will be an investment that will help you to retire. Saving for emergencies can also be instrumental in raising your credit score and lowering your interest rate. Win-win situation, you have money for emergencies and better credit.

6. Live within your means. There is always the matter of wanting what everyone else seems to have. You should reconcile yourself to buying only what you can honestly afford. You really don't need a Beamer that runs 130 miles per hour. You must recognize the difference between what you want and what you really need to make yourself happy, not to impress those around you. Credit cards and auto loans used for unnecessary things is ruining the life of many people in this country and undermines America financially. When we all start living within our means, America will be able to recover from the credit crisis a little at a time leading to better times for all of us.

7. Be wise and frugal about your everyday expenses. Do you really need that $3 latte every morning? Your cup of coffee on the way to work every morning costs between $60-70 a month. We must start to consider such things. If you drink a cup of coffee at home and save the difference in cost, in ten years you could take a trip around the world, or buy a hybrid car to save even more money, and perhaps help save our planet. One cup of coffee is just one example; there are many ways to curb your everyday expenses. Use your saved money to put in your savings account or pay off debts with high interest. Let's get this country out of debt through some frugal living...we can do it!!

8. Maximize your loan dollars. When it comes time to take a loan for a new car, do not only shop for the car, shop for the loan, this applies to many loans. If you can, join a credit union in your area which is a great way to save money and get a good interest rate. Check your area out to see what is available. Check out different avenues on the interest you can earn on money saved too, they will be very competitive but you want your money where it earns the most interest. Some of these things take time to investigate, but in the end, you will be the winner when you stay on top of maximizing your dollars.

9. Earn interest, don't pay interest whenever possible. Department store credit cards are an absolute no-no, no-no! We cannot stress this enough because these cards are only good when you shop in their store, and the rates are always higher than a good bank card. One payment on one card is almost always easier to make than several, and it is definitely simpler to make one payment on time. Late payments can double your interest rate in no time. By putting money in savings and not paying interest to department stores, you can help strengthen the American economy and earn interest from the banks. Win-win situation for all.

10. Create a budget and live by it. Everyone should live on a budget, a loose plan or very tight restrictive budget according to each person's need. You can get good ideas at www.smartaboutmoney.org. Financially, everyone needs to have a plan of how to get where you want to go or need to go. Those people you see on vacations and doing things you want to do have prioritized their income to allow for the good things in life and still be able to respond in money emergencies. If your neighbor who makes close to the same amount of money you do is leaving on an Italian vacation while you are going to your mom's lake house, you need to pay attention to what your neighbor is doing right. Take classes in money management at a community college if you are having troubles budgeting, this will be money well spent.

11. <u>Look before you leap into home ownership.</u> As mentioned earlier, your home will be an investment to help you toward financial stability. Keep in mind there are many pitfalls to purchasing a home. Educate yourself on how to buy a home that meets your needs and your checkbook. Presently, all across this country, our citizens are losing their homes because they did not do their homework before signing on the dotted line. You must realize when you agree to pay monthly installments for thirty years that you must be able to afford that payment. Therefore, check on everything that pertains to this contract; how high are the closing costs, the interest rate, occupancy permits, etc. If you don't know how much this is going to cost, do not sign. Make sure you never take an interest only loan; you must begin to build equity immediately. Do business with only very reputable mortgage brokers. The closing cost and title insurance vary tremendously from company to company; there can be as much as 100% difference. Please never let anyone talk you into including your closing cost and title insurance in the mortgage, you will be paying interest on these costs. These charges can be as much as the first three years payments against the equity on your amortized mortgage. If you cannot afford a down payment, closing costs and a private inspector for your purchase, you cannot afford to buy this home yet. Waiting for the right time financially can alleviate a lot of stress for you in the future. Home ownership should be a happy time not a stressful financial burden.

12. <u>Be aware of the responsibility of home ownership.</u> While we are still on the subject of buying a home, please make sure this home meets your needs and not those of your friends. Do not buy on the assumption that it will impress your family and friends. Responsibility impresses more than showing off. Keep in mind the cost of home ownership goes well beyond the mortgage payment. You are now the one to make repairs and improvements (that emergency fund can come in handy again). You will also have the cost of landscaping,

lawn mowing, and seeding. You will also need tools for these jobs. You will need to plant trees and other general lawn maintenance. Before you buy a normal suburban home, decide if you have the time and the will to take on the job of a single family home. Sometimes a condo is more practical. For those of you who go this route, you must familiarize yourself with the cost of assessments and covenant of the condo association. Whether you decide on a single family home, a condo, or even manufactured housing, make sure you are aware of all costs involved in the purchase and make sure it fits your needs and your budget. Home ownership is a great pleasure and responsibility, and a big part of the American dream because everyone wants their own space; please be sure you are ready to take on this responsibility before signing on the dotted line. Stabilizing our country's economy is a must and one way you can help "Take Back America".

13. Drive an automobile that fits your checkbook. Ah! The automobile, the stuff of all young men's dreams. The only problem is that in their present form, they are killing our planet; then again, they can also be a budget buster, so I guess there is more than one problem. What you drive is not who you are, it does not necessarily reflect your income or your status in the world. It should, however, reflect the level-headed hard-worker you are and a person who is trying to save Mother Earth while stashing some cash to have more fun. Let's face it, if you are driving a car you can't afford to drive, you are not going to have much fun with it; chick magnet or not. Be financially responsible by driving the most economical car for your budget and the environment.

14. Stop shopping for fun. Shopping is not a form of recreation. We Americans are the only people in the world who shop for clothes to go shopping in. We build giant energy-consuming temples to rampant consumerism, and we call them malls. Our children go to cruise the shop and lust after things that should never be in a thinking person's home. You want to make a difference in the world, stop being a mega-consumer.

Buy American made goods, you may not be able to afford as many things, but then again we all have more things than we really need. Find a healthier more productive form of recreation; the options are endless.

15. Consider a one-income family unit. Today's family has more problems than the generations before in many ways. It almost always takes two to make ends meet, this is the general thought afloat in most minds today. After studying the matter and doing a little research, I truly believe that one income family units can or may save money when their salaries range from $45,000-$65,000. I think there could be a little latitude in salaries. We contend that the wife staying home actually saves money by giving her the time to shop and prepare meals from scratch, no child care, and only one car insured for commuting. Other benefits include lower taxes and a stay-at-home mother having time to deal with school matters and all that is involved in educating a child. Most educators in the system say that more parental involvement is needed to help our children achieve in school. You may want to check into this way of life. We all know the better the children are educated the better chance we have to "Take Back America".

16. Shop for your food wisely. The news is reporting a 5.7% rise in grocery costs; we who shop know it is closer to 20%. These prices are enough to drive you to shop at Wal-Mart. Don't! You can do better by shopping smarter at other stores. There has to be a strategy to buying, storing and cooking the food you purchase. For many, meat is the big ticket item. In my home, it is produce in the winter. In the summer, I try to grow as much myself as is possible. Those who say you should plan a week's menu in advance are thinking too short. Menus or outlines of such should be for a month to allow you to take advantage of sale cycles. Basics that you keep on hand such as pasta, beans, rice and tomato products such as tomato paste and sauces can be building blocks that you plan a month worth of meals around. With the cost of all things that depend on corn going

ever higher (thanks to some very short sided politicians and greedy farm associations), we shall have to plan meals with less meat and more protein from sources such as bean and soy products. If there are box stores in your area, you will want to check them out; I find very good savings at Aldi's and Sav-A-Lot. I don't mind bagging my own stuff since I like to handle my costly groceries. Shop for your staples at the box stores; in some cases the savings can be as much as 50%. Plan one week a month when you do the staples; that week there will be less to spend on other things. Coupons are another way of saving, but only if the purchase is one your family will use. Newspapers are a good source of coupons, but you can also go on-line and print your own according to your own needs. By using all resources, you can come up with as much as 50% savings, it is more work but make it a treasure hunt with your children and savings can become a game. Maybe you could even award a monthly prize to the child that comes up with the most savings each month. Find ways that work for your own family and share ideas with family, friends, and neighbors. We are all in this mess together, and we can help each other beat this bad time in American history. We may even come out stronger for it and I am sure, much smarter.

17. <u>Stay healthy for financial advantages.</u> Health insurance, shriek! If there are two more hated words in the English language when used together, I can't think of what they are unless it is Cheney and Bush. Insurance companies own this country, so let's all make a pledge to bankrupt them; stay healthy and put the money in savings. If you have employer provided health care, use the system as little as possible. Instead stay healthy, eat right, stay slim, don't smoke or drink to excess, and indulge in healthy and safe exercise. Do all the things insurance companies want you to do, but go one step further and drop them. The satisfaction alone should be good for a year's mental health. Seriously, I am just kidding about living without insurance, but by living a healthy life, you may be able to negotiate a better premium.

18. Home school your children. Consider home schooling your children, they will get a better education. It is a big savings on commuting, clothing, and school lab fees, etc. Your children will grow up with more of your ideas and avoid the dangers that seem to plague public schools such as drug usage, communicable diseases, and the bullying that often causes public school massacres. There are many advantages to home education, getting to spend more time with your child and know them better is a priceless reward. The education system in America has fallen behind most other industrialized nations. By home schooling your children, you can rest assured they get a better education without all the hazards of public school. Learn how to get started with your child by going to www.homeschooling.about.com. To make it easier for you, you will also need to add /od/gettingstarted/p/homeschool/101.htm. I will say it again, our futures lie in our young, and their education is vital to "Take Back America".

19. Downsize for financial advantages. When it is time to retire, make up your mind to enjoy the years of freedom, but also know even though you did your best to plan, prices will continue to rise. You will have more medical bills, more prescriptions, and possibly hospital stays. So watching your budget will still be necessary. You can live well on less money if you are not afraid to downsize. A smaller home or a condo with lower taxes, insurance, and utility bills will make your money go much further. Use the equity in your large home to pay cash for a smaller place and fix it to your taste with money leftover from the sale. Any money over the price of your new home can be used to establish a savings account to pay insurance, taxes and emergency repairs. Smaller home, fewer expenses. Win-win situation.

20. Plan well for an enjoyable retirement. When you are older and live in the area you intend to stay in, there are many important things to do. If you have insurance that will allow you to have home health care, you should find the home health care companies in your area and investigate for reputation,

cost and the insurances they accept. If you are not insured for in-home health care, investigate the convalescent homes in your area. Now would also be a good time to sign your assets over to trusted children or grandchildren. If you have managed to have money put aside, check into tax shelters and trust funds to limit the amount of estate taxes your family will have to pay. By doing these things, you will make it easier for yourself and your family. Death of a loved one is always difficult, but with good planning you can make it bearable for them. For more ideas on how to prepare for retirement, go to www.ehow.com.how_543_retirement.html. Enjoy your retirement by doing things you never had time to do; spend time with your family, spoil your grandchildren or perhaps your great grandchildren, and just smile when their parents complain because your children will do the same with their grandchildren, and so the cycle of life continues.

There are no cut and dried ways to be a financial success in this old world. Perhaps there are a few concepts in this chapter that will help you start your road to financial responsibility. The idea of this book is to help and inspire Americans to make some changes that will enrich the lives of all Americans. If we can do that for just a few or hopefully a nation, we will have been successful. Just remember that a good strong economy is created by people who save money and live independent lives. So give it your best shot, this country needs responsible people like you to help "Take Back America".

Chapter 15

Have Faith and Practice What You Preach

"When one door of happiness closes, another opens; but often we look so long at the closed door that we do not see the one which has been opened for us."

Helen Adams Keller (1880-1968)

Originally church and state were supposed to be separate. This has never really been true. Many similarities exist. We have decided to take a different approach in this chapter to show you some of the similarities and how they coincide to make our lives better. Because there are so many religions and faiths, we decided to use the Ten Commandments as the first ten suggestions because they apply to how all of us should live our lives, no matter who we are and no matter what our beliefs. The Bill of Rights ensures our freedom of religion, our freedom of expression, and the freedom of the press. The laws of our land reflect the consequences for those who do not abide by the Ten Commandments. We hope you see the similarities and that the analogy will help you see that these values have always been an important part of making our country what it is. Let's all put our faith in our country, our family, and each other to help "Take Back America", and let's all practice what we preach in order to bring back America's honor.

1. Have no other God before me. In general, everyone believes in the religion they were born into and that is important because religion and faith hold a family together. Our own constitution guarantees the freedom of worship. Dedicate each day to God. Wake up and thank the Lord. On a beautiful

fall day, wake up in the morning with a wonderful sense of anticipation. Go outside and see the trees in their fall colors, and thank the Lord for this bounty. It is my sincere wish that everyone in this nation rejoices in the beauty we have been provided. Being alive on God's beautiful green earth is a wonderful thing. When you dedicate each day to your faith, you will lead a very fulfilling and satisfying life. In the end, isn't that what it is all about?

2. Have no other idols before me. Have you ever tried to convince someone that your God is better than theirs? Beliefs are tied to your religion and we all have unique views on this subject. Whatever you call your God, he should be your one and only God. Put your faith in His hands for comfort and the answers you need help with to deal with everyday life. When you do this, it gives you faith in yourself to help you make better decisions. Believe in the value, truth, and trustworthiness of your being. You are an important significant piece of the puzzle that makes up this big world. Allow yourself to be the best you can be, practice what you preach and faith in yourself will follow. Your confidence will take control allowing you to accomplish the goals you set. America needs self-assured, honest people to help "Take Back America".

3. Do not take the name of the Lord in vain. Cursing your situation or losing faith does not solve anything. By owning up to your mistakes, you can find many answers to your problems. The gift of faith eases the mind, so pray for faith. Many people blame others for the way their life turned out. I was one of these people for years, take my word for it, you will feel better if you take responsibility for your life. Admit it, and then fix it. Admit to yourself you cause most of your own problems and figure out a way to change those habits. When you take responsibility for your actions and realize the consequences, your world can change for the better. America would definitely benefit if more of us would own up to our mistakes. It would stop many problems in work situations; especially it seems to me in the government. Placing blame

is a waste of time and unethical if you know you are the one who is at fault. Own up to your mistakes and help "Take Back America".

4. Remember the Sabbath, keep it holy. Sunday has definitely divided the church and state. No matter what your religious belief, not many can get every Sunday off. Many religious holidays are rendered meaningless and Sunday is no longer a day of Sabbath due to commercialism. The almighty dollar has taken precedence over religion. Remember, the Bill of Rights guarantees your freedom to worship, do not let anyone take this away from you. Do what you can to worship on the terms of your faith. But remember, religion like integrity, will be recognized whether you attend church on Sunday or not. Be proud of your faith.

5. Honor your father and mother. Our parents are the most influential people in our lives. They are responsible for mapping out the values that will help build the foundation of our futures. Realize your parents sacrificed much to raise you and they deserve to be honored. On Mother's Day and Father's Day, find the time to make sure they know how much they are loved and honored or pay tribute to their memory. If you haven't had a real father or mother figure in your life, learn from the elderly that you respect. Always honor the elderly because our history anchors and charts our future. Raising children is a tough job, hats off to those parents who sacrifice much to raise well-rounded responsible individuals. Remember to always honor your parents.

6. Do not commit murder. Of course, this is so obvious if we want a better society for America. Even though we have the Right to Bear Arms, we must only use those rights the way they were intended, to protect ourselves. The Right to Bear Arms does not give you the right to play God with somebody's life. The loss of life affects many, not just the victim. Don't be pacifists; use your faith to do whatever is necessary to right these wrongs. Be involved in neighborhood watches, notify

the police when you know of criminal actions, and protect yourself and others from the criminal element. All of this is so necessary in our goal to "Take Back America" and will restore faith in the American judicial system.

7. Do not commit adultery. To begin with, the word commit and adultery should not be in the same sentence. Just the word "adultery" leaves a bad taste in your mouth. Commitment is too easily broken in today's world. Have faith in marriage. To do this, you must believe in marriage which is very difficult when divorce has become an easy out. Before the marriage ever happens, most have decided if it doesn't work, I'll just get a divorce. In some instances admittedly, bad decisions do need to be corrected however. Not everyone is suited for marriage, so before you decide to take a walk down the aisle, review your marriage vows, and make sure you can practice those vows for the rest of your life. Marriage needs to be taken more seriously; you are taking a partner for life. Vows are spoken and not to be broken. When you promise to love, honor, and cherish, use your faith to practice those vows the rest of your married days. You must be loyal, faithful, devoted, trustworthy, and so much more. It is not easy by any means, but a lifelong companion by your side witnessing your life is a precious gift. Having someone to share all your hopes and dreams is invaluable. When you realize this and you have faith in your marriage, you can get through all the hard times together, the way a marriage is meant to work. Strong marriages create strong families; strong families create strong individuals with faith in marriage, a much needed value in America today!

8. Do not steal. The Constitution established institutions for our protection from those who steal. We have local, county, and state police to help us with such matters. When matters really get out of hand, we have the National Guard. We should not need these institutions to stop the stealing of money, material items, and our identities. Why would anybody want to take something from somebody who has probably worked very

hard to achieve it? If it is not yours, do not take it. God has asked you to not steal, and you must not if you want to stay in His grace and the grace of all people. Again I will say we need to unite together as a nation to help "Take Back America". We will not be able to do this if we steal from each other.

9. Do not bear false witness against your neighbor. Being neighborly is difficult to do anymore; it is almost a form of art. In our busy, hectic lives, it is hard to find the time to be neighborly. It is important to find the time to get to know your neighbors so that we can all watch out for each other. As we begin to accomplish this, our neighborhoods will be stronger, safer places to live. We will also be more informed about our neighbors allowing us to make better decisions. God says do not bear false witness against your neighbor. If unjustly accused, our constitution entitles everyone to an impartial jury, the right to representation, and a speedy trial (like that happens anymore). Time has not changed corruption obviously, but society will always work toward eliminating corruption when at all possible. Integrity and faith will help us accomplish this in all of our endeavors. It is really a step in the right direction, and we need to step forward to "Take Back America".

10. Do not covet your neighbor's house or wife. We need to stop the green-eyed monster. If your neighbor has a nice new car, be happy for them, not jealous because you drive a ten-year old wreck. Jealousy can be very destructive because "keeping up with the Jones" can be very expensive. Is this foreclosure mess created by jealousy? We should be happy for the success of our friends and family. When you are doing the best you can do and being a responsible person, be proud of yourself, not envious of others. Again, it basically comes down to commitment, dedication, integrity, and trust for all of us to have faith in each other and come together as a Nation.

11. Have faith in your country. Today this can be a hard thing to do. I struggle with it everyday as I watch the news in horror.

But as I continue to watch the news and see the problems other countries face, I realize how lucky I am to live here in the United States of America. I realize how lucky I am to have my family and friends and that I can see them whenever and however I choose. I realize how lucky I am to be able to get in my car and drive wherever I want to drive (as long as I can afford it). I realize how lucky I am to be able to vote (even when my candidate is not elected). I realize how lucky I am to choose my religion and that gives me all the faith I need in my country. All Americans need to realize how fortunate we are to live in such a free country. We need to realize that when we all pull our faith together, we can overcome anything. We are Americans who live in the home of the free and the land of the brave for those full of faith.

12. Practice kindness to everyone. When you do kind things for God's children, and we are all God's children, the Lord smiles. Treat his creations with respect and empathy. When you practice these things, the Lord smiles upon you. Let's make kindness contagious. Give it to everyone who will accept. Have you seen the bumper sticker that says, "Practice random acts of kindness everyday"? Corny? You bet! But still a great idea, the ultimate "pay it forward". Include your neighbors in this because you should love your neighbors as yourself. Everyone deserves kindness, compassion, and thoughtfulness. The best part is when you give it, it is sure to come back to you. So go for it, you can make the world a better place by sharing the art of kindness; it can enrich so many lives including your own.

13. Let charity begin at home. Charity does begin at home and also in your town, your state, and your country. Why did it take hours for us to send help to the victims of the Indonesian Tsunami, but it took days for our government to get water to its United States Citizens after Hurricane Katrina? Do you find this odd? I find it unacceptable!!! We must not stray from helping the world, but when the citizens of the United States are in need, our tax dollars should make us the number one

priority. No questions or red tape needed. We need to put our people first, the people who have made this country what it is by being law-abiding taxpayers. When our government does this, much faith will be restored to the American people, a faith needed to help all of us believe that charity begins at home.

14. Keep Christ in Christmas. Commercialism has taken this holiday over. Even people with no religious beliefs are probably thinking we have gotten side-tracked on its meaning. We need to quit teaching our children about the materialistic side of Christmas and teach them about the religious content. To those of us who believe, it is the day our Savior was born. The Christmas season is for rejoicing and celebrating with Christ in our hearts and minds. For everyone, it should be about the joy of spending time, sharing meals, and making memories with your family and friends. Those memories should not include going into debt to make sure everyone has something special. Remember that there is no greater gift than one from the heart. Instead of saying "Happy Holidays" try to say "Merry Christmas", and may all we say it to recognize that we are reminding them it is about Christ. Not everyone will agree with these thoughts, but before you completely rule them out, take some time and think about it. Please remember why we celebrate Christmas, observe your faith's rituals, and make this a special time to spend with family and friends.

15. Do not gossip. Live your life for the joy in your life, not the dirt in other people's. Even listening to this type of talk makes you less than you should be. The tabloid papers and celebrity news give us insight into the lives of people we don't know and shouldn't want to know after hearing their secret lives. I do not read these things or watch programs about them. These things cheapen life and by listening to them, you cheapen your own. The rest of the world sits back and watches our lives as we listen to celebrity gossip, no wonder they laugh at us. We do not want our reputation to be as inhumane, shallow self-

indulgent robots. We need to impress with our intelligence and willpower and make our country known for its humanity and sincerity.

16. <u>Act instead of criticizing.</u> Many times you see things not being done in the way you think they should be done. Just because someone is doing it differently, doesn't make it wrong. If you think you can do these things better, volunteer to help do the task instead of being critical. It may get done better, and everyone will have a much better opinion of you when they see you in action. Otherwise, the example you set by just criticizing is generally bad; people just think your plain crabby, too picky, or just lazy. A job done right sets a good example for all Americans to see. When you act instead of criticize, you are practicing what you preach, something all Americans need to do to help "Take Back America".

17. <u>Read and study the Bible.</u> Today we have many choices when we are ready to read and study the Bible. The Bible is printed for all age groups and in a format that is easily understood. This Holy Book is available on CD, Audio, DVD and the world-wide-web. The Bible is not just for a certain religion or group of people, it is for all people believing in Christianity or wanting to know more about Christianity. If you are a person that does not believe in God, but may have a curiosity about this book, you should feel encouraged to read it. I believe it has a detailed knowledge of good and truth that all of us can relate to. It speaks of how we should treat each other and teaches us how to live our lives as honest, kind human beings. A lesson we could all learn despite our religious differences. Take a look around at the events happening in our world today, and you will find many of them down right terrifying. Change in our lives is desperately needed, changes that range from personal decisions (possibly turning to God) to the big changes that affect your whole family. I think we would all do well to think about the direction we are headed as a nation, and make a decision to change that direction. Whatever decisions we need to make the Bible will be available to give

comfort and support in its teachings. If you haven't tried that route, maybe you should. It couldn't really hurt, could it?

18. Have faith in family. The family unit is a strong bond between individuals connected by blood or marriage, but it can also be individuals well acquainted with good and complete knowledge of each other. Families do come in all shapes and sizes these days. The most important thing about a family unit is being able to have faith in those involved. Faith doesn't always come easy in families, faith must be earned, and at times you must forgive in order for faith to be restored to your family unit. But when you can rely on those family members to be there for you through thick and thin, you are truly blessed. When you can rely on those family members to be honest with you even when it hurts, you are truly blessed. When you can rely on those family members for love and support, you are truly blessed. Faith doesn't get any better than that.

19. Preach. PREACH! When you hear that word, what does it bring to mind? For most people, it reminds them of going to church. To others, it may mean Mom and Dad giving you a lecture. To a few, it may mean speaking out on something they believe in. Like so many words in our English language, it can have many meanings and uses. The meaning I found in the dictionary describes it as giving moral or religious instruction, to proclaim or put forth in a sermon, to advocate by urging acceptance or to speak out in support of something in a moralizing way. If the definition just described is true, we should all have something to preach about. Preaching is an age-old practice, and I imagine it always will be as long as we always have something to believe in. So the next time you feel you are getting preached to, remember it is not necessarily a bad thing. It could simply be someone letting you know how they feel and not being afraid to voice it; there is certainly nothing wrong with that.

20. Practice your beliefs. Let's face it, everyone is not going to have the same beliefs when you live in a world that has billions of people. However, you can still be true to your own beliefs, and that is what I would like to discuss. No matter what your religious preference, you should be dedicated to that belief. No one should have the right to criticize you for it, nor should you criticize anyone else. If your church meets more often than mine or less than mine, it doesn't make you more religious or less religious. It simply means your way of worship is different and works for you. The important thing is to go to the services and try to live those convictions on a daily basis. None of us are perfect, but what counts is the true effort of trying. Remember you can pray anywhere and at anytime, you don't need an appointment with God, and He happens to be a very good listener. I haven't met anyone who hasn't needed to talk to Him once in a while. I think one of the mistakes we make is only calling on Him in our time of need instead of talking with Him everyday. Being diligent about out practices will convey our passion for our faith and benefit us in so many ways. Don't let the stress of every day life pull you away from something so important. Staying focused and having faith will give you strength to handle the stressful times we all encounter at one time or another.

To respect your fellow man's beliefs and have him do the same is a wonderful part of living in America. In many countries in this big old world, freedom of religion is not even remotely possible without violence. So, as Americans, we should be soooo grateful for the rights our constitution ensures us and do whatever is necessary to make sure it stays that way. Americans will never let this happen as long as all of us "Have Faith And Practice What You Preach".

Chapter 16

Have a Healthy Mind and Body

"A good conscience is a continual Christmas."
Ben Franklin (1706-1790)

When you add the word "body" to the above quote, you definitely have a continual Christmas; there is nothing better than a good healthy mind and body to help a person accomplish all the tasks we face day after day. America has the highest rate of obesity in the world. We also lead the world in heart and lung diseases mostly caused by lifestyle choices. In order to change this, we need to make better choices in our diet and in our recreation. We will continue to have high insurance and poor medical services until we make the better choices in the way we live our lives. A healthier society both in mind and body will benefit the whole country by helping our medical system not get bogged down with what are mostly preventable health problems. A healthy mind and body will definitely benefit you and your family–when you feel better, you are more outgoing and more fun to be with. It creates a positive, self-confident person needed to help "Take Back America".

1. Have regular check-ups. Have you ever thought of a medical check-up as a road map? As we become ever more vigilant (I hope) of our health as a way towards a better society, our doctors can draw us a map of where we have been and where we need to go with our health based partially on family medical history. Keep in mind that certain medical conditions are hereditary and your doctor needs to have that information for proper diagnosis. When you know your problem is high cholesterol, you know where to change your diet and may

be able to achieve better numbers without expensive and often harsh drugs that have many side effects. Friends and family may give suggestions on how their handling their high cholesterol, but only your doctor knows what is best for you (what works for one, does not always work for another). This is only a few examples why you should have regular check-ups. Keep track of your own medical records at home so you can track your progress to good health and hopefully a better, healthier America.

2. <u>Be prepared when you visit your doctor.</u> When you visit your doctor bring a list of questions you need answered, discuss them with your doctor; after all, that is why you pay them. If you see a good physician, they will be glad to answer your questions. Most people know their body much better than their doctor does. Pass your knowledge of your body to your doctor to make their job a little easier; and by doing so, you will get more complete health care. As mothers and wives, we know we need to persuade our children and husbands to do the same (or make the damn list ourselves). It truly is important for us to teach our families to practice being responsible for their own health–because only you know what's going on with your body. Insurance is forever changing, be responsible for knowing what yours will cover in case your doctor orders tests that you know may not be covered, it may save you money and time, and cut down on the paper work for the doctor's office (which in turn saves them money and you, again, in the long run). Also, bring a list of prescriptions you may need refilled to prevent later phone calls. If you are changing physicians, always make sure to bring all pertinent information with you such as allergies to medications, medications you take, and as mentioned above, your family medical history. Be a good scout, be prepared.

3. <u>Exercise regularly</u>. In order to achieve and maintain good health, everyone should have a daily exercise routine. One should start the day with some stretches while the coffee is brewing for instance, just a few to get your body limber (ok,

maybe that doesn't work for you, but you can come up with your own ideas too). Find ways to work stretches and exercise into your work, play, and rest; a simple thing such as reaching further out with the broom or mop as you do housework is simple and beneficial. There are many ways to exercise regularly. See what your community offers or figure out your own routine; the more it works for you, the more likely you will make it a healthy habit. Think of how you work and add some fun exercise to it. Maybe you can grab a friend and get moving; the buddy system works well for motivation (do you want to be the one to call and say you can't make it?). The benefits from exercising are limitless and are a big part of making America healthier in mind and body.

4. <u>Expand your horizons, read!</u> There is nothing better to expand your mind than to read a good book. Anytime you read, you learn something, even if it is just sentence structure and a few new words. The world can become a more familiar place and you can learn to understand other cultures by reading. Reading is still one of the best entertainments in the world. If you use the public library, you can have the whole world at your fingertips for little or no money. All parents should take their children to the library and encourage them to read all types of books, there are many great adventures between those covers. The entertainment value is definitely the best for your buck. The educational value is immeasurable. The health benefits for the mind are priceless.

5. <u>Find a reason to laugh everyday.</u> A study I read some years ago states that laughter (even if it's faked) makes you feel better. The very act of laughing releases endorphin, a chemical in the brain that gives you a mental and physical lift. Laughter shared with friends and family is among the most priceless things in this old world. Whatever makes you happy and hurts no one is good for you (having fun at someone else's expense is not healthy). The expression "live, love, laugh, and be happy" could be the motto of all happy Americans.

6. Take a walk. A walk is the easiest and cheapest form of exercise, also happens to be one of the best for mind and body. As I am sure you know, exercise releases endorphin in your brain that gives you a physical and mental lift at the same time. To learn other benefits of walking, go to www.mayoclinic.com. The very fact of being outdoors in the sun is also good mental stimulation, and you get your daily dose of Vitamin D. Make it a family practice to take your family on nature walks; children will never learn to value Mother Nature and the world around them unless you as parents teach them. Plan a weekend day at a state park. Bring a list of trees, plants, birds and other wildlife common to the area; see how many of the listed items you and your children can find to mark off the list. By searching for them, you get a triple benefit–exercise, knowledge, and a great way to spend time with your children. Make it fun for everyone involved and create memories so that your children will look forward to nature walks and learn the benefit of exercise (which never had to be taught before the invention of video games).

7. Spend time in the sun, but do it safely. Stressed out, depressed, nerves stretched to the max? There are things you can do to unwind without the use of drugs. Many people become depressed in the winter and do not know why or what is causing it. The lack of sunlight is often the culprit for winter blues, the shorter winter days mean less natural light. Even in the winter, everyone needs to manage some time outdoors. Bundle up and take your dog for a walk (having a pet is considered by many to be one of the best ways to de-stress, pets can actually add years to your life by lowering your blood pressure) or go window shopping, but spend some time in the sun every day you possibly can. It does wonders for your state of mind. On the other hand, wear sun screen; we all know it is the correct thing to do. There are some brand names that are better than others, consult your doctor for the best type for your skin. Put it on children too young to do it for themselves (remember sun damage received early in their lives can effect

them for years to come). A lot of exposure to the sun can cause a lot of damage to your skin and even worse, cancer. Skin cancer can almost be totally eliminated by limiting the skins exposure to the sun. So when long sleeves and long pants are not practical, use sun screen. Along the same lines, it must also be remembered that everyone including children of all ages should wear sunglasses when outdoors even when it is cloudy. Sun damage to the eyes is on the rise all over the world. Inexpensive sunglasses should be by the front and back doors of everyone's home, so those leaving the house can put them on each time they go outdoors. Sanitize them often, but always have them ready and available for your family. Wear hats to shield your face from the sun, hats are fun and back in fashion. More information on sun care can be found at www.skincancer.org. Fun in the sun is healthy and can be accomplished without risking your health.

8. Use your medication safely. In the rush to bring new medications to market safely, safety is not always a priority. In the past few years, there have been many recalls of drugs that have caused death and many serious conditions. Always read the entire enclosure that comes with prescriptions or over-the-counter medications, call your pharmacist if you have any questions. Be aware of the side effects and how they can affect your health. Did you know that if you are on certain meds, you cannot drink milk? With others meds, you need to stay out of the sun or you cannot eat grapefruit. All medications can cause interactions with other drugs or food, you need to know what effect the medications have on your diet or on meds you already take. If a medication is new on the market when prescribed, ask your doctor for a sample so you can read the enclosures and try it before you buy it. This can save you money if you can't take it and possibly save your health. As you may know, a lot of medications that were previously by prescription only have become over-the-counter. This is not for your convenience; this is to save insurance companies

money. Always consult your doctor by phone before trying any new medications. Better to be safe, than sorry.

9. Keep good health records. You should be able at any time to look in your family's file and find everyone's health records and prescription drug information. You should also keep track of what vitamins and supplements the family is taking and how well they work for those family members. While this may seem like a lot of trouble, it can save you money and time when you need this information. This can also save money if you know something is not working for a family member; you can skip buying it and try something different that may work. Keeping good records can help keep you and your budget healthier.

10. Get ideas for better health from books. There are always plenty of books on the market or at the local library to help you solve many of the questions that come around in your life (this is one of those books). I am sure you see them everywhere from the grocery store check-out line to the more expensive book stores plus on-line sites such as Amazon.com. Please check the subject matter and the reputation of the author before you spend money on these, as there are many people who write only to make money, not to help their readers (we are not those authors). That being said, there are many self-help books that can help you address your concerns, but always combine reading and common sense to get the most from these books. If you find something that makes your mind and body healthier, you are the winner along with the America.

11. Overcome the stigma of mental disease. Many people in the world consider psychiatry a form of voodoo or something on that same level. Please understand that psychiatry is another level of medical practice. Mental illness is sometimes caused by chemical imbalances in the brain which is often heredity and is as treatable as Type 2 Diabetes. Do not suffer because you are too embarrassed to seek help, ask your family doctor for a referral. If you get a disease or you are in an accident,

you seek medical help. Mental illness is no different, you can be helped and go on to live a very full productive life. So take the plunge if you need to, it can truly change the way you live and the lives of those you love. Mental health is essential for a healthy mind and body.

12. Keep the family support system in place. In earlier times, the family was often the only source of support for those who needed help. Times have changed, but the family is still the most important support system in most cases. Moms, dads, aunts, uncles, brothers, sisters, and cousins need to be there for each other. If you do not have family members to count on, create your own family system with friends and others who do not have their own family. Families do come in all shapes and sizes. The world has become a more mobile place, families are often scattered all over the world making it a bit more difficult to be there to help family members in need. You may have to use letters or e-mails, cards, and phone calls to bolster a person's spirit. So be there for your family and in turn they may be there for you when you have a problem. If your family does not communicate in this manner, be the one to take the first step, it will strengthen your family ties. Family ties will help "Take Back America".

13. Be aware of recalls. Noticed anything funny about our children's toys lately? It doesn't stop there by any means. Our imports are not monitored as well as they have been in the past because import ratio has increased tremendously while exports are at an all time low (it doesn't take a rocket scientist to figure out how that happened). Look for a recall list that is regularly updated because we all need to beware of the dangerous things on the market. I suggest that as you hear of new recalls, you e-mail your family and friends to keep everyone aware as the recalls occur. If you and the people around you watch a different news cast or read different papers and exchange information, you can be more informed than trying to monitor everything yourself. A recall list that I have used and found to be pretty accurate is www.Recalls.gov.

14. Make food choices carefully. By following the food pyramid and selecting the amount of foods recommended in each group, you can live a happy and healthier life. To learn more about the food pyramid among other really helpful information, go to www.mypyramid.gov. Vegetables should be the main part of everyone's diet, vegetables give your body most of the vitamins and minerals that it takes to control the body's repair system. Did you know that your heart beat is controlled by calcium and potassium? Without these minerals, your heart stops. There are many choices in the dairy part of the food pyramid; cheeses, yogurt, milk, ice cream, and on and on. The main thing to remember is that your body cannot absorb calcium without Vitamin D. Vitamin D can be made by your body if you spend time in the sun; it only takes a few minutes a day. Most homogenized and pasteurized milks contain Vitamin D in the proper amount, other dairy products often don't. Check to see if your product choices contain Vitamin D. In truth, it had never occurred to me that as crops grow they deplete the minerals in the soils. Fertilizer helps crops grow, but do nothing to replace the trace minerals that we depend on to be healthy. If you buy organic foods that are grown without fertilizers, pesticides, and herbicides, you will get produce grown in fields enriched naturally, in ways that actually replace the minerals in the soil. Natural crop rotation and compost applications replace mineral value. By eating foods grown in a healthy natural way, you can keep your body in good shape and a healthy body is good for your mental health. In short, track the amount of vitamins and minerals in your food choices to make sure you are getting all the recommended daily doses. Better food choices can make a big difference in your health, mind and body, because when you feel better, it truly reflects in everything you do.

15. Plan and shop for nutritious food. It can be a real adventure. Try new things, I am sure that there are many foods you have never tried. If you have not tried something, you cannot possibly know if you like it or not, so try just one fruit or

vegetable of a different kind each week as your budget allows. You could create some new favorites this way and get better nutrition by doing so. In the summer, check out your farmer's market; it is a wonderful way to get fresh fruits and vegetables locally grown, and you can freeze the naturally grown fruits and vegetable for later use when they are not available. When you plan well, you can make one meal into two, planned leftovers are a great way to save time and money. A good example is to roast two large chickens on Sunday and use the leftovers for chicken salad on Monday evening and freeze a portion for later use. If you are always rushed, planning around major meals just three or four times a week can be a lifesaver, it also saves energy and that also saves money and greenhouse gases. Give planned leftovers a try; I am sure you will make this habit a part of your life. Make weekly menus and stick to them. Be sure they include the food pyramid in proper portions, and they are things your family will eat. I know there are many picky children out there, but if you start them eating properly when they are very small, most will learn to like many foods. Learn more about nutritious food at www.nutritiondata.com. Proper nutrition is important for achieving in school and sports, and it could play a major role in our battle to "Take Back America".

16. Make sure your food is safe and healthy. If you have room, grow some of your own produce, it is much healthier for you and your family and saves money. If you do not have the time or space for this, shop at local farmer markets or the Whole Earth Food Market. The FDA requires dating on all egg cartons so always check the expiration date. Be aware of the practice in some chain stores of putting outdated eggs in cartons of fresh eggs that have had some breakage. When you open a carton to check for breakage, look to see if there are signs that there have been broken eggs in this carton and do not buy the carton even if all the eggs are whole. When buying meat, be aware of the tightly sealed package that has a lot of space over the meat. This is often filled with gases to make the

product appear much fresher than it really is. This practice is often seen in the big super centers (you know what company runs these stores). The meat can sit in the case for days and retain its bright fresh look; don't be fooled, a good part of the time you are getting stale meat that will taste strong and be less nutritious. So avoid buying meat packaged this way, we pay too much for these products that are of inferior quality. To avoid this problem with meat, buy whole cows and pigs from a reputable local farmer and split with friends, family, and so on. When you buy local, the benefits are many; saving gas not only for you but for trucking companies which in turn helps the environment, helping local farmers and the local economy, making fewer trips to the grocery store, and most importantly, having safe food for and your family.

17. Beware of contaminated food. Many items on the market are cause for concern now more than ever. Check foods for the label that says this product has been irradiated. This process exposes food to high levels of radiation equivalent to millions of chest x-rays and it is used to kill bacteria. This process also destroys the nutrients in food and leaves the toxins and carcinogens that remain. It also perpetuates dangerously unsanitary conditions in meat-processing plants. Beef and chicken are a major worry because of the way they are raised. The practice of using growth hormones and antibiotics is a real point of concern. However, chickens can be purchased that contain no hormones or antibiotics; they are often labeled free-range chickens. Bell and Evans out of Pennsylvania is one company that does this, learn more at www.bellandevans.com. You also have to worry about the contaminants and diseases. Please keep in mind mad cow disease is an irregular protein called a prion, not a germ or a virus. No amount of cooking can eliminate it. Also please be aware of seafood imported from China, it is not raised in sanitary conditions and can be contaminated with e-coli and listeria. Farm-raised salmon from our northwest contains elevated amounts of mercury, always check and buy the label that says wild salmon. When

in doubt, always look for USDA inspected labels or check with the store manager. These are just a few examples of the foods we should have on our conscious. Stay healthy by being aware and informed of what foods can harm you and your family.

18. Be aware of bottled water. While we still need to drink water more than any other beverage, it has recently been in the news that clear plastic bottles most water is sold in can present a major health problem. The chemicals used to make these bottles have cancer-causing agents that seep into the water. For more information about the harm from plastic bottles, go to www.snopes.com. It is now considered safer to carry a clean stainless bottle with filtered water from your own sink. As most of us know, bottled water is no more than glorified purified tap water anyway. So save your health and space in the landfill, quit buying bottled water.

19. Join a support group. In these days of rush, hustle and often bad times, everyone can use some help. There are many support groups, even in smaller towns, to help you overcome some of your problems. Never be afraid or embarrassed to reach out and join one of these groups; all the members in the group are there to work their way through the same type of problem you have (that is the wonderful thing about support groups). Sometimes sharing your problem can help others in the group, and that can also help your moral. Give it a try; nothing ventured, nothing gained. If it eases your mind, you will be healthier for it.

20. Never stop learning. As we grow older, some of us grow complacent. We have lived a full life, and we are wiser than the young (well maybe), but continue to learn throughout your life. Take courses that interest you at your local community college and courses offered by your employer when possible, nothing you ever learn is ever wasted. Learn first-aid or to arrange flowers, the art of learning can keep your mind supple as exercise keeps your body. So take the time to feed and exercise your mind because **a mind truly is a terrible**

> **thing to waste**, and come to think of it, a waist is a good thing to mind. Sorry, I couldn't help myself.

In summary, there are so many things to be worried about in today's world that we must become well-informed about our health. We can better cope with the problems of today's society when we are healthier and at peace with ourselves. If all Americans practice a healthy lifestyle and attain good health, the cost of health insurance, while it may never come down, will not rise at such astronomical rates. The cost of health care (by doctors, hospitals, and insurance companies) is one of the things taking up so much of the American budget and causing American companies to move overseas. By keeping these costs under control, we can all help "Take Back America". Best of all, you will be a healthier person!

Chapter 17

Have Common Courtesy, Use Common Sense

"If a man can have only one kind of sense, let him have common sense. If he has that and uncommon sense too, he is not far from genius."

Henry Ward Beecher (1813-1882)

Something is missing in most of our country, something very important, in my opinion. Most of our country does not understand what common courtesy really is. It can be so many things, as simple as smiling in recognition when you make eye contact with someone to the more complex part of common courtesy which is basically "do unto others as you would have done unto you". It is really very simple and so very important that we all get along and stand together to "Take Back America". We also need to sharpen our brain and use our noggin. Common sense does not come easily to all; it is hard to learn common sense, but it can be done. You always hear how this country was built by the common man, I'll guarantee you he also had common courtesy and common sense. The people of this nation have to start treating each other with respect; let's stop pissing off each other and learn to respect each other's differences. Just because you got up on the wrong side of the bed does not give you the right to take someone else's sunshine away. I've always heard and always thought it so true, "if you can't say something nice, don't say anything at all." So, if nothing else, be nice to your fellow Americans so we can bring back a common bond that has been missing between all true Americans.

1. Drive Friendly. We all know what road rage is, most of us have been guilty at one time or another. Try to remember that everyone shares the roads, most of us have to spend way too much time in a vehicle, and that all of us basically have the same goal in mind–get where we're going!! Have some common courtesy out there on the roads!! It is really quite simple–learn the laws and obey them. Stop at stop signs (not ten feet pass them so that others don't know what to do), stop at red lights (this means when the light is yellow and about to turn red, stop so that the people who have waited patiently for their light get their fair turn, this also helps the flow of traffic), keep a safe distance between cars (you never know what will happen on a highway or street, do you really want to be responsible for someone's life if you don't have the room to stop), obey the speed limit (and if you don't want to, don't be mad because others do). I could go on and on, but there is no need because we all know what I am talking about. Let's stop breaking the laws and drive like we have sense, yes I do mean common sense!! Just think how many accidents would be alleviated, insurance rates could go down (well, it sounds good anyway). Most of the stress we all feel while driving would be minimized. And I suspect it could be good for our pocketbooks by saving some gas---aggressive driving has been said to waste a lot of fuel. Benefits galore, basically no side effects.

2. Be flexible. Don't get bent out of shape, be flexible! I know it's aggravating when plans don't go as you would like; it's happened many times to me, and I'll be the first to admit it bends me out of shape. All of our lives are basically so out of control that when something fails, we feel it messes up everything. Be flexible. Go on with other things. When the shoe is on the other foot, you will be grateful that others are flexible.

3. Be polite always. Whether someone is annoyed with you or you are annoyed with them, try to correct the situation with please and thank you. Most of the time manners will go a long way. Does this always work? Do we live in a perfect world?

NO!! But can't we all try and give it a whirl. Starting today, plan to be polite in every situation whenever possible. Smile, be polite, and touch someone's world.

4. Use grocery store etiquette. Most people who are reading this book have to grocery shop sometime; that is why this is pretty important. Let's face it, this is not the way most people like to spend their time. It is definitely on my top-ten list of things I hate to do the most. So, of course, this would be the best time to put our common courtesy and common sense to good use so that grocery shopping can become a little less stressful for the common soul. Let's start with the parking lot; everyone needs a space, please limit yourself to one with your vehicle in between the lines; there is a reason those lines are there. Next, on your way in, if someone is unloading their groceries and about to take their cart back, take it for them since you probably need a cart anyways (is it really that much extra work?) This courtesy also saves your store money which in the long run saves you money. While in the store, keep your cart with you and to the right side so that others can pass easily (we all have seen a shopper bent over on the left side with the cart on the right side and no way to pass, it simply isn't fair). However, if you do run into this problem, please refer to the above rule of "Be Polite Always". While in the checkout line, please try not to halt the flow of traffic for other shoppers, try to make all your transactions as quickly as possible (putting your groceries onto the conveyer belt, payment, allowing enough room for others to do the same), and again be polite to the cashier and bagger (working in retail is tough–politeness can go a long way in making their job better and in the long run better customer service for us all). On the way out, don't drive your cart down the middle of the lane, walk down the side your car is on so that other cars can get through (you can easily drive your cart by cars and keep moving, cars can not so easily pass). Return your cart to where it belongs. And if you really want to go the distance on this shopping trip with the common courtesy, common sense thing, if you see an elderly person struggling

to put their groceries in their vehicle, stop and help them–it means so much!!!

5. <u>Insist on manners from everyone.</u> Teach this by example. Most of us know what manners are; we just do not use them. Of course, we all know thank you, your welcome, and please, but do we know acknowledgment is a form of manners? Hello and good-bye are examples of this. Opening doors for people or holding it open longer for the next people, allowing the elderly to be comfortable before the young, and asking before taking are common forms of manners that don't get used much anymore. For more information on this subject, go to <u>www.FunEtiquette.com</u>. Using manners is the right thing to do!! Use your manners and inspire others to use their manners whenever possible so that America can gain a better reputation as a country full of upstanding individuals who care about each other.

6. <u>Have common courtesy and use common sense when in public places.</u> Just because you don't get good service at a restaurant for example, doesn't mean you have to stoop to that level and make the situation worse. Instead use your common sense that tells you there is no sense arguing with someone who treats customers in such a manner. Use common courtesy to deal with this unruly customer service representative–let them know you will continue to treat them with respect and they should learn to do the same. If this doesn't work and the customer service representative is completely rude and offensive, speak to a manager so that this unruly person knows that they cannot continually get away with treating people that way. America needs a better image, do your part to make public places a better place for all.

7. <u>Control your children in public.</u> Everyone has seen this in so many different places; church, grocery stores, restaurants, parks, etc. Sure, the parents are annoyed by their children's behavior, but it is also affecting those just unfortunate enough to be in the same place at the same time. Please do not let your

children ruin other people's time, it is just not fair. Parents, you can get some good ideas on controlling your children while in public at www.education.com. Most of us have had this happen to us with our own children and it is rather embarrassing. Just make a concerted effort by taking the child aside and explaining why this behavior is unacceptable–it shows the people around you that you are at least making an effort to get your child under control. I can remember being on a tour bus with about 50 other people in Washington D.C. with a child who would not stop crying. In the end, my stories of Washington D.C. are about that child crying not about my tour of the White House. We all know it is not completely possible to keep your children under control at all times, but how parents respond to the situation is what can make the difference to those that are around you. Do your best to teach your children how to act in public so that everyone is happy.

8. Use sporting event etiquette. From the small little league game to professional sporting events, somewhere somehow somebody is going to offend someone else. Sports should be about sportsmanship which can be defined as fair play, the ability to win or lose graciously. The media is full of stories about unsportsmanlike conduct that make Americans look quite petty and it is a disgrace to have this image. Parents should control themselves at their children's sporting events and realize there are more important things than winning; children should be in sports for fun, companionship, competitiveness, and many other reasons that help your child develop into a well-rounded individual. At other sporting events, be sure to have common courtesy so that others can enjoy the event too. Sit in your seats, take your turn going in or out during parking, and use your manners so that everyone can have a good time at the events that they so love. You can get more advice on sports etiquette at www.associatedcontent.com. Most importantly, stand and remove your hats during the singing of the National Anthem and never forget to cross your heart if you are a true American.

9. Refrain from foul language in public. Most of us have been in public and had our ears violated many times. I am as guilty as the next, even though in past years I have tried to do better. The problem with foul language in public is that children over hear these words and think it is acceptable. What's more, a lot of people think it is acceptable. I don't know about you, but I would rather America did not have the image of a foul-mouthed people. One of the great things about our country is that we are free to express ourselves, but let's express ourselves with a degree of dignity.

10. Allow others to finish speaking. Let's talk about me, let's talk about me, let's talk about me!! Does this remind you of anyone? We've all heard these people ramble on forever not giving anybody the chance to speak. Interesting conversation is very stimulating unless you are the one who doesn't get to converse. Don't hog the conversation; allow others their time to talk also. And don't just allow them the time to talk, really listen to them. Listening is a common courtesy many of us have left behind. We tend to hear but we do not listen. Use your common sense to know when to take your turn speaking. Who knows, you may find out a lot of things you didn't know that could change your life for the better.

11. Use your attitude to your advantage. Making a difference can begin in what we may consider to be a very small thing, but in fact, it has a huge impact. Your attitude, my attitude, and those attitudes around us impact Americans every day. If we wake up everyday already thinking it's going to be a good day, could that soon become a habit? Could that have an effect on shaping our days from then on? If you dread the next day or don't make an effort to turn around your negative feelings, you have already set the mood for the day. The people you deal with in business and those you encounter throughout the day don't always have a good attitude and it seems to be contagious. Instead, imagine our good attitudes infecting them. I would love to be around more positive people and work with people where negativity is not the norm. And

please do not ruin my fun shopping day with bad customer service. If it is something you have to do anyway, why not make the most of it. This topic is endless, but I am sure we can all relate because of our own personal experiences. When we use common courtesy and common sense with a positive attitude, many great changes could come to this great country of ours.

12. Pay back money you borrow. No matter whom you borrow money from, whether it is your parents, brothers or sisters, or friends, pay it back. It is plain common sense that everybody works hard for their money. It is plain common courtesy to return their hard-earned money to them after they have been nice enough to loan it to you. It would be great if we lived in a world where people could just give money to us when needed, but we don't. Have some common courtesy and common sense; pay back the money you borrow. Many unresolved conflicts in many lives would not exist if everyone lived by this rule. It could help Americans get along better, and we all need to unite to "Take Back America".

13. Do your part at social gatherings. Know when to take your children, and when you do, control them so that all can enjoy the event. Call and ask what to bring if you don't know and make sure you make enough for all. Help with the organization before, during, or after the gathering if you are able. Common sense should tell you that everyone could use a little help from their friends in the clean-up department. One person should not have to do it all while everyone else is having all the fun. Just remember, many hands make lighter work and more enjoyment for everyone.

14. Use restaurant etiquette. Restaurants are too much a part of our lives not to address this issue from both sides. Customers need to realize that working in a restaurant can be very stressful at times; many responsibilities can be flying at you from all directions. Be patient, be ready to order when your waiter is at your table, be polite, and use your manners; more times

than not, these directions will get you much better service. Remember everybody needs to be treated with dignity. For more information on dining in public, go to www.starchefs.com. All restaurant employees should use that same advice and realize that we are using our hard-earned dollars to eat at your restaurant. As a customer, we deserve the service for which we are paying. Please be punctual with our needs, don't bring us cold or inedible food, and don't ignore us. You will reap the benefits of these directions. Restaurants can work for both sides as long as each side has common courtesy and uses common sense.

15. Return what you borrow. When you borrow something from someone, return it as soon as you are done with it and return it in the same condition you received it. Common sense should tell you that the person you borrowed the item from bought it for a reason and paid good hard-earned money to buy it. No one minds loaning out their items to help a friend or relative, but to not get the item returned is almost like having it stolen because you never get to use it when needed. I'm sure all of us have been guilty of not returning borrowed items at one time or another, but let's do our best to have the common courtesy to return borrowed items in a timely manner.

16. Have common courtesy and use common sense as customer service representatives. If you are a public servant in any aspect of customer service, please treat your customers with the respect they deserve when they are paying for your services. Please remember we mostly just want the bang for our buck. When the general public feels like they are not getting the bang, hard feelings occur. What ever happened to the days when the customer was always right? Customer service representatives should put more effort into making their customers feel wanted and needed, instead of wanting to make them feel confused, discarded, and unimportant. It seems to be fine with employers when their employees are rude, roll their eyes, or use sarcasm. Such qualities should not be the standard that good Americans aspire when at their jobs

where they make an impression on many during their work day. Americans should aspire to be the best that they can be while in the public eye, rather they are serving hamburgers, selling cars, or working the front desk of a hotel. Please go to www.ehow.com to learn how to be a good customer service representative. Our reputation as a country is counting on your winning attitude!!

17. Value the small things in life. Among the things that one must learn in life is that little things mean a lot. A beautiful sunset is free or a day with your grandparents. Life moves quickly, before you know it, life has passed you by. Don't take life for granted, live it to the fullest by valuing the small things in life. We could all benefit by doing this. We could live in a world less materialistic–a world where common courtesy and common sense would prevail because so many attitudes would hopefully be changed. Give it a try and share your small things that make you happy with someone to see if they can do the same.

18. Say what you mean, mean what you say. Sounds quite easy, but it is a big problem with our society. Too many people believe that they can say whatever they need to in order to pacify someone at that particular time. Please use your common sense and avoid such ideals. Be honest with yourself and the person with whom you are talking. A lot of misunderstandings in this crazy old world could be eliminated by using this common courtesy.

19. Clean up after yourself. No matter what anyone says, I do not believe that some of us were put here on earth for the sole reason of cleaning up after others. It is just not fair for anyone to expect others to pick up their trash, dishes, clothes, or whatever; with these kind of people the battle is never-ending. Attitudes like this can sometimes be attributed to the parents who allowed this to happen. Whatever the reason, it is inexcusable. Be a responsible American with common

courtesy and clean up after yourself, your image will change for the better.

20. Be punctual. You have always heard that being punctual makes a good impression. How true that is, but it is so much more than that. Certainly being on time for a job interview or to clock in at work is a big deal, but so is being thoughtful of other people's time. Teaching our children this skill is so important. Make them accountable for not being home on time or having a chore done within a time frame. If you can explain and teach them in their young world how it can make a difference, maybe just maybe, they will grow up and realize the importance of it. We all hate to be kept waiting. At the doctor's office, being late for the appointment not only affects the doctor and staff, it also effects the appointments that follow you. This applies to many areas because these days everyone is so busy running here and there. We spend so much time coordinating schedules that when a person consistently runs late it throws everyone off. Are you one of those people? Don't get me wrong, sometimes it is unavoidable, but when it becomes a habit, it is problematic and sends the wrong message. It doesn't instill confidence in how others see you. Just allow a few minutes extra. Maybe set your watch and clocks a few minutes ahead, then forget you did it; otherwise it defeats the purpose. Get more ideas on how to be punctual at www.howtodothings.com. I think all anyone expects is an effort, some common courtesy, and some common sense.

Having common courtesy and using common sense could go a long way in helping "Take Back America". The examples above just touch the surface on this broad subject. The main point is that if we all make a joint effort to be kind to our fellow Americans and extend all courtesies here in the United States, we will all benefit in so many ways. First of all, we will all get along better. Second, our reputation as rude, uncaring individuals will be a thing of the past. And most importantly, being able to work and play together is the only way we can truly "Take Back America".

Chapter 18

Wake Up! Reduce, Reuse, Recycle!

"Courage consists in equality to the problem before us."
Ralph Waldo Emerson (1803-1882)

It is beyond my imagination that Americans do not understand how important this topic is. America produces somewhere around 20% of the world's trash; however, Sweden recycles approximately 97% of their trash. Do you not find that staggering? Why are we trashing the land that feeds us, the land that we live upon, the land we love? Our beautiful land is not infinite; WE WILL run out of places to put trash, especially in an age where new electronics become obsolete before you get them home, that is an exaggeration but not far from the truth. Do we really want this for future generations? If our country does not start reducing, reusing, and recycling, there will not be a need to "Take Back America" because America will only be a trash dump. It is not always easy to reduce, reuse, recycle, but here are some simple ways to get started.

1. <u>Reduce driving by 40 miles a week for each driver in your household.</u> This can be easily accomplished by car pooling, taking public transportation one to two days a week, mailing instead of driving, making one less trip to the grocery store, going as a family (like the old days) instead of everyone driving for their own convenience. I'm sure the statistics here would be staggering if every driver did this in America. Unfortunately, we do not have the money for such research. What's more, do we really need that kind of information? It doesn't take a genius to figure out that we all need to reduce our driving. Reducing fuel consumption is so important in

our task to "Take Back America" because America will be less dependent on other countries for our oil and hopefully drive the gas prices down so that we can all afford to drive when necessary.

2. Reuse household items worth reusing. Reuse dryer sheets for dusting clothes. Use rags instead of paper products. Many items used in everyday life could be reused if we learn not to live in a throw-it-away world. Reusing items will help reduce the production of new which has so many consequences; less products from other countries, less energy to produce new products, less fuel to haul new products, etc. Every one of us needs to reuse whatever whenever possible because individual households will prosper economically and it will keep unnecessary items out of our landfills as long as possible. For more ideas on reusing household products, go to www.realsimple.com. Positive effects on the environment are so important if we want to be a prosperous country with a bright future.

3. Recycle the easy things. Start with the easy ones--aluminum (you can actually make money with this one), paper (so important), plastic, and glass. For those of you who do recycle, thanks so much for doing your part–keep up the good work and move on to bigger and better things. If you have never recycled, begin by taking one step at a time. Go to www.ecologue.com for recycling basics. Start with cans, get the routine down, go to bottles, get the routine down, then paper, etc. Make it a family project because we need to be responsible adults and teach our children how important it is to recycle. Recycling has so many benefits to the environment; less trash in our landfills, less pollution from factories reproducing what is thrown away, less energy used by not reproducing what is thrown away, and the list goes on and on. To learn more, call your local city halls, look up recycling on the internet, read local papers, and watch the local news. Recycling is an important part of taking our country back because it reduces the amount of trash we send to our landfills and will help

keep us independent in the future of requiring other landfill sites abroad that may cause problems. Besides, don't you want to KEEP AMERICA BEAUTIFUL!!

4. Reduce the energy you use in your home. Thermostat down, lights off, TV's off when not being watched; you have heard it all before. But seriously, all of this adds up. Use crock-pots, pressure cookers and microwaves instead of conventional ovens. Insulate your water heater. Caulk windows and doors. You can find many more ideas at www.smartenergyliving.org. We all know the benefits from doing all these things, yet we tend to ignore these simple solutions. Make these kinds of things priorities, it is just not that hard to do and if we all do it as a nation, the benefits could be endless.

5. Reuse packaging products that you receive or give to someone who will. This applies to work and home. If you see something at work you can use at home and is just going to be thrown away, ask if you can take it home to reuse. Others see this and may come up with other ideas to use other things at work that are just thrown away. At PPG Industries in Mount Zion, they used the Styrofoam blocks used to package glass for seeding at soccer fields, backstops for the goals, and also for archery backstops at local schools. Outdated electronics were refurbished and donated to schools. E-bay is such a big thing now; we can re-use packaging to send packages. So, encourage all these people to recycle their packaging and boxes, and reuse, reuse, reuse, and then recycle.

6. Recycle while traveling. While traveling, I am always amazed at how difficult recycling can be. Rather you drive, fly, or stay at a hotel, it seems you cannot find a way to recycle all that can be recycled easily. So, put a basket in your car of some kind that matches your personality or vehicle. Use it to put recyclables in so that you can empty once or twice a week at home. When you fly, ask that your trash be recycled; if they do not recycle, suggest that they do while making obvious to all around you that they are not environmentally

friendly. It is the big companies that don't recycle that cause so much waste. Enough is enough, insist that they do. While staying in hotels or resorts, inquire where the recyclables go and if they do not have programs for recycling, use the above suggestion again. Also insist that hotels have a linen reuse program, energy-efficient lighting, low-flow toilets and showers, and alternative energy sources. Research this before you travel; please frequent establishments that are green and do not frequent those who do not follow green procedures. If we all keep voicing our opinions and insisting on easier ways to recycle everywhere we go, the waste this nation is knee deep in can at least be somewhat controlled. If we don't do something about this kind of waste, well, I hate to even think of those consequences.

7. Reduce your garbage by one bag a week. Of course, you can only do this by recycling. You will be amazed how little trash you will have after recycling. Another way to reduce your bags of trash is to compact your trash--no...you don't have to get the appliance. You can compact on your own. When you are done with an ice cream carton for instance, stuff trash inside and seal. My husband hates when I do this because I will leave whatever I am stuffing on the kitchen cabinet until I can no longer put anything else in it. He should really love it because he doesn't have to empty the trash nearly so much. My husband and I wish the trash companies would charge by the bag or trash can because we pay the same price for trash as our neighbors; we recycle everything, they don't, yet we pay the same. It is hardly fair–to us or the environment.

8. Reuse by re-gifting. If you have a gift from Aunt Bertha that you cannot use but know someone else would love it, re-gift it. This is becoming more and more socially acceptable, especially with the economic woes everyone is experiencing. When you re-gift, it saves you money because you are not purchasing another gift, the item that has already been purchased will hopefully be used, and over-consuming is kept under control.

Many more ideas can be found at www.regiftable.com. Such a simple thing, so many benefits.

9. Recycle automotive parts and oils. Junkyards have been doing this great work for years, and yet, we need to do better. Unfortunately, you can see the need for this by taking a Sunday drive nearly anywhere in our country. Dumping tires, whole cars, and batteries must seem easier than paying the small fees charged to legally recycle where it ends up being reused for good purposes. Oil is just easier to pour out than to recycle where it does not get into our streams, creeks, and rivers when rain washes it down. Well, that is just plain hog wash. We are better than that and our land is tired of being abused. Stand up and be responsible for your waste. Old tires have all kinds of purposes-- playground material, energy sources, etc. Oil can be recycled for many other uses. Old cars can now be given to the Salvation Army or Goodwill and will actually get you a tax write-off. And there are so many other reasons to do these things, just think about it and act responsibly. To find out how to recycle your oil and why you should, go to www.recycleoil.com.

10. Reduce your consumption of water. We've all seen the scary stories lately. Stranger things have happened; don't think that running out of water can't happen. Think about some of the major disasters that we have seen in recent years. One of the first things that come to my mind is the severity of water distribution; you have seen the desperation on many unforgettable faces. Now, imagine that as an everyday problem. Now, remember that water is not only important for body hydration but it is also needed for body hygiene, eliminating body waste, and most importantly perhaps, to grow the food we need to nourish our bodies. So, start with the simple things: turn the water off while brushing your teeth, reduce shower time, just be aware of your water consumption. Every household's water consumption is different, just think about it and you can find easy, simple ways to cut back on your personal water consumption. To find out how to use

water wisely, go to www.wateruseitwisely.com. Mother Earth thanks you, I thank you, and future generations will thank you.

11. Reuse your yard scraps by composting. This is a pretty simple one and does not apply to all, of course. No yard, no yard waste. But to all of us who do have yards, we know this can be a big problem. Composting has been around for centuries but just in a more natural way and a more natural process. Composting helps soil becomes richer in a natural way, the way soils used to be enriched. There are reasons for all things basically and there is a reason that the earth's natural waste can be so helpful to the earth. So, find an area out of the way and pile that yard waste up, turn it over from time to time, and use it for enriching your yard in needed areas.

12. Recycle electronic products. Computers, phones, stereos, receivers, and TVs have become disposable items somehow. Therefore, they have become an environmental hazard not only because they are filling our landfills but because of leaking hazardous materials in these electronic devices. For more information on where to recycle your electronic products and why you should recycle them, go to www.eRecycle.org. Just imagine the last time you were in a large office setting, think about all the electronic devices in that office, now imagine all of that being thrown away instead of recycled. Technology moves so fast anymore that these items become obsolete quickly. WASTE, WASTE, WASTE!!! When buying electronic devices, check with the retailer about recycling. Also, many electronic recycling businesses are popping up that charge fees to take your electronics. Please remember that the recycling of these products requires a lot of work, the devices must be broke down and separated into parts, so if there is a small fee please don't sweat it–it will be completely worth it. Recycling electronic devices has many benefits for this country; less unnecessary trash in our landfills, less hazardous materials in our landfills, jobs to those who are responsible for the recycling of these products, recycled parts

means less manufacturing which is always environmentally friendly.

13. Reduce your gas consumption by changing your driving habits. Aggressive driving consumes more gas. Take the extra five minutes it will take you to drive if you drive non-aggressively. When you are coming to a light you know is red, slow down ahead of time so that you are not sitting idle at a stop light and not having to accelerate from a stop. Think of other things you can do in your driving habits and share these ideas with others. Together we can consume less gas as a nation when we change our driving habits.

14. Reuse plastic water bottles. This is similar to reducing the use of unneeded bottles but deserves its own highlights. These bottles have become a national hazard. Manufacturing bottles uses energy and resources needlessly. Transporting water from other countries uses gas and makes us rely on other countries resources. People buy them, drink a few sips, and dispose of everything or worse, litters by leaving the bottles sitting somewhere. I know, I am one of those "I can't go anywhere without my water" kind of people. The waste of it all is as stated before, a national hazard. So this is what I have done. I only buy bottled water when I am totally without. All those bottles are my bottles I refill at home and then I try my best to remember to take them with me. When the bottle is worn out, it is then recycled. It is not the best solution, but it does slow down the process somewhat. Also, reduce the use of unneeded bottles. Buy bigger refill bottles to refill your small ones, and of course, recycle the bigger refill bottles. This can apply to household cleaners, beauty products, food, etc. Your budget will also benefit. Two small ideas, but environmentally huge.

15. Recycle ink cartridges. Many options are now available in this area. Envelopes are available at your post office; insert ink cartridge, seal, and mail. Retail stores are refilling ink cartridges while you wait; save money and help the earth.

Retail stores are also offering savings on other items if you bring your used ink cartridges in for recycling. Simple for you, saves you money, helps the environment.

16. Purchase recycled products whenever possible. Products that are made from recyclable goods are not of much use if people don't buy them. You can buy recycled products at www.earth-huggers.com or www.greengiftquide.com. E-machines are electronic devices that have been refurbished and sold in many stores at lower prices; the buying of these products saves you money and keeps our landfills clear of hazardous waste. Fleece clothing is made from recycled soda bottles, stay warm and help the environment. You can see how fleece is made and buy fleece products at www.patagonia.com. Research this issue and see what recyclable goods you can incorporate into your life and your work if possible.

17. Open your mind to the fact that recycling is absolutely necessary. Once you do this, it becomes easier or it did for me anyways. Constantly I am coming up with new things that can be reused, recycled, or reduced. Little things, but little things can make such a difference when you have a nation behind you. Little things can keep this country beautiful for future generations.

18. Identify an effective approach for you to incorporate these ideas into your life. What works for some doesn't always work for others. How many times have we heard that? The reason we have heard that so many times is because the statement is absolutely true!! Our nation is made up of all kinds, one of the things that make this country so wonderful. Find out what works for you by discussing other ideas and options with co-workers, friends, and family so that you can find the most efficient way to recycle. The more efficient you are at recycling, the easier it is.

19. Don't buy disposable products unless absolutely necessary. Having the immediate family over for dinner? You probably

have enough serving plates to use and if you have a dishwasher, it is not that much extra work. Having a party for 50? Pretty necessary to use paper plates. Too many times, however, we use disposable items when it is just not necessary. Use your conscience, do what is best for the earth when at all possible.

20. <u>Start local programs for items not recycled in your area.</u> Educate yourself on local recycle programs. See what is needed and find a way to begin a new recycle program that benefits your community. Anything anybody does, no matter how small, helps the process move toward less trash in our landfills which is the ultimate goal to keep this country beautiful.

It is probably not too hard to figure out that this is a subject very dear to me. Years of experience have made recycling just a natural part of my life so I have a hard time understanding how others don't see the importance of this controversial subject. Why would you want to throw something away that could be reused or recycled? It is so wasteful and should not be "The American Way". Reducing what we use is just as important, if not more important, because resources run out!! Please consider all these suggestions and do your best to reduce, reuse and recycle. When we do this together as a nation, we will make America beautiful and "Take Back America".

Chapter 19

Be Aware of How You Affect Global Warming

"The time to repair the roof is when the sun is shining."
John F. Kennedy (1917-1963)

Well, I realize that this topic is one that is very familiar. We all hear how urgent it is, and I can honestly say it can be quite overwhelming. It is all the reports say and more! I thought I knew a lot about global warming, but I learned so much more while doing research for this chapter. The impact of global warming is caused by individuals, families, businesses, and communities. It is time to really take a close look at how we are affecting global warming, not just what global warming means. Hopefully we can give you a few ideas that can be helpful so that we can make informed choices and decisions. Each and every one of us has a responsibility to stop this process. If we want the earth for our children and grandchildren, you must get involved now!!

Global warming has a huge impact on bringing about the changes in our weather. By definition, global warming is caused by the emission of heat-trapping gases produced by vehicles, power plants, industrial processes, and deforestation. It is on the rise; increasing at an alarming rate. To learn more on the latest studies, just get on the internet and do a search. We will name some informative web sites that can educate you and your children during this chapter. You'll be startled at the wealth of information you can find and the severity of the problem.

1. Light up your house more efficiently. These next few ideas, which you may or may not be doing, are things we can do easily around our own home. Replace incandescent light bulbs with compact fluorescent bulbs, especially those that burn the longest each day. They will produce the same amount of light, but use about a quarter of the energy and will last ten times longer saving you up to $30 a year in energy costs. Over the life of the bulb, you will save about 100 pounds of carbon for each incandescent bulb that you replace with an energy saving bulb. You reduce the amount of fossil fuels that the utilities burn. Each time you switch to one of these energy saving light bulbs, you help clean the air today and you will save money on your electric bill. You don't have to run out and buy all new bulbs if you don't want to, just keep replacing them as they burn out. It is a start and can have a huge impact when more and more people start participating. Here is an interesting tidbit I found at www.fightglobalwarming.com : if everyone in Memphis, Tennessee would replace just two regular 60 watt bulbs with compact fluorescent, the savings would power Hartford, Connecticut for three weeks. Go to www.msnbc.msn for more information about florescent light bulbs and how you should dispose of them. It really gives you something to think about.

2. Turn down the heat and turn up the air conditioning. Heating and air conditioning use more than half the energy in an average home in the United States. Buying and installing a programmable thermostat can save money and carbon, you can find out more at www.toolbase.org. Some people are very good at remembering to turn down the thermostat when gone from the house or going to bed, some of us tend to forget. Purchasing a programmable thermostat can make a difference, the cost of one range from $30 to $250 depending on the desired features, but it will certainly save you money over time. You program the temperature desired to your schedule and it automatically will do it for you. These are readily available and installing is not difficult. Your unit

will work less and the result will show on your bill and the environment. Old thermostats keep the house at a certain temperature until we physically adjust the thermostat; so you can see the difference a programmable thermostat can make. Virtually all of us share in the responsibility for greenhouse gas emissions, whether in our car or homes, this small step can make a tremendous difference.

3. Maintain your home for energy efficiency. Check in attics, around pipes and duct work, and under flooring on the ground floor if you have an unheated basement for inadequate insulation. Correct any problem you see; you will only benefit from this project. Insulate the pipes that carry hot water throughout your home. If your water heater is more than five years old, wrap it in an insulating jacket and turn down the thermostat if it's set higher than 120 degrees. You really won't notice a big change and again, it can save you money. If you think about it, most of the suggestions that have been researched and passed on have an impact on how we affect global warming and help us by saving money. Air leaks that cause drafts can not only cost money but contribute to global warming. You can increase your energy efficiency as much as 30 percent by plugging air leaks. That is a significant number! To find out more on making your home more energy efficient, go to www.usagreen.org/homeEnergy.html. Already I can imagine putting the money I save into a vacation fund I can't afford at the moment because household expenses are so high. Seriously, after this chapter, you should be able to see how much money you will save over the course of time by using these suggestions and how it helps global warming is just as obvious.

4. Don't waste energy. During certain months of the winter, my electric bill is normally higher than the rest of the season. By caulking and weather-stripping the windows and doorways, I can cut down on drafts and air leaks that we talked about earlier. Each degree you lower your thermostat in the winter, cuts your energy bills by three percent. In addition, you can

have your utility company do a free energy audit of your home to show how to save even more money. It may be a small investment of your time, but after all, it's free and will show you how to save more money. What's not to like? Unplug things you are not using. Turn off those lights and TV's. Be aware of the waste happening in your family. Take clothes from the dryer when they are dry instead of letting it go till it beeps. There are so many easy things we can do if we want to make a difference and these changes also help our pocket book. Go to www.sierraclub.org for more information on how you can save money by improving your home and making it more energy efficient. Turn that heat down, throw on another blanket, or better yet, snuggle up to someone (see there are other benefits, too).

5. Don't take water for granted. Americans tend to waste a lot of water. First thing, as a family, you should take a look at where your family is wasting water that can be easily remedied by simply changing your habits. To figure out much water your family is wasting, go to www.wateruseitwisely.com. On a personal level, we can change a few things. When you brush your teeth, keep the water off till it's needed, or use a glass of water instead of leaving the water running. Leave the water off while washing your face; it is not needed during the cleansing process only during the rinsing. When shaving, guys should put a little water in the sink for their needs. Only use the running tap when you really need it. Keep drinking water refrigerated so you won't leave the tap running to let the water get colder. It would be wonderful to use any water we do run out of the tap for another purpose. To become aware of how much water is wasted; keep a bowl in the sink to catch unused water and then see if you can find appropriate uses for that water; no wasted water, that's the idea.

6. Bathe Efficiently. Two words, quick showers. Quick showers use less water than baths. Save baths for a treat–a good soak once in a while does wonders for many. In the meantime, cut down on the time of your shower. For more info about

water usage, go to www.twdb.state.tx.us/Data/Drought/save_water2.asp, it will show the difference between showers and baths. Water from the city uses energy before it gets to us, we use energy to heat the water; so shorter showers reduces energy too. Even if you have a well, you are still using power to pump and heat the water, and you are depleting your valuable resource when showering too long. There are many other options to cut down on the water you use while showering. Install low-flow showerheads and faucets, you will use half the water without decreasing performance. Turn down your water heater to 120 degrees, your hot water expenses may diminish by as much as 50 percent. A family of four showering daily instead of bathing can save the cost of heating approximately 200 gallons of water every week some studies have shown.

7. Do sweat the small things. Don't pay to heat or cool an unused room, close the registers or turn off the radiators. It can save 5-10 percent on your bill. Turn off exhaust fans as soon as need for them passes. Open the doors to the rooms in use to maximize heating and cooling efficiency. These suggestions help the environment and keep money in your pockets. Although we think we know all these things, I am not certain we practice them. Why not start by doing some investigating? Get on-line, go to the book store, go to the library, and call utility companies for any suggestions to help eliminate wasted energy. The utility companies may have printed information or direct you on the most current recommendations. With very little effort and very little money up front, the changes you make could pay for themselves over and over.

8. Minimize energy used in your kitchen. Get rid of your power hungry kitchen tools. Save money and energy by putting your juicer, electric can opener, and egg beater in the cabinet. Defrost food in the refrigerator overnight or at room temperature, it cuts the cost of cooking by 30-50 percent. Match the pan to the burner. Bake an entire meal at one time to save. Cook with microwave or crock pots whenever possible, it draws about one-third of the electricity compared to a conventional oven

while also lowering air conditioning consumption by keeping the kitchen cooler on hot summer days. Resist peeking into oven during cooking; you lose valuable heat each time the door opens. Use lids on pans to same time and money. For more ideas on minimizing energy used in the kitchen, go to www.googobits.com. If you think about it, I'm sure you can come up with many ideas to make your kitchen more efficient and break traditional habits that waste too much energy.

9. Help your state adopt California car standards. In the automobile industry, the U.S. is number one in the top five polluters effecting global warming. We need states to force automakers to build cleaner cars for America. America's cars and light trucks emit 20 percent of the nation's greenhouse gas emissions, the heat-trapping gases that cause global warming. For decades, the Federal Government has done nothing to reduce the global warming pollution; so states are being forced to take action. Some states have adopted California's car standards while others have not; for more info, go to www.edf.org. This will push automakers to the tipping point because it will force them to build two sets of cars; whereas if all states adopted these standards, it would be easier and cheaper for automakers to build one clean line of automobiles for the entire country. Write your state officials and U.S. auto builders to encourage them to take action. This cause is worth getting "on board". So please take the time to research your state's policies; if your state still needs input, take time to write a letter to voice your opinion.

10. Minimize the carbons your vehicle uses. Driving maintenance and habits also play a part in how we affect global warming. A web site to calculate your carbon usage is www.terrapass.com/carbon-footprint-calculator/. http://www.fightglobalwarming.com.After checking this out, you will want to make sure that your tires are inflated properly. It is estimated that 32 million U.S. cars and trucks ride on at least two under-inflated tires, wasting 500,000,000 gallons of gas annually. Those numbers are staggering for something

so easily checked, monitored, and corrected. Keeping wheels aligned and your engine tuned along with your tires can save you up to 165 gallons of gas per year; so mind those spark plugs, oxygen sensors, air filters, hoses and belts. Now keep in mind all those things benefit our impact on global warming while protecting our vehicles, making them last longer which in the long run, saves us money. Combine trips into town for less driving. Buy in bulk to eliminate extra trips which saves you time as well. Park at a central location and get some exercise by walking. There is no down side to any of these ideas, only benefits. The trick is to start doing them and make them habits.

11. Recognize the changes in our environment. With each of us helping, we can reduce the impacts the climate changes have on our lives, environment, and on generations to come. For a better understanding about how much our environment is changing, go to www.earthobservatory.nasa.gov. Global warming is changing distributions of plants and animals. It is also changing our weather with storms that destroy, droughts like we've never seen, and fires that burn millions of acres of forests. It is raising the level of the oceans because of melting glaciers. Deforestation is the second leading contributor of carbon emissions worldwide; the burning of fossil fuels being first. Deforestation is finally gaining attention in international discussions on climate change. It must be part of a comprehensive global climate change strategy. We need to encourage our leaders to take immediate aggressive action. Reforestation projects represent the most cost effective way to reduce greenhouse gas emissions. We need to take part in earth day or any community projects that plant trees. Please plant trees on your own property or that of loved ones. Donating to organizations who are doing their part to address this problem is a great way to help; a web search will allow you to pick one in which you'd like to participate. You will be astounded by the choices you will have. Even though I was

aware of global warming, all the studies and evidence makes me realize even more the urgency of this situation.

12. Use Energy-Star appliances. Buying energy-efficient appliances can save you money each year. If just one in ten homes used Energy Star qualified appliances, the change would be like planting 107 million new acres of trees. When buying an appliance, remember that it has two price tags: what you pay to take it home and what you pay for the energy and water it uses. Energy Star qualified appliances incorporate advanced technologies that use 10-50 percent less energy and water than standard models. The amounts of money you will save on your utility bills will more than make up for the cost of a more expensive, but efficient, Energy Star appliance. Look for the Energy Guide label on appliances, and it will have all the information about what you could save, etc. Replacing your old refrigerator or air conditioner with an energy-efficient model will save you money on your electric bill and cut global warming pollution. Visit www.energystar.gov to find the most energy efficient products. I don't know about you, but I certainly don't mind saving money and the environment.

13. Be aware of energy alternatives. The term "green power" generally refers to electricity supplied in whole or in part from renewable energy sources, such as wind, solar power, geothermal, and hydro power. More options are increasingly being offered for our power needs, for more information on different energy options, go to www.eere.energy.gov. If retail electricity competition is allowed in your state, you may be able to purchase a green power product from an alternative electricity supplier. Some states have already done this. If your state is not implementing electricity market competition, you may still be able to purchase green power through your regulated utilities. More than 600 regulated utilities spanning more than 30 states offer "green pricing" programs. The term "green pricing" refers to an optional utility service that allows customers to support a greater level of utility investment in renewable energy by paying a premium on their electric bill

to cover any above-market cost of acquiring renewable energy resources. In the future, I believe we will see this more and more, which is critical to relieve the effect we are having on global warming so that we have a bright future.

14. Watch or read *An Inconvenient Truth.* A viewer of the movie said, "This film is not a story of despair, but rather a cry for a rally". How true that statement is! If you have not seen the movie yet, please watch it with your family. Don't just watch it, talk about it. It is a powerful movie with real statistics. For example, the ten warmest years in history were in the last 14 years. Last year South America experienced its first hurricane. An Inconvenient Truth is based on a presentation that former Vice President Al Gore has been working on for years. The movie is supported by dramatic visuals and disturbing facts. The message is that global warming is real, and it is caused by human activity. It doesn't matter whether you believe in the same politics as Al Gore; you should view this as a fellow human being speaking out to raise awareness on global warming. He did receive the Nobel Peace Prize for his part and rightly so; you can learn more at www.algore.com. This may seem like a film that would be boorr-ing, after all it is talking about the environment. It is not boring; remember the film won two Academy Awards. It is interesting and relentless in getting the information to you, and also produced by E-bay billionaire and philanthropist Jeff Skoll. A portion of the film's profits went right back into the fund created specifically to fight this crisis. You owe it to yourself and the world to see this movie.

15. Be aware that natural resources are not infinite. Around the world, people depend on natural systems for their economic survival. For example, an estimated 500,000,000 people rely on coral reefs for their food and livelihood. Likewise, over one billion people around the world, many living in poverty, depend on forests for fresh water, food and fuel. We all know what is happening to these resources. It has been happening for a long time. These natural systems and the lives that they

support are being threatened by the impacts of climate change fueled by corporate greed. We need to establish protected areas to strengthen our resiliency to climate change. It will help ensure food security for millions. We have to protect these precious resources; go to www.nature.org for some examples on our resources that are not endless. Millions are depending on us. We have to become more involved. Everything we do has an impact, so please remember to make a donation to such charities when you can and as much as you can comfortably afford. We can't do it all, but any effort and action is a beginning. Encourage others around you to do the same.

16. Try to build a green home. Whether remodeling or building, many home improvement stores now have aisles reserved for green building materials. Some of these green building supplies could be legitimate and others could be questionable, depending on which environmentalist you ask. If you are like most Americans concerned about global warming and protecting the environment, do your homework. Investigate the origin, harvesting methods, and production of green materials before purchasing. Go to www.homebuying.about.com for guidelines on building a green home. Here are some options now available to us. Green floors are typically made from recycled products. These non-toxic flooring materials are said to be safe for the environment and for people; and they can be installed in an eco-friendly manner without harmful gas emissions. Cork floors, bamboo flooring, linoleum floors, and eco-friendly wood flooring are a few choices available. Carpet made from recycled plastic food and beverage containers tends to last longer than nylon carpets. Reclaimed or salvaged lumber can be used to build walls as support beams or in roof construction. Solar energy using the sun's power can be used in many different ways. Energy-efficient windows help reduce lost heat and keeps cool air in during the summer. There are many resources available if you do your homework before building or remodeling.

17. Make suggestions at work to help your business be more environmentally friendly. Is your employer doing all they can to recycle or "be green" at the work place? If not, ask why? Take a look around and see what can be changed or go to www.earth911.org to see how your business can become more environmentally friendly. One suggestion is to turn all computers off at the end of the day. When you are going to be away from the monitor more than 20 minutes, turn it off. Make machines last. Try to get one more year out of existing machines. When cleaning the office, don't use conventional cleaning products that contain known carcinogens; water is a great cleaner along with vinegar and borax. Use recycled paper products if your business is not paperless. Recycle ink cartridges. Learn to fax using the computer instead of a traditional fax machine. Pack your own lunch to cut down on waste related to disposables and packaging; this will save you money and you will not be driving to restaurants also saving your gas and emissions from your car. While doing research on this, I found many web-sites dedicated to helping businesses become greener. As an employer or employee, I encourage you to look it up and take action!!

18. Incorporate global warming into school curriculums. During their school years, my children did not have much of a curriculum concerning global warming. There may be public schools throughout the U.S. that do address this in a satisfactory capacity, but I don't think we are doing enough of it yet. In my eyes these children are our future, and we have left them a huge threat which they will deal with for years to come. I know we can't scare the pants off them by giving them all the staggering statistics, but they hear people talk on TV, the news, and read current articles (or at least I hope they do); they are affected already. Some of our children will be the very ones who may impact global warming. Who knows what will be demanded of them to reverse its effect. So it stands to reason, it needs to be addressed in age-friendly ways during school. By the time they graduate and reach

adulthood, they need to be educated with the information that can help them make adult decisions on what they want to do to change what's happening. Recycling, renewable energy, and sustainable resources are just a few subjects that should be taught while they are in school.

19. Shake up your town. Taking action locally can be more rewarding and more immediate than pursuing change locally. Attend town or city meetings to bring up environmental issues. Many town and city meetings have dedicated time for citizen communication. If your does not, contact your representative. When writing them, be specific as possible. Let them know in detail what your concerns are and why. It may save time by giving them the information they need up front. Get involved in decision making. Vote on issues, sign petitions, and join advocacy groups. Talk to people about inexpensive changes such as using non-toxic cleaners. Talk to people about major changes such as local government offices "going green". Reach out to your neighbors. Do you know information that may help them to save money, energy, or lessen their impact on global warming? Don't be afraid to open a line of communication with them. Suggesting something or sharing ideas you have implemented is not being bossy. Just by letting someone know the benefits you are getting by becoming more environmentally friendly may be all it takes to inspire change and actions.

20. Recycle paper and plastic bags. It takes over 500 years for a plastic bag to break down, including the bags that are in our rivers, lakes, streams, landfills, and your own backyard. The U.S. uses 100,000,000,000 plastic bags yearly; get more facts on plastic bags at www.slate.com/Id/2169287. You can easily reduce the use of these environmental hazards. Just say no. If you only purchase a couple of small items, do you really need a bag? Reuse your plastic produce bags or bread bags. Use the plastic bags you have at home in trash cans. You can find many uses for them if you give it some thought. Use canvas bags for all shopping; they are reusable and hold more. Some

> stores offer incentives to shoppers who bring their own bags. Store your canvas bags in your car so you always have them or by the front door so you can grab them on your way out. Buy Bio-bags. You can find them at natural food stores and they work like plastic bags. They are made from soy and cornstarch and are biodegradable. Take your unwanted plastic bags to stores that recycle them. If stores that use plastic bags will not recycle them, encourage them to do so. These are very simple ideas that just require changing the way we do things.

Take the time as individuals and as families to discuss what you can do. Identify the problem, form an effective approach to the solution, and work your plan. After determining what you want to begin with, it is time to make it a goal. Implement a strong plan. Give other family members their responsibilities. Let's work together and start saving money to help stop this global crisis. None of us can do it all, so start with baby steps. When you have accomplished your goal, begin another and so on. Hold each family member accountable and please explain the important reasons for this. We are doing this for our future generations.

Global warming is a real threat. I'm sure you can tell how passionate I am about this subject, or at least I hope I have conveyed my passion. I truly worry for our children and grandchildren. If you are a person of faith, I encourage you to pray for action from our leaders, manufacturers, automakers, businesses, families, and individuals globally. It will take every last one of us to create a change and turn this crisis around. I implore you to use any of these suggestions, do your own research, pass the word along, and to please take action now.

Chapter 20

Pass Your Enthusiasm Along

"Tomorrow is a new day, Gonna make these dreams come true. I'm gonna believe in myself; I'll tell you what I'm gonna do, I'm gonna stop puttin' myself down; I'm gonna turn my life around."

From the album Scarecrow from 1985
Lyrics from the song Rumbleseat
Written by John Mellencamp

As individuals, we can all make a difference, but as a nation, we can make major changes. America should not be a nation divided; we should be a nation that stands by "all for one and one for all", even though what is best for some is not always best for others. Our common goal should always be what is best for the citizens of the USA–one and all. If some are so rich they can't find enough ways to spend their money while others are so poor they can't feed or cloth their families no matter how much they work, we can never reach that goal. Loyalty to each other should not be replaced by the bottom line.

In the pages of this book, you read many suggestions that we can all incorporate into our daily lives to "Take Back America". Can we do them all? NO WAY!! We are only humans–not super heroes!! What we need, however, is for all of you to take some of these ideas and make them your obsession and "Pass Your Enthusiasm Along" to others–make patriotism contagious.

If you are a person that can easily convince others, use your voice to inform and convince people so that they "Realize One Person Can Make A Difference", especially when Americans stick together.

If you are highly educated, "Educate Yourself and Your Family" by being involved–involve yourself and others into changing our education system; better education for all societies is detrimental to our futures.

If you have political savvy, convince others to "Be A Responsible Voter"–we need voters to do their part to take this country back from lobbyists and special interest groups. Because of this, everyone has to "Be Aware Of The Opposition", knowing the difference between our enemies and the people who want what is best for our country is instrumental if we want our country to continue to be a leader of the world. It is hard to be a leader of the world when the world has no respect for your leader.

All Americans need "To Be Proud You Are An American". How can we do this when faced with such difficult times? Remember this; we do live in a FREE land full of opportunities. Since this country was famous for civility and opportunity, we all need to "Take Pride In Your Work". Our impression on the world as U.S. workers should not be lazy slackers (people who work harder to get out of work) or rude customer service representatives (this includes all who work with the public); it should be an impression that includes respect, appreciation, and production.

As a nation, we have to band together and "Be An American Consumer", the importance of bringing manufacturing back to America is of grave concern to our economy and the world's environment. As we accomplish this, we will be able to "Put Americans First". Why should any country be more important than ours? America is run by our hard-earned tax dollars. It is a disgrace to see our people wait for necessities in a crisis when a helicopter goes into unreachable parts of the world in a mere instance by the same military our taxes support; this is completely and totally unacceptable.

All cultures have something to offer, but it is time for Americans to stop allowing other cultures to take over ours. We must demand that anyone walking the land that we love "Respect American Cultures and Languages"; if you live in America, speak English!! If you can't speak English (or worse, just plain don't want to), go home and speak your language in its country of origin. Americans must demand customer service from anyone who represents America speaks in plain English that we can comprehend. If we all stand together in this belief, hopefully it will force companies to be choosier in their hiring process and force immigrants to learn our language so that we can all communicate. If these immigrants have no desire to do this so that they can be a part of America and its communities, they do not need to be in our country. America has always been known as the melting pot, the problem is the immigrants no longer want to melt together. Demand they start melting!

A big part of eliminating the language barrier is to "Help Secure Our Borders". Illegal immigrants are bankrupting our country. There is no easy way to deal with this problem, but we must start somewhere. All illegals that do anything criminal should be the first to go–why should our tax money pay for them to sit in our jails. The laws need to be changed so that illegals cannot have babies here that are instantly a US citizen. What can we do as individuals? Be aware, report anything that helps secure our borders and keep illegals out of our country; if we have to be tattletales, so be it.

"Don't Be Bitter, Be Pro-Active" connects with the border problem but applies to so many other issues, issues that can make such a difference in our everyday lives. Everyday life is so busy for all of us, but sometimes you just have to get involved and apply yourself to the issues where you can make a difference. One area we can all make a difference is to "Commit To Family Integrity"; even those in our country who may not know their true families can adopt others in the same situation and make their own families. Having someone to rely on, a shoulder to cry on, or just someone to love is priceless; we all need that in our crazy hectic lives.

"Be Involved In Your Community" so that you are aware of problems and anything unusual. You never know, you could be the key to stopping something horrific!! Or you could be a part of big changes that create something wonderful–either way your accomplishments will not go unnoticed and you will be rewarded by a deep feeling of self-satisfaction, a quality all productive Americans crave. Win-win situation!!

If we want to get past the present hard times and the difficult decisions the future holds, we will all have to "Commit To Personal Financial Security". Facts are facts, Americans have too much debt and it is hurting the whole world. So if you are particularly savvy with finances, make it your mission to help others who do not quite get it; be an advocate for putting Americans back in black.

America would not be America if past Americans didn't "Have Faith and Practice What You Preach". This country was basically built with these two qualities. Many people think promises are made to be broken–but that should not be the American way. There is a lot to be said for trust and integrity–how could anything be accomplished if nobody could count on someone's word. In early times, a handshake meant it was a done deal and you would not have to worry whether your deal would be honored; I doubt that is possible today, but we must aspire to be truthful and honest.

To accomplish most of the aforementioned, you must "Have A Healthy Mind and Body". A peaceful revolution on the American System cannot be accomplished by the weak-minded or the unfit. Besides, we need all Americans to be more responsible for their health by doing the right things for their mind and body so that we can get our medical system out of its current crises and under control. And if Americans stop irritating Americans, we could eliminate a lot of the stress we are under and possibly get to a common bond that would bring back America. Therefore, let's all "Have Common Courtesy and Use Common Sense". We are all in this together; let's fight with our enemies, not each other. Let's use our common sense to find solutions for what is ailing America so that all of us can find the American dream. Remember, healthy minds and bodies make better decisions!

And in our fight to "Take Back America", let's also make America beautiful again because we all need to "Wake Up! Reduce, Reuse, Recycle" and "Be Aware Of How You Effect Global Warming." You have heard this many times in this book because it is so important. The benefits are huge in so many areas: financially, economically, and environmentally. Gaining independence from other country's resources is invaluable. Americans have sense; reducing, reusing, and recycling only make sense!

All these issues connect together in many ways. As you start to accomplish one or two things, you will notice it helps you accomplish other issues. And the next thing you know, you are a true upstanding productive self-satisfied American. As soon as this happens, "Pass Your Enthusiasm Along" so that we can create a true "Pay-It Forward" America!! Because when we smile, the whole world smiles with us.

Thank you so much for reading our book, we hope you enjoyed it or at least learned something!

20 Not So Simple Ideas To Help "Take Back America"

"The ultimate measure of a man is not where he stands in moments of comfort and convenience, but where he stands at times of challenge and controversy."
Martin Luther King, Jr. (1929-1968)

Challenge: A test of one's abilities in a demanding undertaking.

1. We challenge corporate America to do something about the pay differential between top corporate executive jobs and rank and file workers. Joe Blow should not earn $3 million for extinguishing 400 jobs. Nor should his pay be 648 times more than Joe Average. At the beginning of the century, the average top-level executive earned between 6 and 10 times the salary of the average worker, now things have gotten totally out of proportion and even executives who have led their companies into bankruptcy are leaving with a golden parachute worth millions. This is unfair; because of their failures, they have lost thousands of jobs for the average worker. Wake up America; it should not be this way. Help bring the labor movement back to our shores and restore equalization in pay throughout our corporations.

2. We challenge American professional sports teams to advertise only with American icons. Baseball, apple pie, hot dogs, and Chevrolet are American standards. I can't hear baseball, apple pie, hot dogs, and Toyota. It just doesn't sound right. So, we challenge all American Sporting Associations to take up our battle cry and only advertise American companies (not companies that have moved to our soil from other countries to take advantage of our diminished economic state). Do you drink Saki while watching football? We, of course, prefer Budweiser (they have great commercials and it's the all-American beer). We may have to wear Chinese-made sporting shoes

because you cannot purchase any made in America, but we still drive to the game in our Chevy, Ford, or Chrysler products.

3. We challenge all branches of government, both state and federal, to recycle everything possible. Once all government employees are required to do so, it will become part and parcel of their jobs and will carry over into their personal lives as well. It is just the responsible thing to do–our government should lead by example.

4. We challenge all celebrities to take one issue from this book and make it their obsession. It is a well-known fact that celebrities influence the way the average American thinks. A good example of this is the work Brad Pitt and Harry Connick Jr are doing to help restore the city of New Orleans (which our government failed to do).

5. We challenge the government to "Put Americans First". We have people in this country that go to bed hungry every night. How can this be in this land of plenty? Our government gives so much to other countries, while Americans who work two or three jobs and pay their taxes cannot afford to purchase healthy food to feed their family. The insanity of it all!!

6. We challenge corporate America to get rid of these computer-aided circle jerks. For those of you who do not know what that means, we guarantee that you have been the victim of one. Does press 1 for English, 2 for Spanish ring a bell? Americans waste so much time trying to get to a customer service representative (who speaks unaccented English that we can understand) that the stress of taking care of personal business has become one of the leading causes, in our opinion, of American stress in the American home. We buy our products from real people, but to get our products serviced, we have to speak to a machine. Shriek!!! How can we put a stop to this? Number one, insist that your calls are routed to an American service center (when more Americans are working, we can buy more of your products). Number two, don't buy the products if that is what you have to endure to do business with that company! Number three, complain to your customer service representative that finally gets on the line; tell them how long it took and demand that your

complaint be sent to a supervisor. Number four, if your CSR does not speak proper English, demand an English-speaking supervisor; if one cannot be provided, e-mail the company with your complaints.

7. We challenge all foreign-born hotel owners in America to provide English-speaking employees in all levels of operation so that your guests can communicate with your employees. We further challenge that these operators stick to the American standards of cleanliness and comfort. Americans are not fond of dirty smelly insect-infested rooms (the spread of bed bugs in America is caused by the hitchhiking bugs from hotel to hotel in the patrons luggage) and we are not too likely to patronize your establishment again as sleeping in our cars is cleaner, better smelling, and in general, more comfortable. Furthermore, we challenge our government to establish a system whereby when making our reservations we can be informed of the nationality of the proprietor. This does not mean we are racist. Americans just want value for their money, to be safe and comfortable when reaching our destination. This is also a challenge to convenience stores across the nations that have been taken over by foreign-born proprietors who seem to have the same standard of operation as those in the hotel business. Where are our health inspectors when we need them?

8. We would also like to challenge the well-known chain hotels that allow this disgusting process to happen. If I visit a filthy motel or hotel belonging to your chain, do you think I will book with your chain again? Not likely, in fact, you can depend on it as a complete fact. As a consumer, we feel we are being misled when we book with an American chain and end up in a war zone. Please find a way to bring all of your hotels up to the standard we have come to expect as Americans and openly let us know when it is owned by a foreign national (this way I can make my own informed decision beforehand, not after I have traveled many miles). If not, you will lose our business permanently and in all likelihood, the business of our friends and family; the word of mouth is powerful.

9. We challenge all American airports to tow planes to and from the runways. It saves gas and alleviates pollution. As an example, Heathrow in London started doing this and cut fuel usage about

20%. It would be a great idea for all American aviation to follow their good example.

10. We challenge all celebrities, sports stars, and entrepreneurs that make more than $1 million a year to start a fund that will earn interest. The interest earned would be given to charities to help the not-so-fortunate. A one time donation from many could keep working for years to come.

11. We also challenge all celebrities, sports stars, and entrepreneurs to realize America needs their help too. All of you are so willing to help other countries, but charity begins at home. America has plenty of needs that could be easily remedied by the support of these kinds of people.

12. We challenge the big-tech companies who say they have no qualified applicants for these jobs and must hire from overseas to start training programs or tech schools to qualify Americans for these jobs. More jobs, more money spent in America on those products.

13. We challenge doctors to change the process by which the insurance companies decide what care their patients need. Doctors know far better what their patients need and should band together to stop this ridiculous health care system of ours. Our diagnosis should not depend on a glorified customer service representative. It would be a step in the right direction for American health care.

14. We challenge all federal, state and local correction facilities to make that facility profitable by having the prisoners sort the area's trash for recycling. If recycling is not practical, the prisoners could worm farm and sell them for bait. The castings from the worms could be sold for fertilizer (very expensive fertilizer). If a prison could do both, trash could be almost eliminated from the land fill because it would be used to feed the worms.

15. We challenge the Government Accounting Office to <u>seriously</u> find a way to eliminate all fraud and waste the American taxpayer is paying for. Losing billions of dollars in Iraq with no explanation

of where the money has gone is completely unacceptable!! Illegal immigrants getting entitlement services are a complete waste of the American taxpayer's hard-earned money! These entitlements should be reserved for US citizens only, the ones who pay the taxes.

16. We challenge municipalities who have to dredge their waterways to use the silt from this operation to mix with the city compost piles to make new top soil. Winds from global warming have caused major soil erosion–this could alleviate two problems at once. The sales from the top soil could pay for the composting site. Cities and towns would save money by not having to pay for sites to dump the dredged silt.

17. We challenge the Pentagon to get your priorities straight and know that we cannot afford to police the world. Nobody asked us to do it and obviously they don't want us to do it. Get your noses out of the world's affairs and take care of our country.

18. We challenge the media to present the news in a way that educates the public instead of shapes the public. This could be so important in educating a public that needs valuable, reliable, and trustworthy information.

19. We challenge the DNC and the RNC to have all primary elections held on the same day some time in the month of May. This could save billions in election funds for the nation and keep the media from being the one to shape our opinions.

20. We challenge all businesses with many locations to always try to keep your employees working in the location that is closet to their home. Such a change would make such a difference! First, of course, and most importantly, is the environmental effect–less gas, less pollution. Second, a financial difference since gas is so not affordable at this point for that employee. Third, probably a better point of view from that employee since he does not feel he is working to pay for his gas and because he is spending so much less time on the road. Grocery stores seem to be especially bad about this ridiculous habit. Change your attitudes for the good of all.

20 Great American Products

Unfortunately, this list was much more difficult to put together than the list for companies that out source. I think this makes a statement all by itself. It is just not right that it is easier to find "Made in China" labels in the USA. Even more disturbing is the fact that China probably does not have "Made in USA" labels in their country. Why do we want to make the products we use in other countries? With the price of oil these days, is it really that profitable anymore? Maybe the fuel prices will bring some manufacturing back to the U.S. Who knows? I know that all Americans need to make deliberate choices about the products we buy and the stores we patronize. Let your wallet (what's left of it) make a statement that will help "Take Back America".

1. Sterilite plastic containers are made here in the USA. It was founded in 1939 by two brothers. The company has gone through many changes since then and has become the world's largest independent manufacturer of plastic for your household needs. Find out more at www.sterilite.com.

2. Marvin Windows is considered by some to be the best in the world. This company won the JD Power Award in 2007 and the 2006 Governor's Award for Excellence in Waste and Pollution Prevention. Their goal is to transform a house into a home one dream at a time. All products are manufactured in the USA except for the entry doors that they make. For more information on this company, go to www.marvin.com.

3. Burt's Bees' motto is to Bee-utify your world naturally. This company began in 1984 by making candles. Today they produce 150 products ranging from face, body, hair and lip care, men's grooming, baby care, and outdoor remedies. They remain committed to the environment and the impact of their company on it. They strive to

do their part and remain very dedicated to this cause by being earth friendly. They have a really great web-site with a lot of information on it. To log on, go to www.burtsbees.com.

4. Chipotle Mexican Grill mostly serves locally grown organic meats and vegetables which is environmentally friendly because of less transportation pollution and more nutritious because of less time in transit. Learn more at www.chipotle.com/fwi.

5. Yankee Candle Company is a true American success story. It began during Christmas in 1969 when a 17 year-old boy didn't have enough money to buy his mother a gift. He proceeded to melt crayons together to make her a candle. A neighbor saw the candle and persuaded him to sell her the candle. He then took the money and invested it in more candles. He made two more candles, one for his mother and one more to sell; that was the birth of the Yankee Candle. With over 150 fragrances and one of the world's largest selections of candles and accessories, they are known world wide today. To visit their web-site, please go to www.yankeecandle.com or call them at 1-877-803-6890.

6. Vermont Teddy Bear Company has homemade bears made in Vermont and guaranteed for life. Making the best bears in the universe for over 20 years, they take great pride in the detail and quality of their work. They have bears for all occasions. To reach them for a Bear-Gram Gift Delivery Service, any other orders, or questions, you can call them at 1-800-829-BEAR or go to www.VermontTeddyBear.com. Browsing their web-site is a lot of fun.

7. Hillerich and Bradsby bats, makers of the Louisville Slugger, have written the history of baseball for the last 120 years. They helped shape our American past time. It is the official bat of Major League Baseball. The story begins with a 17 year-old son and his father. They crafted the first Louisville Slugger for Pete Browning and the rest is history. They have expanded well beyond bats; today they sell equipment and accessories for the game. It is truly a fascinating story. You can find out more at www.slugger.com.

8. Ben & Jerry's use all natural American grown ingredients other than vanilla. Go to www.benjerry.com for more information on a great American company.

9. Silk, an organic soy-based milk product is a wonderful company that is the world's largest user of U.S. food-grade organic soybeans. It is a very healthy product without the side effects of dairy milk and is produced using 100% wind energy which is a great way to save the environment. You can learn about Silk at www.silksoymilk.com.

10. Texas Jeans are "Made In USA". You can find Texas Jeans at www.texasjeans.com. Jeans are also sold in stores (but you won't find them at Wal-Mart, wonder why?), just go to the web-site for locations. From the web-site, you will see that this is a great American company wanting to keep their manufacturing base in the United States. So the next time you need a new pair of jeans, please consider shopping with Texas Jeans.

11. All American Outfitters is an on-line store that has a mission. "The goal of All American Outfitters is to provide our customer a quality American made product with cutting edge style at a great price. 100% satisfaction is always guaranteed." You can find this great company at www.allamericanoutfitters.com or by calling 1-800-392-9098.

12. United States Playing Card Company makes Bicycle cards right here in the U.S., the best selling cards for more than a century. Since 1867, this privately held company has been based in Cincinnati, Ohio. They have a wonderful web-site where you will find many interesting facts along the way. Find out all the details of this company's journey at www.usplayingcard.com.and have fun at the same time.

13. Kitchen Aid Appliances have spent decades creating products so our kitchens will be well-equipped. They have a wide range of products to make our lives easier. They have acquired other companies along the way and incorporated these ventures into their company on the road to success. Their journey began in 1919. The kitchen mixer became very popular during the 1920's and the 1930's and continued

to grow in popularity. For more information and to check out their products, log onto www.kitchenaid.com.

14. Red Wing Shoes are built to fit and built to last here in the U.S. Boots were their first product. These boots were made back when people still rode a horse to work. For 95 years they have maintained a quality product and today they sell their products all over the world. To contact Red Wing Shoes, call 1-800-359-BOOT or log onto www.redwingshoes.com.

15. Merle Norman Cosmetics has their headquarters in Los Angeles, California. They make and distribute a full line of skin care and color cosmetic products. It was started in the 1920's when Merle Norman created a line of cosmetics. She began offering samples to neighbors and soon she had paying customers. It is a family owned business dedicated to quality. To find out more, go to www.merlenorman.com.

16. Slinky Toys invented the Slinky back in 1943. Today, it is considered to be one of the greatest toys ever made. Over 300 million Slinky have been sold world wide. It is still made in Holidaysburg, Pennsylvania, where it all began. The equipment used to manufacture these toys is still the same today. Very little has changed with the Slinky in over 60 years except the ends were crimped for safety purposes and maybe its colors. It still remains valued-priced for children of all ages. Check out their web-site at www.poof-slinky.com.

17. Merillat Industries was started in 1946 in Adrian, Michigan. This cabinet company employs over 5000 people. They have eight manufacturing plants, all located in the United States. They have become a respected leader in their field, known for quality and service. The web-site for this company is www.merillat.com.

18. B & K Components began in 1981. They are known for making great sounding audio components and keeping the price reasonable. Critics have taken notice and have given the company excellent reviews on these products. Everything they make is designed, engineered, and made in Buffalo, NY and is engineered to be up-graded. Their focus

is on quality, and they strive to earn loyalty. The web-site for this company is www.bkcomp.com.

19. Cabela's Inc is the world's foremost outfitter. In 1961, their journey began at a kitchen table where a dream was launched. The founders voiced a dream that has survived the test of time to become a very successful world-famous catalogue business. A leader in outdoor equipment, they have grown to be the largest mail order, retail, and internet outdoor outfitter in the world. They produce more than 76 different catalogs and mail more than 120,000,000 catalogues each year, and those numbers continue to grow. To learn more about this, go to www.cabelas.com.

20. Aegis Bicycles believe that "Made in USA" still matters. They make handmade carbon fiber bikes that are made in Maine with dedicated craftsmen. They strive to produce the best product they can. These bikes are built to last as long as you do. Aegis continues to produce the fastest and most comfortable carbon frames, hats off to their dedication to quality. Go to www.aegisbicycles.com for more information.

Find out more at http://www.bloggingstocks.com and use key words "products made in America". If you want to help "Take Back America", patronize these companies and find others that make their products in the United States of America. It may seem like a small step, but it can make all the difference for our country, both environmentally and economically.

20 Well-known American Companies That Out Source

The following list does not of course represent all companies who out source, but they are definitely the more recognizable companies. As you look down this list, you will notice that most of these companies sell products that are pricey. Our opinion is that if these companies did not pay their corporate employees so much, these products could be just as affordable to make in the USA. Corporate greed has made these people forget who made their companies so successful in the first place, the people of the United States of America. These companies were built with American sweat and patronized with American money. By moving their services and factories to other countries, they have put America in a horrible situation. We have lost our good-paying jobs and we can no longer afford to buy the products that we used to make. Who is really the winner here? You can confirm all these companies and a whole list of other companies that out source at www.cnn.com.

1. Mattel

2. Bassett Furniture

3. Levi Strauss

4. Nike

5. American Greetings (another oxymoron, why can we not get American greetings made by Americans).

6. Carter's

7. Maytag

8. Hewlett-Packard

9. General Electric

10. Best Buy

11. Black and Decker

12. Walgreens

13. Union Pacific Railroad (is there anything more American)

14. Toys "R" Us

15. Radio Shack

16. OshKosh B'Gosh

17. Nordstrom

18. Nabisco

19. Microsoft

20. Halliburton (Sound familiar? It has been rumored that someone in a very high position is linked to this company.)

Please try to let these companies and all companies that out source know the American public does not approve by calling and complaining, and most importantly, by using our pocketbooks and not purchasing their items if they don't change their ways!

Bibliography

Chapter 1: Realize One Person Can Make a Difference

Quote

About: Quotations
www.quotations.about.com

Web Sites

The Great Idea Finder
www.ideafinder.com

Andre Agassi Charitable Foundation
www.agassifoundation.org

About: Women's History (Susan B. Anthony and Carrie Chapman)
www.womenshistory.about.com

Annenberg Political Fact Check
www.FactCheck.org

About: American History (Watergate and William Felt)
www.americanhistory.about.com

Apollo 30th Anniversary
http://nssdc.gsfc.nasa.gov

Beer History
www.beerhistory.com

The Greatest Inventors and Inventions
http://library.thinkquest.org/5847/ford/htm

International Brotherhood of Teamsters
www.teamsters.org

Audie Murphy Memorial Website
www.audiemurphy.com

John Edward's 08
www.johnedwards.com

CNN (John Kerry)
www.cnn.com/2004/allpolitics

Lou Dobbs
www.loudobbs.com

We Have Seen Better Days
Interests and Irritations
www.hecubus.wordpress.com

Defending Those Who Defend Our Borders
www.fobpnews.com

America's Most Wanted
www.amw.com

Harry S Truman Library and Museum
www.trumanlibrary.org

Associated Content (Rev. Larry Rice)
www.associatedcontent.com

Suze Orman
www.suzeorman.com

Nobel Prize
www.nobelprize.org

CNN (Cindy Sheehan)
www.cnn.com

CNN (Dr. Sanjay Gupta)
www.cnn.com

CNN
Planet in Peril
www.cnn.com/SPECIALS/2007/planet.in.peril/

The Warbird Forum (Todd Beamer)
http://warbirdforum.com/beamer.htm

Info Please (Amy Vanderbilt)
http://www.infoplease.com/ipea/A0880203.html

Jeff Corwin
www.jeffcorwin.com

Al Gore
www.algore.com

Fight Global Warming
www.fightglobalwarming.com

William J. Clinton Foundation
www.ClintonFoundation.org/Giving

Clinton Foundation
http://en.wikipedia.org/wiki/William_J_Clinton_Foundation

William J. Clinton Presidential Library
http://www.clintonlibrary.gov

Books

My Life by Bill Clinton
Alfred A Knopf, New York 2004

Giving
How Each of Us Can Change the World

By Bill Clinton
Alfred A Knopf, New York 2007

Amy Vanderbilt's Complete Book of Etiquette
50th Anniversary Edition by Nancy Tuckerman and Nancy Dunnan
Double Day

Readers Digest May 2008
Hal Colston Page 108
Dayna Steele Page 111
Valerie Sobel Page 115
Avery Harston Page 104

Retirees News
The Teamster Retirees Newsletter
James P Hoffa General President
February 2008

Documentary

An Inconvenient Truth
Directed by Davis Guggenheim
Presented by Al Gore 2006

Chapter 2: Educate Yourself and Your Family

Quote

Benjamin Franklin (1706-1790)

Web Sites

Mind Tools
www.mindtools.com

Rosetta Stone
www.rosettastone.com

University of Minnesota Extension
www.extension.umn.edu

Professor House
www.professorhouse.com

Psychology Today
www.psychologytoday.com

Kids Health
www.kidshealth.org

Books

Winning Words by Allen Klein
Portland House, New York 2002
Quote by Frank Smith

Documentary

An Inconvenient Truth
Directed by Davis Guggenheim
Presented by Al Gore 2006

Chapter 3: Be a Responsible Voter

Quote

Preamble to the Constitution
Written by Thomas Jefferson (1743-1826)

Websites

On the Issues
www.ontheissues.org

A Service of U.S. Government Printing Office
www.gpoaccess.gov

Government Made Easy
www.usa.gov.Agencies/Local.shtml

Annenberg Political Fact Check
www.FactCheck.org

I school
www.ischool.zm

Telling America's Story
www.America.gov

The Eighties Club
http://eightiesclub.tripod.com/id296.htm

CNN
http://archives.cnn.com/2000/ALLPOLITICS/stories/11/16/recount.chads/

Chapter 4: Be Aware of the Opposition

Quote

Born in the USA, album, 1984
Dancing in the Dark, lyrics from song
Words and music by Bruce Springsteen

Websites

A Chronological History of the New World Order
www.constitution.org/col/cuddy_now.htm

The Knight's Templar
www.ancientspiral.com/templar.htm

The Dark Ages: A Brief History
www.geocities.com/soho.square/8171/dark.html

The Trilateral Commission
www.trilateral.org

The Trilateral Commission and the New World Order
www.antiwar.com/berkman/trilat.html

The 2005 Trilateral Commission Membership List
www.conspiracyarchive.com/NOW/Trilateral_Members.htm

Source Watch Encyclopedia
www.sourcewatch.org

The New World Order: An Overview
www.educate_yourself.org/now

Center for Responsive Politics
www.opensecrets.org/pacs/pacfaq.php

Democracy in Action
www.democracyinaction.org

The New York Times (3/12/2008 edition)
www.nytimes.com

Human Events
www.humanevents.com

New York Times
http://nytimes.com/2004/10/31/books/review/31SCHILLI.htm

The American Resistance
www.theamericanresistance.com/sovereignty/sovereignty.htm

Stop the North American Union
www.stopthenorthamericanunion.com/NAU

CBS News
www.cbsnews.com/stories/2003/10/02/60minutes/main576332.shtlm

Books

How to Talk To a Liberal (If You Must)
The World According to Ann Coulter
By Ann Coulter
Crown Publishing Group 2004

Chapter 5: Be Proud You Are an American

Quote

Bill Clinton (1946-Present)

Web Sites

About: American History
www.americanhistory.about.com

Flag Store USA
www.flagstoreusa.com

History
www.history.com

Litter. It costs you.
www.litteritcostsyou.org

Military Site Map
www.military.com/veteransday/history.htm

The History Place Tourism Guide
www.historyplace.com/tourism/usa.htm

Family Search
www.familysearch.org

The St. Louis Post Dispatch (4000th soldier)
www.Stltoday.com

Washington DC
www.thedistrict.com

The Pledge of Allegiance: A Short History
http://vineyard.net/pledge.htm

Chapter 6: Be an American Consumer

Quote

Scarecrow, album, 1985
Minutes to Memories, lyrics from song
Written by John Mellencamp and George M. Green

Web Sites

The Side Road
www.sideroad.com/Self_Help/being-let.html

Task Force on the Future of American Innovation
www.futureofinnovation.org

BNET
www.findarticles.com

After Downing Street
www.afterdowningstreet.org

Report Illegals
www.reportillegals.com

Chapter 7: Be an American Consumer

Quote

Born in the USA, album, 1984
My Hometown, lyrics from song
Words and music by Bruce Springsteen

Web Sites

MSN
A Mother's Quest to Boycott China 11/21/2007
www.msnbc.msn.com

PharmTech
http://pharmtech.findpharma.com

Local Harvest
www.localharvest.org

Greener Choices
www.greenerchoices.com

Environmental Career
www.environmentalcareer.com

U.S. Winery, Vineyard and Wine Festival Directory
www.officialwinery.com

Chapter 8: Put Americans First

Quote

Thomas Jefferson (1743-1826)

Web Sites

Fox News
www.foxnews.com

National Coalition for the Homeless
www.nationalhomeless.org

America's Second Harvest
www.secondharvest.org

Angel Food Ministries
www.angelfoodministries.com

Rumor Has It (Kurt Warner)
www.snopes.com

Chapter 9: Respect American Culture and Language

Quote

Theodore Roosevelt (1882-1945)

Web Sites

American Family Traditions
www.americanfamilytraditions.com

What Would Our Forefathers Do
www.whatwouldourforefathersdo.com

U.S. History Map
www.learner.org/interactives/historymap/index.html

Litter. It costs you.
www.litteritcostsyou.org

The National River Association Headquarters
www.nrahq.org/education/guide.asp

The Story of Independence Day and America's Birthday
www.holidays.net/independence/story.htm

Family Search
www.familysearch.org

Chapter 10: Help Secure Our Borders

Quote

Uh-Huh, album, 1983
Golden Gates, lyrics from song
Written by John Mellencamp

Web Sites

Report Illegals
www.reportillegals.com

U.S. House of Representatives
http://forms.house.gov/wyr/welcome.shtml

CNN
www.loudobbs.tv.cnn.com

CNN
www.cnn.com/CNN/anchors_reporters/cafferty.jack.html

Gov Tracks
www.govtracks.us

New York State Attorney General
www.oag.state.ny.us

Chapter 11: Don't Be Bitter, Be Pro-Active

Quote

John F. Kennedy (1917-1963)

Web Sites

Ezine Articles
www.ezinearticles.com

The Internet Consumer Recycling Guide
www.obviously.com/recycle

Real Simple
www.realsimple.com

The Natural Conservancy
www.nature.org

Adopt a Highway Maintenance Corporation
www.adoptahighway.com

Meals on Wheels Association of America
www.mowaa.org

Chapter 12: Commit to Family Integrity

Quote

Martin Luther King Jr. (1929-1968)

Web Sites

Technology
www.teach-nology.com/tutuorials

Helium
www.helium.com/items/810208-teaching-ethics-childrenteach-example

How to do Just About Everything
www.ehow.com/how_2108829_b-good-friend.html

The Online Self Improvement Encyclopedia
www.selfgrowth.com/articles/how_to_develop_a_sincere_personality.html

About: Parenting of K-6 Children
www.childparenting.about.com

Chapter 13: Be Involved in Your Community

Quote

R.L. Stevenson (1850-1894)

Web Sites

National Neighborhood Watch Institute
www.nnwi.org

American Red Cross
www.givelife.org and www.RedCross.org

New York State Attorney General
www.oag.state.ny.us

Be Ready
www.ready.gov

Chapter 14: Commit to Personal Financial Security

Quote

William A Ward (1921-1994)

Web Sites

National Endowment for Financial Education
www.smaraboutmoney.org

Social Security Retirement Planner
www.ssa.gov/retire2

Your 401K Portal to the Web
www.401khelpcenter.com

About: Home Schooling
www.homeschooling.about.com/od/gettingstarted/p/homeschool/101.htm

How to Do Just About Everything
www.ehow.com.how_543_retirement.html

Chapter 15: Have Faith and Practice What You Preach

Quote

Helen Adams Keller (1880-1968)

Chapter 16: Have a Healthy Mind and Body

Quote

Benjamin Franklin (1706-1790)

Web Sites

United States Department of Agriculture
www.mypyramid.gov

Nutrition Data
www.nutritiondata.com

Bell and Evans
www.bellandevans.com

Mayo Clinic
www.mayoclinic.com

Skin Cancer Foundation
www.skincancer.org

Rumor Has It (bottled water)
www.snopes.com

Illinois Product Recall
www.Recalls.gov

Chapter 17: Have Common Courtesy, Use Common Sense

Quote

Henry Ward Beecher (1813-1887)

Web Sites

Fun Etiquette
www.funetiquette.com

Together, We'll Learn
www.education.com

Associated Content
www.associatedcontent.com

The Magazine for Culinary Insiders
www.starchefs.com

How to Do Just About Everything
www.howtodothings.com

Chapter 18: Wake Up! Reduce, Reuse, Recycle!

Quote

Ralph Waldo Emerson (1803-1882)

Web Sites

Real Simple
www.realsimple.com

Ecologue: Green Living Made Easy
www.ecologue.com

Smart Energy Living Alliance
www.smartenergyliving.org

Re-gifting
www.regiftable.com

American Petroleum Institute
www.recycleoil.org

Water Use It Wisely
www.wateruseitwisely.com

U.S. Environmental Protection Agency
www.eRecycle.org

Earth Huggers
www.earth-huggers.com

Green Gift Guide
www.greengiftguide.com

Patagonia
www.patagonia.com

Other

Living Green: 365 Ways to Make a Difference
2008 Page a Day Calendar
Workman Publishing, New York
www.pageaday.com

Chapter 19: Be Aware of How You Affect Global Warming

Quote

John F. Kennedy (1917-1963)

Web Sites

MSN
www.msnbc.msn

Fight Global Warming
www.fightglobalwarming.com

Tool Base Services
www.toolbase.org

American Evergreen Foundation
www.usagreen.org/homeEnergy.html

Sierra Club
www.sierraclub.org

Water Use It Wisely
www.wateruseitwisely.com

Texas Water Development Board
www.twdb.state.tx.us/Data/Drought/save_water2.asp

Independent Articles and Advice
www.googobits.com

Environmental Defense Fund
www.edr.org

Terra Pass: Restore the Balance
www.terrapass.com/carbon-footprint-calculator

NASA Earth Observatory
www.earthobservatory.nasa.gov

Energy Star
www.energystar.gov

U.S. Department of Energy
www.eere.energy.gov

Al Gore
www.algore.com

The Nature Conservancy
www.nature.org

About: Home Buying and Selling
www.homebuying.about.com

Earth 911
www.earth911.org

Slate
www.slate.com/Id2169287

Books

136 Best Ways to Save on Your Home Energy by Sunset
Menlo Park, California
Sunset Books, September 2001

Documentary

An Inconvenient Truth
Directed by Davis Guggenheim
Presented by Al Gore 2006

Other

Living Green: 365 Ways to Make a Difference
2008 Page a Day Calendar
Workman Publishing, New York
www.pageaday.com

Chapter 20: Pass Your Enthusiasm Along

Quote

Scarecrow, album, 1985
Rumbleseat, lyrics from song
Written by John Mellencamp

20 Great American Products

Web Sites

All web sites listed with companies.

Blogging Stocks
http://www.bloggingstocks.com

20 Well Known American Companies That Out Source

Web Sites

All information found at www.cnn.com/CNN/Programs/lou.dobbs.tonight/popups/exporting.america/content

www.ingramcontent.com/pod-product-compliance
Lightning Source LLC
Chambersburg PA
CBHW061343280526
45784CB00001B/114

* 9 7 8 1 4 3 4 3 9 3 7 1 5 *